The Ten-Dollar Wildcat

J. P. ALLENBRIGHT

THE TEN-DOLLAR WILDCAT

HOW TO PLAY AND WIN UNCLE SAM'S OIL AND GAS LEASE LOTTERY

ARLINGTON HOUSE PUBLISHERS
WESTPORT, CONNECTICUT

This book is dedicated to
my daughter, Dawn, a budding oil scout

Copyright © 1979 by J. P. Allenbright

All rights reserved. No portion of this book may
be reproduced without written permission from the
publisher except by a reviewer who may quote brief
passages in connection with a review.

Library of Congress Cataloging in Publication Data

Allenbright, J P
  The ten-dollar wildcat.

  Includes index.
  1. Oil and gas leases—United States. 2. United
States—Public lands. I. Title.
HD242.5.A76   332.63'242   80-12845
ISBN 0-87000-475-1

Manufactured in the United States of America
P 10 9 8 7 6 5 4 3 2 1

Contents

Preface　　vii

Part I: Introduction and Orientation

1 / The Black-Gold Rush	13
2 / The Federal Oil and Gas Leasing System and Its Management	20
3 / Land Classifications and Types of Leases	25
4 / How the Lottery System Works	33
5 / Considering the Odds	44
6 / Oil and Gas Geology for Beginners	66

Part II: Choosing a Parcel

7 / Where's the Action?	81
8 / Your First Decision	106
9 / Using a Filing Service	110
10 / Zeroing In on Your Own	132

Part III: Filing for Your Parcel

11 / How to File	157
12 / What Not to Do	167
13 / Winning and Losing	173

Part IV: Selling Your Lease

14 / Reevaluating Your Lease	187
15 / Tax Considerations	193
16 / The Buyers	198
17 / Some Selling Tips	203
18 / Assigning Your Lease	212
19 / Thinking Big	215

CONTENTS

Appendix A / Filing Agents' Recommendations for the July 1978 Wyoming Posting ... 219
Appendix B / U.S. Crude Oil and Natural Gas Production by State, 1975 ... 221
Appendix C / Federal Land Acreage ... 223
Appendix D / Bureau of Land Management Offices ... 225
Appendix E / Resource Index ... 227
Appendix F / Directory of Filing Services ... 233
Appendix G / Decision of the Department of Interior Board of Land Appeals Reversing a BLM State Land Office Rejection of a Winner's Offer in a 1978 Oil and Gas Lease Drawing ... 247

Index ... 251

Preface

Play not for gain, but sport.
Who plays for more
Than he can lose with pleasure
Stakes his heart.

GEORGE HERBERT

Want to try your luck at a monthly lottery run by the United States Government? The $10 entry fee could make you an oil-rich tycoon. Each month the Bureau of Land Management holds a lottery to determine the approximately 1,000 winners of oil and gas lease rights on federal lands. Winners may sell their lease rights to oil companies who bid upwards to hundreds of thousands of dollars for the leases, plus pay an overriding royalty on any oil or gas they find. What's the catch? Well, not all of the leases offered are for potentially valuable lands, some are for hopeless "goat pastures" on sides of mountains. As a matter of fact, only a small percentage of the leases have commercial value, and it takes some expertise to determine which leases may be worthwhile filing for. Also, the number of entries that are submitted for some of the more desirable leases often run into the thousands. But if you are speculatively-minded the risks may appear low and perhaps worth taking, especially when viewed in light of the potentially high financial rewards.

R. J., a retired San Antonio, Texas, businessman, was the winner among 3,500 entrants for a 1,922 acre lease in Wyoming. His $10 gamble netted him a $144,000 offer from Marathon Oil Company. It was his second big win in two years. Patricia, from Chicago, had considerably better odds going for her when she won a valuable New Mexico lease in a drawing from only 217 entries. Of course, for every winner there are many losers. And contrary to popular belief, the odds of winning are *not* the same for everybody. Also, there are pitfalls that need to be avoided.

The purpose of this book is to share with you the knowledge that I have gained about the federal simultaneous oil and gas leasing system, to show you the pitfalls, guide you past the rip-offs that lurk to ensnare the unwary, and to help you develop a playing strategy which will minimize your risks and enhance your chances of winning. I have attempted to be as fair, factual, and unbiased as I could be. You should know that since writing this report I have started my own oil-lease filing service. Also, I have been participating in the oil and gas lease lottery on a regular basis. How successful I might have been in the drawings I prefer to keep between myself and the income-conscious IRS.

It is not my intention in this book to entice anyone to participate in the oil and gas lottery. Whether this game is for you needs to be your own personal decision and one which I certainly do not want to bias. This is not a get-rich-quick scheme; it is an informational report. In order for you to gain the maximum benefit from this information I suggest that you put any gambling impulses aside and keep them aside as you study the following pages. The learning experience and any subsequent decisions or actions should stem from a keen intellect and not from flared-up emotions. Do not feel rushed. Take a couple of weeks, or even several months, to consider if this oil and gas lease lottery is for you. Think rationally, considering your spendable income, the time and effort involved, your family temperment (no sense in straining family relations), your business philosophy, and, of course, your religious traditions and morals on gambling.

If you determine that this game is for you and you're ready to kiss at least a $10 ante good-bye, then I trust that this book will provide you with the orientation and information that you will need to prudently participate in what may ... perhaps may ... turn out to be a profitable venture for you. On the other hand, if this book provides you with the knowledge and insight to discourage you from participation in the lottery, and thereby saves you filing service fees, time, effort, and possible grief, then I feel that I will have been of equal service to you.

Important, Late-Breaking News!

On September 28, 1979, the Department of the Interior published a set of proposed changes in the rules governing the simultaneous oil and gas leasing system. Most of these proposals were designed to prevent abuses of the lottery system. On February 29, 1980, Secretary of the Interior Cecil D. Andrus ordered a temporary suspension of the oil and gas lease lottery to permit investigation of alleged widespread fraud within the lottery system and implementation of the proposed rules to prevent recurrence of such fraud. The proposed rules and the fraudulent practices they are intended to curtail are discussed in detail throughout this book. *In April 1980, the secretary ordered that the lottery be resumed by June 16, 1980, with all of the proposed antifraud rules put into effect. In addition, he directed that the criminal warnings on BLM forms be strengthened, highlighted, and more plainly stated; that a brochure be prepared that plainly states the statutory and regulatory requirements for lottery participation; that a toll-free number to provide information on the leasing program be set up; that a new system for assignment of the record title to a lease, using serialized assignment forms issued only after a lease has been issued and usable only for assignment of a particular lease, be established; and that the state BLM offices more closely monitor the lottery system.*

Part I
Introduction and Orientation

1
The Black-Gold Rush

Remember waiting in long lines to buy gasoline when tempers of idling motorists were fueling faster than their gas tanks? That was in 1974 and again in 1979, when the Organization of Petroleum Exporting Countries had a showdown with the world, asserting that they were no longer going to "give away" their natural resources. In 1974 alone, the OPEC nations quadrupled the wellhead price of crude oil. The era of cheap oil was over. Americans were shocked to realize how dependent their economy and national security were on the OPEC cartel. The higher crude oil prices created an inflationary explosion, simultaneously plunging the United States into a recession with aftershocks promising both a marked deepening of the U.S. trade deficit and a drop in the value of the dollar in international money markets to new lows. Compounding the problem was the fact that the energy needs of our nation were growing. Earlier, in July 1971, the National Petroleum Council's study of the U.S. energy outlook revealed an annual growth rate of approximately 3 percent to 4 percent in our energy demands for the next three decades. By the year 2000 Americans were expected to be consuming annually an amount of energy three times greater than the amount they consumed in 1970. It became obvious that for economic survival the U.S. had to become energy-independent. With this rude awakening the scramble for alternatives to foreign imports had begun. The government was faced with a series of options.

It could impose restrictions on the use of energy. However, this would be a detriment to our economy, employment, and basic freedom. Anyway, even with restraints, it is unlikely that the American life-habits of abundant energy use could be sufficiently modified for a timely impact on the energy crisis. My neighbor was not about to give up his gas guzzler and I could not forego my long, hot, massaging showers.

Perhaps we could be more efficient in the use of our energy. However, testing and implementing new technology is a long-range and also costly process. Long-term capital equipment expenditures have already been committed. Corporations, like individuals, are reluctant to change over to new technology. If, for example, a highly efficient automobile engine were to be developed, it would be at least five years before we would see it in sufficient quantities to impact our energy use. Any impact on the energy crisis through capital equipment changeover would be slow, costly, and minimal.

Another option is to accelerate the development of our domestic energy resources. This covers a wide range of alternatives, for example, enhancing oil recovery from existing oil fields. Currently, we can extract only about one-third of the oil out of a well, which leaves nearly 300 billion barrels in currently known reservoirs. A report by the National Petroleum Council states that most of this remaining oil is not recoverable under any foreseeable conditions. So again, we need more research and more time before enhanced recovery processes can impact our energy needs.

We could develop our coal resources which we have in abundance; 3.2 trillion tons of it, according to the U.S. Geological Survey—enough coal to meet our energy needs for about 500 years. But, again we are faced with the problem of modifying our energy using machinery to be able to utilize coal. Coal mining is more damaging to the earth's surface than oil drilling. And since coal pollutes the air when burned, technology must be developed to control emission of the pollutants, which means more time before coal utilization becomes a viable large-scale alternative source for our energy consumption.

Nuclear power is another option. According to the Atomic Energy Commission we have 2.3 million tons of readily available proved uranium resources, a supply which should be sufficient to satisfy our needs for several decades. However, widespread use of nuclear power plants will take a long time to implement even under the best of circumstances. Environmental factors, safety considerations, nuclear waste disposal, and security requirements hamper implementation. After the mishap at Three Mile Island, officials are taking a long hard look at the nuclear energy option. Also, construction of additional energy plants could lag until the breeder reactor, a new type of nuclear power reactor that produces more fuel than it uses, is fully developed and tested, which could be some time yet.

According to the National Petroleum Council, the U.S. has 1.8 trillion barrels of crude shale oil of which about 7 percent (129 billion barrels) is concentrated in easily accessible areas. Nevertheless, oil shale processing technology is still in the developmental stage. More processing plants need to be constructed and the feasibility of oil shale processing demonstrated before large-scale operations would be undertaken. Further, water, which is essential to the extraction process, is scarce in the areas of oil shale deposits, an obstacle which needs to be overcome for long-term production efforts. And there is the uphill battle against environmentalists.

What about sunshine power? Did you know that enough sunlight falls on Florida in one day to power the world for nearly a month? Solar energy is our most feasible new power source. It is clean and virtually inexhaustible. However, the solar state-of-the-art is still in the infant stage. Much research and development still needs to be done. The problem of efficiently collecting solar energy and storing it for use on cloudy days needs to be overcome, and transmission systems for efficiently distributing solar power still need to be developed. Another angle to harnessing solar power is through its effect on organic compounds. The sun can be used to gassify organic compounds, such as cow manure, a process which yields useable by-products, for example, high-nitrate fertilizers. Unfortunately, the methane gas generated from this process requires a costly chemical cleaning process. Therefore, as promising as sunshine power may be it is unlikely that we will see it in widespread use for another decade or two.

Is the answer blowing in the wind? The federal Energy Research and Development Administration spent $24 million in 1978 on wind-energy research in order to answer this question, and their test windmills are beating away in Ohio and Colorado. NASA is testing a 125-foot-diameter wind turbine in Ohio and the U.S. Bureau of Reclamation is considering a proposal for a $77 million, 49 unit, wind generator network in Wyoming. General Electric is planning to construct the world's largest windmill, a 200-foot-diameter, two-bladed turbine, in North Carolina, and other major test projects are spinning away in Puerto Rico, Rhode Island, and New Mexico. However, more research and development is needed and initial capital outlay for wind-powered systems is high. Research thus far indicates that wind could never satisfy more than a small fraction of the total U.S. energy needs and it would take another twenty years before we could fully exploit our wind resources.

Another alternative is "moon power," offering us a tremendous energy source through its effect on our oceans. We could harness the movement of waves and tides. But, as with so many other options, more time is needed for more research to be done, and the initial capital outlay is high. Also, the geographical requirements would limit applications to the coastal states.

Maybe we can all run our cars on water instead of gasoline? That's not as farfetched as it may at first seem. There is a municipal bus in Provo, Utah, that uses water for its energy. The water is the source of hydrogen gas which serves as the fuel to power the engine. The Billings Energy Corporation in Utah has developed a simple and inexpensive modification which can convert any gasoline powered engine into a hydrogen-burning vehicle. Not only are the converted automobiles safe and nonpolluting, the major auto manufacturers are backing the project, and Mercedes-Benz has announced that it expects to offer a hydrogen-powered car within five years. The major obstacle is to streamline the technology for producing hydrogen gas so that it can be readily available at local "gas" stations. Eventually, every family could have their own hydrogen producing plant. Several factories have already switched to hydrogen power and there is also an experimental village under construction which will have all of the houses powered by hydrogen. Hydrogen energy applications technology may be a viable solution to our energy problem, but switching over to a new energy source on a grand scale takes time.

There are other options such as geothermal energy which is produced when subterranean water is heated by the earth's molten core. The heated water escapes as steam through geysers, which can be used to drive steam turbine generators. Widespread application of subterranean steam power is not technically or economically feasible. Neither can we appreciably affect the energy crisis by expanding our hydroelectric power through new dam constructions because most of the suitable dam construction sites have already been utilized. Use of synthetic fuels is another answer, but like the other options it will not make visible inroads into our society for some time yet. More research is needed, more money and more time.

Last, and least, but worth a mention, is "flower power." Some agronomists believe that we can help solve the energy crisis by growing fuel-producing flora. The euphorbia plant produces a gasoline-like fuel and the xguayule plant produces a latex-like product. By far the best fuel producer is jojoba, an evergreen shrub which can yield two tons of oil-nuts per acre. Jojoba oil is claimed to be manifold superior to presently available engine and transmission oils and has many other uses as a lubricant. However, it takes fifteen years for a jojoba orchard to fully mature, and little acreage is being cultivated. Then, there is the problem of more research to validate the uses of flora-extracted oils, and the need to overcome the inertia of public acceptance of this source. Wouldn't you be reluctant to run your car on nut oil?

Regardless of the options we consider, we are faced with the same theme: more research to improve the technology so that energy utilization can be made economically feasible, and more time to do research, build models, test theories, and implement technology. But there is no time. The energy crisis is here and now and requires an immediate solution. Notice also, that there is no energy shortage. We have a huge and virtually inexhaustible supply of energy currently available to us in varied forms. The problem is a lag in technological development to be able to efficiently and sufficiently utilize the abundant energy surrounding us. As long as oil was cheap and readily available from overseas there was no need for the United States to consider alternative sources and new technology. Through our own lack of foresight we created a gap between our increasing demand for energy and a self-sufficient means to fill our energy needs. How long it will be before the energy gap is closed is difficult to forecast. Many factors are involved: government policies, environmentalist debates, priorities of projects, appropriation of research funds, national and international economics, future OPEC pricing policies, and the like. I venture to say that it will be another five to eight years, at the earliest, before we begin to see our way out of the energy crisis and another ten to twenty years before we are independent and energy-comfortable. In the interim, until we can phase in new technology, we need to either continue to rely heavily on energy imports or expand our own oil and gas production. The latter is obviously the better choice. In spite of the shortcoming of deepening our dependence on the use of fossil fuels we need to expand the use of such fuels as a necessary temporary stopgap measure. The technology for oil exploration and drilling is already there. Adequate transportation is available; pipelines, railways, and truck routes are, for the most part, established. Refineries and processes are available and already proven. For the short-term the most logical step to take in order to help narrow the energy gap is to expand our drilling program to extend and develop existing oil and gas fields, and to locate new oil and gas fields.

Fortunately, the United States has an enormous oil and gas energy resource base. The National Petroleum Council Committee on Possible Future Petroleum Provinces of the United States (NPC) concluded, in part,

> The ultimate petroleum potential of the United States including known reserves and past production, and assuming median estimates of potential and 60 percent recovery of 720 billion barrels of oil-in-place, may exceed 432 billion barrels of crude oil, 1,543 trillion cubic feet of natural gas, and 49 billion barrels of natural gas liquids. The amounts that *will* be discovered are not ventured, but if discovered and produced future production of crude oil would be 346 billion barrels (4.0 times past production); future production of natural gas would be 1,195 trillion cubic feet (3.6 times past production); and future production of natural gas liquids would be 38 billion barrels (3.5 times past production).

Other sources of hydrocarbons such as oil shale, tar sands, solid hydrocarbons, and coal were not considered in the NPC's study and report. The NPC report further indicated that over half of our nation's remaining oil and gas resources are on federal lands.

In its report to the President, the Public Land Law Review Commission stated, "The Federal Government generally should rely on the private sector for mineral exploration, development, and production by maintaining a continuing invitation to explore for and develop minerals on the public lands."

Now let's recap and examine what all this means to us as potential oil speculators. The United States is currently dependent upon foreign powers for its immediate oil needs; oil prices are being raised by the OPEC nations; the U.S. economy and security are being threatened; the U.S. must move quickly towards energy independence; new technology will not be available to alleviate the oil and gas crisis for another five years or so; the best interim option for the U.S. is to develop its own supplies of oil and gas; oil and gas supplies are enormously abundant in the United States, most of which are still to be discovered; over half of our nation's remaining oil and gas resources are on federal lands; the federal government's policy is to rely on the private sector for development of its oil and gas resources. To these factors, add the fact that the government is allowing oil and gas prices to rise. When oil companies receive more for their oil and gas (either directly or through tax incentives) they have the necessary profit-motive stimulating them to expand exploration for new fields. Expanded exploration increases the demand for oil land, and the black-gold rush is on.

The Arizona Oil and Gas Conservation Commission reported that vast amounts of acreage are under lease by both major and independent companies and considerable exploration activity is anticipated in the near future. Wyoming, one of the more advanced oil and gas exploration states, reported that it had about 135 drilling rigs in constant operation throughout the year, resulting in the discovery of 40 new oil and gas fields. The Oil and Gas Commission of Arkansas reported that the 549 oil and gas drilling permits it issued in 1977 was the largest number of permits it issued in the past 16 years. Likewise, drilling activity has been high in Colorado during the last few years and is expected to remain at a high level in the near future. Colorado reported 56 new oil and gas field discoveries in 1977. South Dakota reported that exploration for oil and gas in 1977 was at the third highest level in the state's history. In New Mexico, gas well completions hit an all time high of 830; up from 518 in 1976. Montana also reported a favorable outlook for future oil and gas development.

This brief perspective spots a trend of increased oil and gas exploration activity following the Arab oil embargo. A more comprehensive summary of states' oil and gas exploration activities is presented in Part Two. This increased surge of activity has been coupled with a greater demand by oil companies to lease the oil-rich lands owned by the government. Most of the choice lands are offered for lease on an open competitive bidding basis. The more speculative parcels, referred to as "wildcat" lands, are made available on a noncompetitive basis via a lottery system. This is where you, the layman oil speculator, can participate. I will cover the details of how you can participate, later. For now we want to develop a big-picture perspective of the oil and gas leasing system. This comprehensive overview will help you later when you formulate your strategy to more effectively participate in the lottery.

2
The Federal Oil and Gas Leasing System and Its Management

The development of the United States began during the 100 years after it became a nation. It was during this time that seven of the original states ceded their western lands to the federal government. These lands generally included those between the original states and the Mississippi River. Subsequently, the federal government acquired the lands west of the Mississippi to the Pacific Ocean. And in 1867, the United States grew to its present size of nearly 2.3 billion acres of land with the acquisition of Alaska. In order to encourage the development of its vast area, which for the most part was unsettled, the federal government adopted a policy of selling or granting away its land to those individuals, corporations and agencies that would make best use of it. Land continued to be conveyed until the Taylor Grazing Act of 1934 brought the era of homesteading to an end. In total, the federal government had disposed of over 1 billion acres of its land. With the settlement and development objectives of the government met, its policy shifted towards the retention of some lands in federal ownership. Today, the federal government owns 755.4 million acres, an area roughly equal to the size of India. Of this remaining public domain 285 million acres have been reserved as national parks, national forests, and national wildlife refuges, and for specific uses by the Department of Defense, Atomic Energy Commission, and other federal agencies. The remainder of the public domain lands—approximately 457 million acres, excluding Indian reservation lands—has not been set aside for particular uses.

Much of the federally owned land is rich in natural resources, including huge concentrations of undiscovered oil and gas deposits. Historically, the government has maintained a policy of not only permitting, but encouraging both individuals and corporations to explore for, and to claim and develop its mineral resources. Initially there were no laws enacted to regulate mineral development. As mineral interest increased in the wild west the need for a code of ethics became evident, and the early western miners established a set of rules and regulations which subsequently became embodied in the General Mining Law of 1872. Under this legal mining system anyone had the right to claim mineral deposits on public lands merely by discovery. By the simple procedure of filing a claim the prospector could extract minerals without any payment to the government in the form of royalty or otherwise. Although this system was generally applied to the metallic minerals, it was also applied to oil and gas.

With the increased industrialization of the nation, the passing of World War I, and improved oil drilling technology, it became prudent for the general welfare of the public interest to exclude certain specific minerals from the General Mining Law of 1872. Such excluded minerals, to include oil and gas, were no longer up for grabs. Instead, they were to be made available through a controlled land-leasing system, and the Mineral Leasing Act of 1920 was born. In general, this act permits the leasing of nearly any public domain lands for minerals covered by the act. It requires the payment of annual rentals until production starts and the payment of royalties thereafter. Lands not within any known geological structure in a producing field of oil or gas must be leased to the first qualified applicant without competitive bidding; lands within a known geological structure are offered to anyone on a competitive bidding basis. (This will be covered in detail in chapter three.) In 1947, the Mineral Leasing Act was amended to include mineral leasing on "acquired lands."

The information presented in this book will provide you with a working knowledge of the Mineral Leasing Act insofar as the lottery system is concerned. However, if you would like to learn more about the regulations pertaining to the oil and gas leasing system you may obtain a reprint of the regulations from any of the state offices of the Bureau of Land Management, or contact the director at the Washington, D.C. Office. BLM addresses are listed in Appendix D, or you may call 202/343-7753. The 24-page booklet will be sent to you free of charge. Ask for "Regulations Pertaining to: Oil and Gas Leasing as Contained in Title 43 of the Code of Federal Regulations (Circular No. 2357)."

The Mineral Leasing Act has some inherent flaws which work to the oil speculator's favor. Under it, the leaseholder can retain the lease for ten years without doing any exploratory or productive work on the land. This loophole enables the acquisition of leases for mere speculation. Also, under the leasing system a distinction is made between "known geological structures" and lands not known to contain mineral wealth. However, some of this "unknown" land is valuable—it becomes valuable when speculative demand for it increases. When many individuals file for such land it is literally given away in a lottery. The winner can then auction the land to the highest bidder. This procedure in effect transfers potential bid-revenues from the government and into the pockets of lay oil speculators. Some major oil companies consider the lottery system a nuisance and feel that it does not serve them. They argue that the volume of lay entries that are filed on some of the parcels minimizes their (the oil companies') chances of winning and they end up bidding for the parcels anyway.

To streamline the administration of the federally owned public domain lands the Public Land Law Review Commission was formed. Their study concluded in 1970 with the publication of a 342-page report which included recommendations to modify the existing federal systems for exploration, development, and production of mineral resources on public lands. The commission recommended that "competitive sale of exploration permits or leases should be held whenever competitive interest can reasonably be expected." To this end the commission also recommended the elimination of the known-geological-structures standard for competitive allocation of oil and gas lease rights, which would eliminate the lottery system currently in effect. The commission further recommended the establishment of performance requirements designed to assure diligent exploration as a condition of retaining and renewing the lease rights conferred, thereby eliminating the speculative holding of leases without development.

Nearly a decade later we still have the oil and gas lottery system. Evidently, there must be some strong supporters backing the system. Perhaps eliminating the system is not a high priority to consider since the revenues generated from the speculative filings are now running at over $25 million annually, a source of revenue that would be lost if the lottery system were discontinued. Maybe it is politics that is preventing changes from being enacted, or perhaps the basic land-law philosophies need to be more carefully considered in light of a more comprehensive plan before any changes are put into effect. In any event, the oil and gas lease lottery system remains in effect, and while it is the modus operandi, those who are interested, and able to, should consider their opportunity to participate in the oil rush at equal parity with the oil giants. It's one of the last of the U.S. government's big give-a-ways, perhaps only remaining with us until our huge bureaucratic system can move to amend the present mineral leasing system.

The one-third of this nation which is federally owned is for the most part managed by six agencies of the federal government. In the order of the amount of acreage managed, they are: the Bureau of Land Management (470.4 million acres); the United States Forest Service of the Department of Agriculture (186.9 million acres); the Department of Defense (30.7 million acres); the Fish and Wildlife Service (26.6 million acres); the National Park Service of the Department of the Interior (23.3 million acres); and the Bureau of Reclamation (8.7 million acres). Other agencies account for an additional 8.8 million acres. The Bureau of Land Management, which has been charged with the land and resources management of over 60 percent of all federal lands has the additional responsibility for the administration of mineral resources on approximately 313 million acres where surface administration is in another agency, or where the land surface has been transferred to private ownership with a reservation of minerals to the government. The BLM received its authority on July 16, 1946, when it was created as an agency of the Department of the Interior through the consolidation of the General Land Office and the Grazing Service.

The BLM is responsible for the identification, classification, use, and disposal of public lands. It administers grazing on the lands under its jurisdiction and is also responsible for the survey of all public lands. It also administers the mining laws to provide for the development, conservation, and utilization of mineral resources on all public domain. In the case of oil and gas development and production, this involves the selection of areas for leasing and the administration of the Mineral Leasing Act to include the conduct of the monthly oil and gas lease lottery. To perform its functions the BLM relies on assistance from other agencies such as its sister agency, the Geological Survey of the Department of the Interior. The Geological Survey supervises geological and geophysical exploration, performs mineral resource evaluations, and supervises the exploratory drilling and production activities on leases. The BLM is also charged with the leasing functions of submerged lands outside a given state's three-mile territorial limit for the recovery of mineral resources. The protection of the environment is the function of all federal agencies in the performance of any of their responsibilities which may have an impact on man's environment.

To conduct its business the BLM has established twelve State Land Offices of supervisory jurisdiction, and a headquarters office located in Washington, D.C. Eleven of the state land offices are located west of the Mississippi. Their geographical distribution is patterned after the irregular distribution of the public domain lands which they administer. Almost all of the lands managed by the BLM are located in the eleven western states plus Alaska. The federal government owns over 95 percent of all the lands in Alaska, about 86 percent in Nevada, and some 67 percent in Utah. At the other extreme is Connecticut, where only 0.3 percent is owned by the federal government. A more detailed analysis of federal land ownership is provided in Appendix C, and a directory of BLM state land offices is provided in Appendix D.

Although all of the BLM offices are governed by the same uniform statutes and rules and regulations, some of the procedures and services vary between the offices. For example, some land offices sell reference maps; others do not. Each office has developed its own packet of informational material pertaining to the oil and gas leasing system. Some land offices provide comprehensive literature, including reprints of articles on the oil and gas lottery. The information is provided free of charge, and you may wish to request a packet from each of the offices. It would be good for you to peruse each of the office's packets for your additional orientation. You will find that prices charged for lists and supporting reference materials differ among offices.

The next chapter provides a detailed analysis of the different land classifications used by the BLM and the various types of leases that it issues to ensure the orderly and profitable development of the oil and gas resources.

3
Land Classifications and Types of Leases

The Bureau of Land Management has classified its lands into three categories: known geological structures (KGSs), open land, and lands in conflict. Access to these lands for purposes of oil and gas exploration and development is enabled by the BLM through leases, a different type of leasing system being used for each category of lease. The types of leasing systems are competitive and noncompetitive. The noncompetitive is further classified into two types, regular filing and simultaneous filing.

All of the leases grant the lessee the exclusive right to drill for, extract, remove, and dispose of the oil and gas deposits that may be found in the leased lands. A leaseholder, however, is not required to become involved in the exploration, drilling, and production operations. The provisions of the lease allow the leaseholder to sell, transfer, or assign his rights in the lease to another party. This provision is one of the key factors that makes the acquiring of a lease so appealing to the layman. You only need to win the BLM's drawing for a much sought-after lease. Admittedly this is a lot easier said than done, but once past this big hurdle the remaining steps are easier. You pay the first year's rental, which is now set at one dollar per acre (formerly fifty cents per acre). You then act as a middleman, transferring your lease to an oil company at a handsome profit per acre. More about these aspects later. Now let's consider in detail each of the land classifications and the respective types of leases that the BLM issues on these lands.

Known Geological Structures

The U.S. Geological Survey (USGS), under the auspices of the Department of the Interior, performs extensive field studies on the more than 755 million acres of federally owned land and as a result of its findings classifies some of this land as being valuable for oil and gas deposits. The name given to this classification is *known geological structures*. Title 43 of the Code of Federal Regulations states: "A 'known geological structure' is technically the trap in which an accumulation of oil or gas has been discovered by drilling and determined to be productive, the limits of which include all acreage that is presumptively productive." The latter part of this definition is important, as it clearly states that any lands that the USGS deems to be even *potentially* valuable would by definition fall within the classification of KGS. It is interesting to note that only a small fraction of all public lands has been determined to offer favorable prospects for oil and gas exploitation. The classification of a land tract as a KGS does not guarantee the presence of oil or gas under that tract. It only states a known geological possibility. Detailed information concerning the procedure used in making the KGS determinations may be obtained from the U.S. Geological Survey, Washington, D.C. 20240.

All determinations of KGSs by the USGS are documented by the filing, in the appropriate land office, of maps or diagrams which describe the structures by legal subdivisions, sections, township, and range. Further, the USGS and some state agencies maintain records on exploration, development, and production activities in a field after leases are issued. This technical information may be obtained from various sources (see Appendix E for addresses).

Any land that is classified as being a KGS may be leased only as a result of competitive bidding. This type of leasing most often attracts only those petroleum firms or individuals who can afford the costs of drilling for, and developing, the oil and gas resources. The BLM determines the location and how much of the KGS oil and gas acreage to offer for lease. The BLM also sets the dates of the lease offerings. Factors considered are the national energy situation, future supply-demand imbalances, environmental factors, public interest being served, profit potential, etc. Eventually, a few land parcels are scheduled for auction to the highest bidders. The offerings are publicized beforehand in the *Oil and Gas Journal*, a regional magazine such as the *Western Oil Reporter*, and the local county newspaper where the leases are offered. Also, the BLM office in Washington, D.C., sends notices of competitive lease sales, to be held throughout the nation, to persons on its mailing list. All such lease sales are specific as to geographic location, sale date, time, and place. The parcels are offered in units not to exceed 640 acres. Each unit is bid for separately. All biddings are by sealed envelopes which are opened and read publicly at the designated time. Bidders are expected to bid the standard two dollars per acre annual rent plus a bonus bid. The lease is awarded to the highest bonus-per-acre bid. Bids often run into the millions of dollars as oil companies compete for the right to drill holes on the prospects of striking oil or gas.

Theoretically, a shrewd opportunist could make a minimal bid on each of the parcels being auctioned, hoping that for at least some of the parcels no other bids would be made and he would be the winner. This possibility heated the speculative fever of two cunning businessmen, a test pilot for a small aircraft firm in Texas, and an Alaskan prospector. They joined their wits in a hopeful scheme to parlay a $7 investment into an oil sheik's ransom, and formed a paper corporation named Champion Oil. Their target was 179 tracts of cold, barren land located in the North Slope of Alaska near the settlement of Dead Horse. (Although this classic case refers to lease sales conducted by the state of Alaska for state-owned lands, the state's rules and regulations parallel those of the federal government. Therefore, the outcome of this case is undoubtedly exemplary of how the federal government would react in a similar situation.) The duo decided to bid one dollar on each of the 179 parcels that went up for bid. To show their good faith they put two thin dimes—the required 20 percent of their bid—into each of 179 sealed envelopes. In contrast, competing against them were the multi-billion-dollar oil giants, whose bids collectively topped $1 billion for the same parcels. As each of the sealed envelopes was opened the bids were read out: Amerada Hess Corporation, $43,500,000; Getty Oil, $53,000,000; Champion Oil, $1. This procedure was repeated for each parcel, and every time Champion Oil's dollar bid was read out and the two dimes tossed on the table government officials and the spectators at the Anchorage lease sales office had themselves a few laughs. By the time the bids were all read out, it turned out that Champion Oil was the only bidder on seven of the tracts. No one was laughing when Champion Oil representatives came forward to claim their leases on 17,900 acres. The state refused to issue the leases, and a legal battle ensued. Meanwhile, a German oil firm offered Champion Oil $500 million for the leases if Champion won its case. After a ten-year court battle the Alaska Supreme Court finally ruled that the state and not Champion owned the leases and that the state does not have to issue leases unless it thinks the bids are high enough or that the sale would be in the best interest of the state. It was a nice try anyway! To keep future "jokers" out, when the seven tracts go up for sale again, $10 million will be required as the minimum bid.

From this case history we know that leases for tracts classified as KGSs are not going to be given away cheap, even if nobody wants them. Anyone who is considering speculating to the contrary should be prepared for a losing battle.

Offshore oil and gas leases fall within the same KGS classification, the only difference being that they are located underwater. Under the Outer Continental Shelf Lands Act of 1953—the only authority that exists for mineral leasing on the OCS—all oil and gas leases must be issued on a competitive bidding basis only. The administration of the leasing functions is charged to the OCS office of the Bureau of Land Management. Incidentally, the OCS leasing process includes the "receipt of fair market value" as one of its goals. It is obvious then, that the leasing of off-shore parcels is meant to be strictly for the major petroleum firms and is outside the scope of the individual oil speculator.

Now let's consider the prospects of oil and gas leases on what is referred to as open land.

Open Land

Most of the federally owned land is *not* known or believed to contain oil or gas. Such land, when it has not been under prior lease, is designated by the government as open land, that is, it is up for grabs by any American citizen on a first-come, first-served basis. Excepted lands are national parks and monuments; Indian reservations; incorporated cities, towns, and villages; naval petroleum and oil shale reserves; lands acquired under the act of March 1, 1911, known as the Appalachian Forest Reserve Act, and other acquired lands; and lands within one mile of naval petroleum or helium reserves. Since open land is of unknown oil and gas potential and usually located in the boondocks, competitive bidding is not required.

Instead, open land is leased by filing a simple form and paying a $10 filing fee plus an annual rental of $1 per acre. Through the "noncompetitive regular filing system" these noncompetitive leases are issued for a primary period of 10 years and so long thereafter as oil or gas is being produced in paying quantities. Over the years oil companies and individuals were willing to gamble that the Geological Survey's inferences were not conclusive and that maybe oil or gas could be found; in many cases their gambles proved fruitful. Some of our major oil fields were the result of speculative ("wildcat") drilling on unproven land. Wildcat drilling has been successful enough to justify its continued use as a valid means of oil and gas exploration. One gusher at today's price of crude can offset the exploration costs of drilling numerous dry holes.

Wherever test drilling begins some speculators rush in to file for leases on the nearby open lands with the hopes that if the test-well proves productive their leases will skyrocket in value. Of course, it is safe to assume that any wildcatter would lease a large area of land around his proposed drill site much in advance of filing for a permit to drill, keeping the hungry speculators perhaps miles away from the action. Theoretically, the strategy of leasing lands ambient to planned drill sites can be a good way to speculate in oil and gas, but one should have a more reliable source of inside information than the local barber. Bankers, securities firms, wildcat crews, drilling rig suppliers, and USGS and BLM employees and all of their families, relatives, and friends get early notice of an oil company's lease, exploration activity, and planned drilling, and can rush to file for a nearby open land lease. There is an old proverb on Wall Street, "Sell on good news," meaning simply that all of the insiders know of that pending new product announcement, merger, or raise in dividends, etc., well before the information hits the news wire. They take an early position. As the news breaks the insiders know that the public will jump in to buy, thereby driving the stock up a few points, and it is at that time that the insiders bail out taking their profits. Likewise, if you happen to find yourself able to lease a tract right next to a *supposed* drill site you had better ask yourself why. I do not want to discount this type of speculating; I merely caution readers to make sure that the company planning to do the drilling is not just a fly-by-night whose directors are more concerned in bilking the investors out of their money than in actually drilling for oil. When a wildcatter decides to begin drilling operations on his lease he must file an "intent to drill" notice with the Geological Survey, a copy of which is sent to the BLM for recording with the lease. However, pinpointing the drilling site is not required. The USGS cannot vouch for the reputability of any wildcatter.

Some con artists file an intent to drill notice solely to draw speculative demand for surrounding leases which they own under different names. They make up and publicize stories about their proposed drilling, and then lie in wait for the greenhorn lease speculators to buy up their marked-up leases in hopes that the "planned" wildcat test will be successful. One rip-off artist made a million dollars promoting and selling goat pasture leases in this manner. So check your information sources, otherwise you may be leasing land next to what was intended to be a shallow dry hole.

Some long-term speculators apply for leases on open land where no drilling activity is planned. They gamble on the hunch that some day some oil company will become interested in the area and will pay a premium to acquire the lease. This is a costly proposition since the leaseholder has to pay an annual rental fee of $1 per acre on a minimum parcel size of 640 acres. Smaller parcels are allowed only when the desired parcel is surrounded by lands not available for leasing. Information on available open land shows up on the individual township oil and gas plats which are recorded with the BLM. Because of the millions of acres in this category, the BLM does not issue handout materials to identify which lands are open. It is up to the potential speculator to review the records and determine what lands are available. Individual township oil and gas plats can be ordered from the BLM, or you can contact a private firm or individual to perform this service for you. It is important to note that the reason millions of acres of open land remain readily available is simply because no one has wanted to lease them.

Lands in Conflict

When an open land lease expires, terminates, or is relinquished or cancelled, the land is classified as "Lands in Conflict" and becomes available for re-leasing. In other words, lands in conflict are those lands which were *previously* leased on speculation but on which no oil or gas has been found, and they are available for re-leasing for any of a number of reasons. The previous lease may have expired at the end of its ten-year term. Remember, open land leases are not renewable after ten years if no oil or gas is being produced or if drilling is not underway. Maybe the lease was terminated by the BLM because the lessee failed to pay the annual rent, which generally the lessee would not neglect to do if he felt that the land had potential. Whatever the reason for the expiration of the lease, the law requires that the lands must be made available for re-leasing, equally to everyone under the leasing system called noncompetitive simultaneous filing. This system is commonly referred to as the "Oil and Gas Lottery," the "U.S. Government Oil and Gas Drawing," the "Federal Simultaneous Oil and Gas Raffle," and by several other similarly descriptive titles. Most of the public interest is directed to this system, which has been in effect since 1960. Prior to 1960, the land parcels which were being offered for re-leasing were available to the first taker. As the value of leases skyrocketed due to increased energy demands following World War II, BLM office business soared. Human nature being what it is, crowds stormed the land offices and fights broke out as people scrambled to be first. In order to assure an orderly, safe, and fair awarding of these noncompetitive leases the simultaneous oil and gas drawing system was developed.

The Bureau of Land Management emphasizes that most of the leases offered under this system are "garbage leases" on "rank-wildcat" lands. A lease only becomes attractive when it adjoins or is in the proximity of either new discoveries or areas where drilling and leasing activity is brisk. The biggest challenge to the oil lease speculator is the selection of the "right" parcel on which to file. This should definitely not be left to chance or guess work. Remember that these are parcels that are being re-leased because they were not productive before. Some of the tracts are known to have dry wells on them.

You might be wondering why anyone would want to acquire a lease that someone else found fruitless. Because a lease is relinquished or terminates after 10 years without being productive does not necessarily mean that it lacks potential. Perhaps the lessee was a speculator who ran out of money to keep paying the rent. Perhaps illness or death prevented further payments from being made on the lease. Maybe the lessee was a wildcatter who went bankrupt or changed his priorities before he could effectively explore his tract. Oil companies like to build huge inventories of land near their current, and prospective, drill sites and in no way can they get around to test drill on all of their acreage within the 10-year limitation. Maybe a tract is given up as worthless on the basis of a test well drilled to 5,000 feet. Maybe at

10,000 feet oil or gas could be found. The reason for the expiration of a lease, the length the lease was held; and the name of the former lessee is on file at the BLM offices and is available to the public. Wildcat oil and gas maps indicating productive wells and dry holes are available from the USGS, BLM, or private sources.

This chapter has provided a thumbnail sketch of the types of land classifications and respective lease plans that are available under the federal oil and gas leasing system. The remainder of the book deals in depth with the noncompetitive simultaneous filing system as your means to speculate in oil and gas leases on lands in conflict. The details of how this lottery system works are discussed next.

4
How the Lottery System Works

At 10:00 A.M. on the third Monday of the month each of the twelve BLM state land offices posts a filing list of all lands in conflict that are available for re-leasing within its jurisdiction. Descriptive titles given to the monthly filing lists vary between state offices. The most common titles used are "Notice of Lands Subject to Simultaneous Filing of Oil and Gas Lease Offers," "Notice of Lands Available for Oil and Gas Filings," and "Notice and Posting of Lands Subject to Simultaneous Oil and Gas Filings Pursuant to 43 CFR, 3112." Not uncommonly, the lists are also referrred to as the "Availability List" and the "Wildcat Filing List."

The availability lists identify, by parcel number, each of the land tracts being offered for lease. Supplementing the parcel number is a legal description of the land pursuant to the "public land rectangular system" (explained in chapter ten), which lists the subdivision, section, township, and range of each parcel. If the land being offered has not been surveyed the legal description is given by metes and bounds. Any special stipulations or conditions that pertain to a parcel are described in detail on the availability list. The list also gives the total acres of each parcel, which can range from about 40 acres to a maximum of 2,560 acres. Also indicated are the county in which the parcel is located and the former lease number ("old serial number") under which the parcel was leased. This number is a handy reference for tracing prior lease ownership. The availability lists can be examined free of charge in the public room at each respective land office. To accommodate those persons who cannot personally come to the BLM office the monthly filing lists can be obtained from the state offices by mail for a small charge. The fee, which varies with each office, ranges from one to five dollars per list.

Following the third Monday's posting of available lands the BLM allows five working days for applications to be submitted on the standard form, the "Simultaneous Oil and Gas Entry Card," which is provided free of charge by the BLM offices. Each person is permitted to file only one entry per parcel. Each entry card must be accompanied by a filing fee of $10 (see Part Three for filing procedures). All applications received during the five-day filing period, which usually ends 10:00 A.M. on the fourth Monday of the month, unless extended due to a holiday, are considered to be filed at the same time ("simultaneously"). In order to fairly determine to whom the lease will be issued the BLM Land Offices conduct a public drawing. The date of the drawing is usually a few days after the filing cutoff period, the actual time being fixed by each BLM office to allow ample time for their staffs to process the numerous applications which often exceed 100,000. All entry cards are sorted by parcel number and then the cards are placed into a three-foot-long revolving drum, one land parcel at a time. A BLM official does the honors, drawing three cards for each parcel. The names and addresses of each winner are called out to the small crowd of spectators. The first card drawn entitles the winner to a ten-year oil and gas lease upon payment of the first year's rental of one dollar per acre. The winner is notified by certified mail and has fifteen days following the notification to make the rental payment. If the first drawee fails to qualify for the lease, the lease is offered to the second drawee, and so on. If each of the three drawees, in order, fails to submit his rent in time or be otherwise disqualified, the parcel will be offered again the following month. Of course, if only one application is received for a parcel then no drawing is necessary, the applicant is notified and is issued the lease upon making the rental payment. If no applications are received for a given tract the land reverts to its previous open land status and becomes available under the applicable procedures for issuing open land leases.

Shortly following the drawing each BLM land office posts a listing of the three successful drawees per parcel. This listing is commonly referred to as the "Drawing Results List" or the "Oil and Gas Drawing Record." Results lists can be obtained from the respective BLM offices for a small fee. All of the unsuccessful applicants are notified by the return of their entry cards.

As this book goes to press, the Bureau of Land Management is proposing to make some procedural changes to its lottery system in order to promote more efficient exploration and development of its land. The BLM wants to conduct its lotteries on a quarterly schedule instead of monthly. The availability list would be posted at 10:00 A.M. on the third Monday in January, April, July, and October. The time periods allowed for the filing of entry cards and the submittal of the first year's rental would be expanded from 5 to 15 days and from 15 to 30 days respectively. Also, the BLM proposes to increase the maximum size of the leases it offers to 10,240 acres.

Lease Terms and Conditions

As a leaseholder your lease grants you the exclusive right to explore and drill for, extract, remove, and dispose of oil and gas deposits that you might find under your land. Your rights continue for 10 years and so long thereafter as oil and gas is found in paying quantities. To retain these rights you must pay an annual rental of one dollar per acre or fraction of an acre. Failure to pay the annual rent terminates the lease, but you are not held liable for the remaining balance of unpaid rent. You simply lose your lease. There is no authority under the law to grant extensions on unproductive leases. You are not obligated to develop your leased land. You can "tie it up" by just letting it sit. Your lease grants you an 87.5 percent portion of the proceeds from any oil or natural gas that is found. The U.S. government retains the customary 12.5 percent landowner royalty on production.

An oil and gas lease conveys no surface rights other than the right to seek and remove oil and gas. You do not have the right to use or occupy the land for residential purposes. You cannot build a house or summer cabin on it or use it for cultivation. Also, your lease does not permit you to exclude the general public from other lawful uses of the public land.

The government has a policy of multiple development for its land. The regulations state: "The granting of a permit or lease for the prospecting, development, or production of deposits of any one mineral will not preclude the issuance of other permits or leases for the same land for deposits of other minerals with suitable stipulations for simultaneous operation. . . ." An oil and gas lease does not permit you to mine sand or gravel or to remove any minerals other than oil and gas from your leased land. As indicated earlier, most minerals other than fossil fuels, such as gold, silver, tin, lead, copper, sulphur, etc., are not mined under a land leasing system. Rather, they are available to prospectors by the process of outright claim. So, while somebody is leasing the oil and gas rights on a tract of land, somebody else can overlap with a claim to the sand, sulphur, trace minerals, or whatever.

"Beating the System"

This multiple development provision, coupled with a lust for money, has set the stage for a handful of foxy operators who decided to try and beat the system.

The best known of these operators is Merle Zweifel. According to an article in the January 20, 1972, *Wall Street Journal*, Zweifel busily raced his pickup truck all over the U.S. for about 15 years, hammering two-by-fours into the ground to stake mineral claims on 2.5 percent (over 20 million acres) of all federal land. Wherever large oil and coal companies were operating on federally leased land, the neck twitching and bald-headed Zweifel came in with his overlapping claims. He staked mining claims on about 465,000 acres of the Piceance Basin in Colorado, where some of the biggest oilshale beds in the country are located. He has 8,000 mining claims in Wyoming, over a half-million acres covered in Arizona, and has staked a whopping 50,000 claims covering 14 million acres in Nevada, about 15 percent of the state. He has staked mineral claims on land in California, Utah, Montana, Illinois, Michigan, Ohio, Kentucky, Pennsylvania, New York, and Massachusetts. When he got to the east coast he just kept right on going, claiming over 1.5 million acres of seabed along the Atlantic coast.

His consistent strategy was to cloud lease titles with his mineral claims wherever he could find federal land that was being used or considered for other purposes. His intent in every case was the same: he would write letters to the leaseholders informing them that their oil or coal deposits were commingled with his locatable minerals and that such oil or coal cannot be extracted without disturbing these minerals. Zweifel's letter then suggested that an agreement be worked out to permit the leaseholder to mine Zweifel's claimed minerals. Otherwise Zweifel would proceed to restrain the leaseholder from extracting the oil or coal, since he argued that such extraction was damaging to his locatable minerals. Needless to say, Merle Zweifel quickly earned himself the reputation of being a pain in the neck, a reputation he hoped would spur the leaseholders to buy him off. But he was wrong. The oil companies fought back by challenging his claims.

HOW THE LOTTERY SYSTEM WORKS

According to the 1872 mining law, to stake a claim one does not have to prove a valuable mineral find unless challenged, although technically he is supposed to stake claims only for valuable minerals he finds. You also need to do some preliminary physical work. Then, after staking the claim, federal law requires that $100 of "assessment work" must be done on the land each year.

Merle Zweifel's overzealous attempt to weave his way through the grey area of the law for a quick fortune turned back on him. The Nevada state attorney general charged him with 16 felony counts of filing a false document. A spot check of Zweifel's 50,000 claims in that state disclosed no evidence of assessment work being done and in most cases even the preliminary work was not done. Zweifel was released on $32,000 bail and faced one to six years in prison and a $5,000 fine for each count. Incidentally, Zweifel, who is reported to have once studied for the ministry, spent some time in jail for a mail-fraud scheme involving some Oklahoma land deals in the 1950s. It would seem that he should have stayed with the ministry. If anyone tries to extort money from you by clouding title to your oil and gas lease, know better than to pay him off. Take him to court.

There are hundreds of thousands of laws on the books, all attempting to shed some light on the Golden Rule. And each time someone comes along and attempts to finagle his way around the law to better himself at the expense of his fellow man, more and more restrictive laws are enacted in an attempt to keep guiding man's behavior according to the Golden Rule. While you study this report perhaps some schemes will come to mind for playing the simultaneous oil and gas lottery by weaving through laws. There are many schemes that can be used, but take a lesson from Merle Zweifel, and do not let yourself go off on any dubious tangents. The simultaneous oil and gas lottery system was established as a service to you and others like you. The United States government is one of the few governments in the world which permits its citizens to own interests in the country's natural resources. This privilege should not be abused. If you decide to participate in this service you have a responsibility to make sure that you do not hurt yourself in the process and to make sure that you do not do anything that would hurt anyone else. You will hurt yourself in the lottery by staking more time, effort, and money than you can comfortably afford. You will hurt others in the lottery by not playing the lottery within the *intent* of the laws, rules, and regulations.

Restrictions, Rights, and Prerogatives

Some leases issued have special stipulations incorporated as part of the oil and gas lease. The text of each of these stipulations is posted for review as part of the "Notice of Lands Available for Oil and Gas Filing." Special stipulations include: need for environmental impact studies; limiting drilling to certain months so as not to interfere with the seasonal life patterns of local fauna; restriction of surface occupancy within delineated ecosystems; no surface use on inventoried archeological sites; no occupancy on slopes exceeding certain given percentages, or on areas subject to landslides; no additional road construction; no surface disturbance near roads, live water, and power lines, and so on. A thorough review should be made of all restrictions pertaining to the parcels you are considering. We will consider these again in Part Two.

I have assumed that it is not your intention to acquire a lease for the purposes of doing the exploration, drilling and production yourself. Therefore, I have excluded from this report such leasing conditions as bonding requirements, drilling operational procedures, plugging of dry wells, etc., which would be of concern only to wildcatters. If you wish this additional information, consult the Code of Federal Regulations.

As a speculator not interested in getting into the oil and gas drilling business, your most important lease right is being able to assign or sublease all or part of your leased acreage for either a divided or undivided interest on it to any person qualified to hold the lease. This provision applies equally to the overriding royalty. Subdividing, assigning, and subleasing is done by paying a nominal fee and filing a simple form with the Bureau of Land Management. This topic is discussed in more detail in Part Four. You also have the right to will the rights to your lease to your heirs and devisees.

Qualifications of Leaseholders

Federal oil and gas leases may only be obtained and held by citizens of the United States, associations of citizens or corporations organized under the laws of the United States or of any of its states, and municipalities. As used in the regulations (43 CFR, 3112) the term *association* includes partnerships. Associations and corporations must file qualification forms with the BLM before filing for a lease in order to prove that they are authorized to hold interests in oil and gas leases.

Minors may not file for, acquire, or hold federal oil and gas leases. For purposes of oil and gas leasing a minor is defined as an individual who has not yet reached the age of 21. Plans are in the works to amend the rules to allow oil and gas leases to be obtained and held by individuals considered to have reached the age of majority under the laws of the state in which the lease-parcels are located. Oil and gas leases may be issued to legal guardians or trustees of minors in their behalf. (However, the BLM wants to amend its present policy and disallow use of *revocable* trusts for participation in simultaneous oil and gas leasing.) Guardians and trustees must file a statement with the BLM to prove their authority to act on behalf of the minor, verify citizenship of both the minor and the guardian or trustee, and to indicate oil and gas lease holdings of the minor as well as those of the guardian or trustee which are being held for the benefit of other minors.

No person, associate, or corporation may hold, own, or control more than 246,080 acres in any one state, of which no more than 200,000 acres may be held under option. This ruling includes "indirect" participation through membership in associations or as a stockholder of a corporation which holds leases or interest in a state. However, in Alaska the acreage limitation is 300,000 acres in the northern leasing district and 300,000 acres in the southern leasing district, of which no more than 200,000 acres may be held under option in each of the two leasing districts.

Regarding aliens' ownership of U.S. oil and gas leases the federal regulations state, "Aliens may not acquire or hold any direct or indirect interest in leases, except that they may own or control stock in corporations holding leases if the laws of their country do not deny similar or like privileges to citizens of the United States." I wonder how much latitude there is in the interpretation of the phrase "similar or like privileges." As I read this regulation, there are several angles by which, say, an Arab could participate in America's oil and gas leasing system. Think about it.

Value of Leases

What is an oil lease worth? Another way of phrasing this question would be, How much can I make at this game? A valid consideration since no one is playing the oil and gas lease lottery just for the fun of it. Estimating a lease's value is one of the major variables that goes into formulating your playing strategy. Others are the odds of winning and the amount of money and time you are willing to risk. For now, let us consider the value of leases.

Frankly, a lease is worth whatever someone is willing to pay for it, and that figure has ranged anywhere from zero to millions. Asking about the value of a lease is similar to asking a realtor what a house is worth. The primary factor that makes a lease-parcel attractive to someone is its location. If the land is near a producing oil field or near exploration already under way, the value will be greater since the speculative interest is greater than it would be if it were located away from any current production, drilling, or exploration. Remember that we are talking about leases on tracts of land that are not known to contain, and are not even suspected of containing, oil or gas. Hence, we are dealing with an unknown which may or may not yield oil or gas. The unknown becomes measurable quantitatively by its proximity to a known geological structure. The escalating price of oil has made wildcatting exploration worth more now than ever before, and there are enough new discoveries being made to keep the speculative fever running high. Statistics published by the American Petroleum Institute indicate that in 1977, of the 9,961 wildcat wells drilled, 27 percent were productive.

Leases on tracts in the proximity of a producing oil or gas field can sell for as much as $100 per acre plus an "overriding royalty." But the number of such desirably located leases is small, only about 100 out of the roughly 1,000 leases offered by the BLM each month. Of these hundred, only about 10 to 15 are sold to the oil and gas industry giants for more than $100,000 each, plus overriding royalty payments. And about 30 to 40 additional leases are sold for around $50,000 each, plus the override. If the maximum lease-acreage is quadrupled to 10,240 acres as proposed, expect to see the choice larger leases occasionally top a million dollars each and a multimillion dollar bonanza coming up on rare occasions.

These are ball-park figures. There are many other factors besides location determining the value of a lease. Again, as in real estate we need to consider the potential for the development of the parcel. Can it be readily explored upon? Is the tract comprised mostly of steep slopes, difficult to work on? Is it easily accessible by road? Is there a nearby pipeline for transporting the oil and gas once it is found? Also, conditions and stipulations on the lease may be so restrictive as to render the lease worthless for drilling, exploration and development, even if it were located next to a gusher. Also to be considered are the more mundane factors which influence lease prices: OPEC oil pricing policies, energy demands, and our government's policies towards domestic exploration.

A magazine recently ran an article on the oil and gas lottery which stated that a winner of a lease would certainly be paid at least 10 times the amount he paid for the lease. Do not believe such propaganda. The minimum that you can get for anything is nothing. There are a lot of garbage tracts being offered by the BLM each month, and the BLM has no responsibility to label which tracts are downright worthless. The simultaneous filing system is designed to make available the re-leasing of parcels on a competitive basis, and that's all. A tract that is worthless today, however, can suddenly jump in value if a wildcat strike occurs nearby. This is true even for those tracts that have had prior unsuccessful drilling on them. In August 1978, a filing service recommended a 2,545 acre parcel in Johnson County, Wyoming. Although there were two dry holes on the tract the parcel was estimated to be worth $25,000 to $50,000 plus an overriding royalty. The basis of the high evaluation was the anticipation of additional exploration in the area of the lease and the fact that the tract was located seven miles from the Flying E oil field.

In the early seventies some goat pasture leases neighboring the Poison Draw field in Wyoming's Powder River Basin skyrocketed to over $100 per acre, plus overriding royalty, when a strike was made in the area. A West Virginia man is reported to have received $500,000 for his parcel, plus an overriding royalty of 5 percent—his lease was located adjacent to an existing natural gas field.

The overriding royalty is what keeps you in the action after you sell your lease. It is part of the agreement you make with the oil company, and it entitles you to a percentage of all the income from oil and gas produced and sold. It is computed on the basis of gross production, free and clear of expenses. Overriding royalty payments usually run between 2 and 6 percent. If you win a lease, and if you can sell it, and if the buyer drills on it, and if they find oil or gas, then your royalty payments could make you rich. The January 19, 1976, issue of *Moneysworth* magazine reported that a 3 percent overriding royalty agreement on a 340-acre tract in Converse, Wyoming, had an estimated worth of $340,000.

To better understand what royalty payments can mean to you let us look at a hypothetical example. Assume that you have a 5 percent overriding royalty agreement on a parcel where an oil well is producing a modest 25 barrels per producing day. (One barrel equals 42 gallons.) Since wells pump around the clock, 7 days per week, 365 days per year, your well would be producing 175 barrels per week, 9,100 barrels each year. If crude oil is going for $16 a barrel, your 5 percent override would be 80 cents per barrel, $140 per week ($.80 × 175), $7,280 per year ($.80 × 9,100). With a dozen wells on your tract producing for 20 years, you could end up a millionaire.

The evaluation of a parcel is a complex matter based on many variables. However, there is a rule-of-thumb that can be applied, and that is that a lease is worth whatever similar leases in similar locations under similar circumstances are selling for. You only need to identify the similarities. It is difficult to come up with exact figures, but there are two sources which will be of help. The *Southwest Oil and Gas News* (P.O. Box 25847, Albuquerque, NM 87125) is a weekly newspaper which includes periodic reports on lease sales and prices. A six-month subscription is $12. The other source is the filing service companies who publish monthly "teaser lists" (tip sheets) of their lease selections. These lists include an estimated dollar value for each of the leases recommended. Although the estimates are rough, they do provide a frame of reference to work from. (See additional comments in chapter 14.) It will not cost you anything to get on the mailing lists of the filing services. The lists of parcel recommendations that they will send you will usually indicate the county in which the parcel is located as well as the legal description of the parcel, but most do not give the BLM filing numbers. These the filing services provide for a fee. You do not need the BLM filing numbers in order to chart the parcel locations on a map, however, and by noting the estimated values you will soon get a good feeling for the market. Incidentally, do not get hooked by the flashy literature of any filing service company, at least not until you have read this book in its entirety.

Thus far I have discussed what values the oil companies place on leases. It is interesting to point out what value the leases have to filing service companies. The filing service companies make their money by selling parcel selection lists and by providing filing services to the public. Assume that a filing service company gets 200 applications for each of its monthly parcel recommendations for which it charges $15 per filing. If it makes 10 recommendations, it will make, regardless of who wins or loses, $30,000. Additionally, some filing services act as lease brokers and earn commissions for selling winners' leases to oil companies. One service boasted earning $100,000 in lease sales commissions for 1978. So, you can see that leases have a high value to the filing service companies.

What are leases worth to the Bureau of Land Management? In 1977, wildcat leases brought the BLM $25 million in revenues from the application fees alone. In addition, the BLM received about $10 million in revenues from rental payments made by lease winners, and stands to receive an additional 12.5 percent as an overriding royalty payment on any oil or gas that is found.

By stating these figures I do not mean to deride the filing service companies or the BLM. I am merely reporting on the value of leases when viewed from different perspectives. Certainly the filing service companies have a right to profit from their research and the services they provide. And certainly the U.S. Government is entitled to its share.

Now let's look at the odds you will have to beat to strike it oil-rich.

5
Considering the Odds

If you bet on a horse, that's gambling. If you bet you can make three spades, that's entertainment. If you bet cotton will go up three points, that's business. See the difference?

BLACKIE SHERROD

Statistically Speaking

The following is a partial winner's list of some of the more valuable parcels that were offered in the June 1978 Wyoming lottery:

Winner's Name and Address	BLM No.	Acreage	No. of Entries	Estimated Value
Russell W. Brown Cheyenne, WY	WY-58	1,826.97	5,404	$136,000 plus $975,000 ORR*
Betty Reeder Garden Grove, CA	WY-60	2,392.29	3,749	$91,000 plus $850,000 ORR
David Rucker Beltsville, MD	WY-61	2,240	3,051	$84,000 plus $700,000 ORR
Carl A. Smith Venice, CA	WY-62	2,406.36	2,901	$85,000 plus $750,000 ORR
Elizabeth Connell Denver, CO	WY-63	1,520	4,292	$73,000 plus $540,000 ORR
Greg Panos Salt Lake City, UT	WY-64	2,545.40	3,260	$92,000 plus $935,000 ORR
Arminda Mancillas San Benito, TX	WY-73	1,280	5,661	$172,000 plus $950,000 ORR
Collins C. Diboll New Orleans, LA	WY-119	1,840	6,135	$143,000 plus $1,000,000 ORR
Evelyn Richards Denver, CO	WY-137	651.75	3,742	$70,000 plus $450,000 ORR

Winner's Name and Address	BLM No.	Acreage	No. of Entries	Estimated Value
Evelyn K. Olds Milwaukee, WI	WY-141	1,613.58	3,277	$62,000 plus $425,000 ORR
Warren K. Burgess Guyman, OK	WY-186	1,200	2,850	$60,000 plus $450,000 ORR
Harry R. Logan Burlingame, CA	WY-188	2,080	1,674	$38,000 plus $350,000 ORR

* ORR = overriding royalty

Additionally, there were dozens of other winners, mostly of smaller, but sizeable nest eggs.

Reviewing the monthly BLM drawing results list is sufficient to excite anyone's dreams. We naturally identify with the winners and visualize ourselves in their place. Allow me to burst your dream bubble and bring you back down to reality. Let's put our fantasies aside and take a good look at the odds of winning this game.

Take, for example, parcel number WY-137 in the table above. Evelyn Richards competed against 3,741 other entries and won a small fortune, an accomplishment we would all like to duplicate. But, what does it mean to be picked the winner out of 3,742 entries? For one thing it means Evelyn was very lucky. She had to be with those odds against her. It also means that 3,741 people were not lucky. They lost. Their dreams didn't materialize. And who knows how many times previously they also lost?

In 1977, about 2.5 million entries were received by the BLM for 9,000 parcels offered in the lottery. In other words, in 1977 there were about 9,000 winners. Of this 9,000 only about 10 to 20 percent won leases that were of mentionable value. Most parcels are worthless. In 1977, there were about 2,491,000 losing entries. Ask any of these losers what it means to be picked a winner and they will probably say, "Lucky!" No wonder, then, that a representative of a major Beverly Hills oil lease brokerage firm I interviewed asserted that his firm does not pay attention to the oil and gas lottery. He stated, "The odds are poor... properties not that great.... It comes out a bummer as far as we're concerned."

But back to Evelyn Richards, the 1 in 3,742. How lucky must she have been to win? On strictly a long-term statistical basis it means that for every 3,742 times she would enter the lottery she would win once, assuming of course that there were 3,742 entries at each drawing and she filed her limit of one entry each time, and all other influencing factors remained constant. Conceivably, she could win ten times in a row or she might experience a very long time of continuous frustrating losses. But, on the long-term average Evelyn Richards would win once every 3,742 times she entered the lottery. To get a more realistic perspective of what this means, assume that she files one entry each month, twelve entries per year. Divide 3,742 entries by 12 entries per year and you get 311 years and 10 months. This is the average length of time that it would take her to win once. With odds of 3,742 to 1 against her, and filing one entry per month, she would have to play an average of about 312 years to win once. Needless to say 3,742 to 1 is a long shot, a very long shot indeed. The odds of dying are better than these odds of winning. Unless you have plans for cryonic suspension or some other gimmick for longevity, your chances of cleaning up at 3,742 to 1 odds before you bid your body adieu are slim.

Not all parcels have thousands of entries. Some of the lower-valued parcels receive only 100 or so entries. If you consistently played the lottery for lower-valued parcels against 100 other entrants, and you filed one entry per month, you would average one win every 8⅓ years, a far more plausible venture. To get a realistic conception of what 1 in 100 means, take 100 pennies. Lacquer or scratch one. The marked penny is your entry, the other 99 are your competition. Now conduct your own lottery. Put all 100 pennies into a sack, shake them, and draw one out. Was it yours? Repeat this experiment 100 times. How often did you win? Perhaps several times, perhaps not at all. Figure that it costs you the minimum of $10 for the BLM filing fee every time you enter, and figure an overhead of at least $5 per entry for maps, geological information, reports, postage, etc. That's a total outlay of $1,500 for 100 tries.

Statistically speaking we have taken a realistic, nonemotional perspective of how the odds stack up in this game. Even at 1 in 100, it's a long-shot speculation. But, considering a $1 million pay-off potential, a $15 flyer, even at 1 in 5,000 odds, is tempting. It is almost odds-on when compared to state-run lotteries. For example, the odds are 1 in 250,000 that you would win the $10,000 prize in the New York State weekly lottery. When Illinois began its state lottery the odds of winning the $300,000 jackpot were 1 in 6 million, and the chances of winning their $1 million bonanza were a mind-boggling 1 in 30 million. Did you ever participate in a retail store's drawing? The odds that you won are remote. For example, the odds of winning the top $2,000 prize at Safeway's Bingo game were 1 in 1,750,000. If the total cost of your weekly grocery bill was increased by just one cent in order to offset the cost of the game, on the average, you would have paid out $17,500 to win the $2,000, and at one grocery trip per week (i.e., one entry per week) you would win, on the average, once every 33,654 years—if the game and you lasted that long. That's mathematical fact.

Odds versus Pay-Off Potential

All other factors being equal the odds of winning will vary in direct proportion to the anticipated financial return. You have already seen what the typical number of entries is for some of the more valuable parcels. The following listing, abridged from the June 1978 Wyoming lease offerings, typifies the number of entries filed on some of the lower-valued parcels:

Winner's Name and Address	BLM No.	Acreage	No. of Entries	Estimated Value
John J. Puhl Portland, OR	WY-10	280	35	$ 750
Jack Mask Roswell, NM	WY-13	356.85	182	$ 2,000
John W. Bierlein Frankenmuth, MI	WY-15	240	122	$ 750
John J. Puhl Portland, OR	WY-17	440	90	$ 1,500
Roger J. Langley Richardson, TX	WY-21	279.65	179	$ 1,500
Marilyn J. Conc Lubbock, TX	WY-25	320	233	$ 3,000
R. B. Sheverbush Cheyenne, WY	WY-28	280.83	123	$ 2,000
Robert L. Connell Denver, CO	WY-29	38.45	71	$ 500
J. D. Wright Casper, WY	WY-33	120	87	$ 1,000

Winner's Name and Address	BLM No.	Acreage	No. of Entries	Estimated Value
Richard J. Swenson Eden Valley, MN	WY-36	40	90	$ 300
Viola J. Kirkwood Casper, WY	WY-37	280	247	$ 1,500
Marcia P. Lane Beverly Hills, CA	WY-40	40	161	$ 1,000
S. A. Cantine Cheyenne, WY	WY-51	640	477	$10,000
Donn R. Swift Hobbs, NM	WY-56	40	166	$ 600
Robert D. Kout Milwaukee, WI	WY-59	880	1,086	$15,000
Arthur E. Rose Ypsilanti, MI	WY-70	320	546	$ 6,500
Bruce A. Blakemore, Tr. Midland, TX	WY-81	200	82	$ 1,000
Nola M. Dippel Eagle River, AK	WY-82	162.03	138	$ 2,500
Irwin Rubenstein Denver, CO	WY-84	320	217	$ 5,000
Marvin B. Gillis Dallas, TX	WY-86	280	905	$ 4,000
Marilyn J. Cone Lubbock, TX	WY-87	40	87	$ 1,000
Laurie A. Volz Cheyenne, WY	WY-93	480	104	$ 1,500
Clifford Park Riverside, CA	WY-99	971.77	663	$20,000
B. A. Blakemore, Tr. Midland, TX	WY-100	278.14	254	$ 6,000
Bernard Halperin Thousand Oaks, CA	WY-104	680	235	$ 3,500
Jon P. Lindstrom Cheyenne, WY	WY-105	320	1,172	$10,000
Harry Zuckerman Chicago, IL	WY-107	240	345	$ 3,500
Nancy S. Nakoa Honolulu, HI	WY-110	239.64	1,245	$ 7,000
Otto G. Green Oakland, CA	WY-114	200	825	$ 6,000

Winner's Name and Address	BLM No.	Acreage	No. of Entries	Estimated Value
E. C. Buell Salt Lake City, UT	WY-116	320	862	$ 5,000
Annamarie Duncan Denver, CO	WY-117	640	161	$ 3,000
Joann Howard Texarkana, TX	WY-120	80	188	$ 2,000
F. J. Bradshaw Salt Lake City, UT	WY-125	520.36	44	$ 2,500
Jay L. Truett Golden, CO	WY-126	2,422.76	321	$ 7,000
Merle C. Chambers Denver, CO	WY-127	149.56	299	$ 3,000
Beverly B. Goodman Cheyenne, WY	WY-133	160	335	$ 5,000
Roger J. Langley Richardson, TX	WY-138	1,548.06	189	$ 5,000
James Barkdull Littleton, CO	WY-139	480	670	$ 7,000
June Oil & Gas Co. Denver, CO	WY-145	219.77	240	$ 2,000
Clotilde M. Young Denver, CO	WY-146	1,280	1,538	$25,000
Ruth Harper New York, NY	WY-147	788.72	1,113	$20,000
Edmund C. Lynch, Jr. Dallas, TX	WY-150	640	1,267	$16,000
Spelman Prentice Casper, WY	WY-151	480	1,243	$15,000
Dorothy G. Harden Broomfield, CO	WY-152	960	913	$20,000
Lawrence C. Harris Roswell, NM	WY-154	360	773	$ 9,000
Edwin W. Mitchell Aurora, CO	WY-155	800	434	$ 8,000
Dyke Lansdale Westminister, CA	WY-156	200	492	$ 5,000
Geoff Panos Salt Lake City, UT	WY-159	627.59	1,212	$10,000
Louis T. Merriam, Jr. Darien, CT	WY-160	480	1,715	$ 7,000

Winner's Name and Address	BLM No.	Acreage	No. of Entries	Estimated Value
Carol W. Fraker Denver, CO	WY-161	937.92	1,976	$15,000
Phillip E. Flanagan Rivertown, WY	WY-162	40	54	$ 400
Henry Oxnard Irvine, CA	WY-163	1,516.40	1,529	$30,000
Celeste C. Grynberg Denver, CO	WY-165	40	138	$ 800
Charles E. Graham Denver, CO	WY-169	80	123	$ 1,000
Randolph Harrison Chicago, IL	WY-170	2,252.87	1,843	$45,000
C. D. Trossen Riverside, CA	WY-172	1,265.99	950	$20,000
Petroleum Exploration Denver, CO	WY-173	2,469.33	1,463	$40,000
Jack B. Gains Cheyenne, WY	WY-174	2,410.23	1,435	$35,000
E. Perry Bolger Midland, TX	WY-175	25.39	57	$ 375
Bryan Bell New Orleans, LA	WY-176	320	547	$10,000
W. N. Kruse Wayland, MA	WY-177	2,559.36	1,496	$25,000
Woodrow J. Gaudet Hamden, CT	WY-178	1,099.85	1,246	$30,000
Harper Oil Company Denver, CO	WY-182	640	775	$11,000
John H. Campbell San Carlos, CA	WY-183	1,280	1,385	$30,000
Robert L. Connell Denver, CO	WY-184	320	762	$ 8,000
Pittsford Oil Investors Buffalo, NY	WY-185	394.64	946	$12,000

The estimated values listed were obtained from consulting sources believed to be reliable. No figures were available on the potential future overriding royalties for these parcels, but it is reasonable to figure roughly 2 to 5 percent. Some of the lower-valued leases might not attract any royalty considerations. Some parcels might not even attract any buyers. Other parcels might sell for considerably more than the estimates given.

The above listing provides a good idea of the odds of winning in this game. Note how the number of entries varies with the estimated value of each parcel, and note how the estimated value varies with acreage size. Larger parcels valued at a few dollars per acre and smaller parcels valued at $10 to $20 per acre draw more speculative interest than smaller parcels valued at only a few dollars per acre. This is understandable since the pay off potential for the smaller and lesser valued tracts is not sufficient for most speculators to risk a $10 to $15 bet. Notice how many of the parcels valued in the neighborhood of $1,000 to $3,000 drew under 200 entries. Not considering the possibility of a royalty payment a $1,500 return on a $15 wager in a 100 to 1 odds drawing, from a business point of view, is not that good. You would have the additional risk of laying out $1 per acre per year on your lease and the uncertainty of being able to market your lease at a reasonable level of profit: From a business investment viewpoint a $100,000 pay-off potential for a $15 risk at 3,000 to 1 odds is a much better prospect. However, the likelihood of winning at such high odds is very small. Unlike the lower valued parcels, the higher valued parcels are sold more quickly and you would probably be able to find an eager investor to loan you the one dollar per acre lease fee until the parcel is sold.

Anybody can win at this lottery. There are plenty of worthless goat pastures being offered by the BLM each month, with few or no takers. The idea is to win a reasonably valuable tract. What value is "reasonable" depends upon your expectations, considering the odds and investment involved.

My review of the BLM winners lists and consultant reports of parcel values shows that some people do not do their homework before they file an entry for a parcel. For example, WY-5, which was offered in the June 1978 lottery, attracted 19 entries. Yet, this 2,176 acre parcel was considered to be virtually worthless by a leading consulting firm because there was no market interest in this tract. The prior lease holder was a professional oil speculator who was relinquishing his lease rights after holding the lease one year. Obviously he could not sell his lease rights within one year and chose not to throw good money after bad with a second year's lease payment. Nineteen speculators—rank novices—had contrary ideas, or dreams.

On the other hand, sometimes a valuable parcel draws little interest. That is rare, but it happens. A 693-acre parcel in Garfield County, Colorado, with an estimated value of $10,000, attracted only 19 entries from the entire United States. In the New Mexico, August 10, 1978, drawing, Getty Oil Co. won nine leases on which they were the only applicant. They won an additional eight leases on which there were only one to three other applicants. Getty Oil came in second and third place on a few other leases where the number of applicants was few. The winners must have done their homework. They won with virtually no competition, and they won parcels which were sought after by a major oil company. We can safely assume that Getty Oil would be willing to pay more than the $1 per acre overhead paid by the winners. Maybe it is only $1.50 per acre which they will offer. Nevertheless, on, let's say, a 2,558 acre parcel the profit would be $1,279. Not bad for a $15 risk at three to one odds. Also, it is likely that the winners could determine Getty Oil's interest in their leases before committing the $1 lease payments to the BLM.

In Arizona, Idaho, and Oregon, where there are yet to be found any significant deposits of oil and gas, there is relatively little lottery interest. At the other extreme are Montana, New Mexico, Utah, and Wyoming, which, due to their continued oil discoveries, are the most active leasing areas, in both the number of parcels offered and the number of potentially valuable parcels available. In Wyoming, where there is an oil exploration boom, the greatest number of parcels is offered. Of these, a good many are valuable. Consequently, Wyoming draws a higher number of entries than do the other states. The following table provides a rough overview of the odds of winning leases at each of the BLM land offices. The list was compiled from the July 1978 postings and subsequent drawing results lists.

BLM Office	No. of Parcels Offered	Total No. of Entries	Average No. of Entries Filed per Parcel
Arizona	6	40	7
California	10	652	65
Colorado	43	6,886	160
Eastern States	16	5,562	348
Idaho	none	—	—

BLM Office	No. of Parcels Offered	Total No. of Entries	Average No. of Entries Filed per Parcel
Montana	162	21,856	135
Nevada	18	442	25
New Mexico	88	32,609	371
Oregon	none	—	—
Utah	96	24,626	257
Wyoming	205	179,013	873

These statistics are a snapshot of the past and do not necessarily indicate what the spread of odds will be like in the future. Circumstances change. For example, the stepped-up exploration activity in Arizona or Idaho, if fruitful, could bring these states into the speculator's spotlight and thereby greatly vary the odds.

About 200 filing service companies concentrate their efforts on the most lucrative states. Their touting and filing patterns greatly influence the odds of winning in the drawings.

Touting Minimizes Your Chances

Some filing service companies advertise the BLM Lottery in widely circulated newspapers and magazines. Their come-on ads are lucrative and tantalizing. Such publicity efforts are responsible for most of the applications that are filed. Recently, the publicity of the filing services has been mounting resulting in more than quadruple the number of entries filed with the BLM over the last five years. The BLM statistics on the simultaneous oil and gas leasing system made available July 1978 are as follows:

Year	Number of Parcels Offered	Acres	Number of Filings
1973	13,038	13,816,182	600,000
1974	11,292	11,571,162	1.2 million
1975	13,355	14,510,844	1.8 million
1976	9,114	59,547,009	1.9 million
1977	9,000*	10,000,000*	2.5 million*

*Approximate figures

The odds of winning are lengthening. Many of the filing agents act as commissioned lease brokers for winners, and the publicity they generate increases their chances of winning at the cost of minimizing yours. The more clients the agents can get to enter on one lease the better the agents' chances that *one* of their clients will win, resulting in a brokerage commission for the agent. These filing services claim to be acting in the best interest of their clients by helping the clients increase their chances of competing with the major oil firms for lease rights. Just how much help some service firms provide their clients is questionable. It is to a service's self-interest to file many clients on the same parcel. Some service companies permit their staff members to file on the same parcels that they recommend to their clients, thereby directly competing in the lottery with their clients. Also, due to the similarity of the promotional material used by some of the filing service agents I suspect that either some services plagiarized their competitors' material or that some services may be working closely together, perhaps coordinating their filings and splitting risks and profits.

Not all service agents are fast-buck operators. There are some excellent services available. Generally, the greater the list of recommendations offered by the service, the wider your choice will be and the better will be your odds of winning. Nevertheless, because filing services usually recommend only the choice parcels you can expect the odds against you to run up to 10,000 to 1 when using an agent. Because of the commission, it is not worthwhile for an agent to recommend the lesser valued parcels. Why would an agent file several hundred of his clients on a parcel that has a potential value of only $1,000 on which he would gain a commission of about $100, when the agent could file his clients on a $500,000 parcel and gain a potential of $50,000+ in commissions? Many agents have thousands of clients and therefore stand an excellent chance that one of their clients will be a winner. For example, assume that an agent wants to take a crack at a parcel that is estimated to be worth $500,000. Assume that this agent has 2,000 clients he will file on this one parcel. Also assume that this parcel will attract 6,000 additional entries from other sources. The chances that one of this agent's clients will win are 1 in 4 (2,000 in 8,000). The agent has one chance in four of making $50,000 commission for finding a buyer for his winning client's lease. Not bad when you consider that the agent has already collected at least $20,000 in handling fees from his clients. Further, if the agent coordinated his filings with that of other service agents, their collective chances of winning would be excellent. With such favorable odds going for them you can see that the filing agents would not waste their resources on the much lesser valued parcels. Be sure to note that the odds of winning in the example just given are 7,999 to 1 against *each* client—sizeable odds to be bucking in this high-stakes game.

To better understand how the touting of parcels affects your odds of winning please refer to Appendix A. I have selected eight popularly advertised filing agents and have compared their lists of recommendations during the same month for Wyoming. I chose Wyoming for the sampling because these eight agents did not make sufficient numbers of recommendations for other states, from which I could make a comparison. The top three touted parcels were: WY-77, recommended by six of the eight agents, with 6,776 entries; WY-126, recommended by seven of the eight agents, with 6,431 entries; WY-153, recommended by six of the eight agents with 5,144 entries. The average number of filings for these three parcels was 6,117. The average number of filings for the next eight most touted parcels, numbers WY-35, 61, 65, 75, 76, 124, 136 and 185, each recommended by four or five agents, was 3,248. Admittedly, this sample is not statistically conclusive, but it does serve as an indication of a plausible cause and effect relationship between the touting of parcels and the number of respective filings submitted. Looking at related values: WY-77 and WY-126 were each estimated to be worth about $100,000 plus an overriding royalty amounting to an additional $900,000. WY-153, being a smaller tract, had an estimated value of about $50,000 plus an overriding royalty potential of about $500,000. The eight runners-up parcels ranged in estimated value from a low of $50,000 to a high of $100,000, plus an overriding royalty potential which ranged from $500,000 to $1 million for each parcel.

In spite of the long odds you face when using filing services, do not discount their use. If you have *extra* money and would love to keep a few dollars riding on a longshot then you should consider using filing services as part of your overall gaming strategy.

Other Influencing Factors

Thus far we have seen how your odds of winning the BLM lottery vary with parcel size, estimated parcel value, and the touting of parcels by filing service agents. There are other factors which can influence the odds of winning.

Any situation which affects the demand for leases will affect the number of entries that are filed, and your chances of winning. Oil discoveries or dry holes, proposed drillings or abandoned efforts, active acquisitions of open land leases or relinquishing of leases—all these affect the market climate for leases; so does the international political arena especially in regard to OPEC pricing policies and another possible oil embargo. Changes to our mineral leasing policies, environmental issues, and domestic energy pricing policies and practices will also affect the demand for leases. New technology for oil exploration and extraction can turn what was hitherto a goat pasture lease into a potential oil tract. Developments in harnessing alternate energy resources and changes in our nation's energy needs, will translate into varying demands for oil leases. Changes in state business laws and policies and their enforcement may affect the operation of filing service companies. Some filing service companies have already been temporarily suspended from operating in some states. Cease and desist orders can change the filing patterns of large numbers of entries. Another major factor influencing the odds is the number of worthwhile lease parcels the BLM offers during any given month. Sometimes the number of parcels is relatively small for a state, yet the number of people playing may be the same. Hence, the average number of entries per parcel would increase and your chances of winning would decrease.

Your odds of winning will also be influenced by factors that affect your competition. The amount of spendable income that is available to oil-lease speculators will have a bearing upon how many competing applications are filed. Excessive inflation will reduce spending power and reduce the number of dollars that are available for speculation. Likewise, a depressed economy will force many of the novice speculators out of the market as they change their spending priorities. Spending patterns also change with seasons. Most people are short of extra money during the December holidays and therefore would be less prone to speculate on oil leases at that time. The summer months also tend to see fewer filings because most people are too preoccupied with vacationing. A mail strike can prevent a lot of competitive filings from reaching the BLM on time. BLM offices operate on deadlines and may not necessarily adjust their calendars to compensate for a mail strike. Under such circumstances whoever can get their entry cards to the BLM can expect minimal competition. The publication of articles and books on the oil and gas lottery is bound to stimulate interest and reduce the overall chances of winning. (This book alone will not do it. In fact, the knowledge gained from it will improve your odds of winning, more than offsetting the lenghtening of odds caused by the publicity from its publication.) Shifts in the emotions, attitudes, and opinions of oil lease speculators are also bound to affect the number of filings submitted to the BLM. We only need to look at the radically behaving stock markets and money markets to see the influence peoples' emotions have on demand and prices.

Expect the odds to vary month to month. Historic patterns do not necessarily predict future trends. At best they provide the speculator with a "feel" for the marketplace. It is this "feel" which will add to your background knowledge of the oil and gas lottery system and help you to develop a more competitive strategy. Your playing strategy is a major contributing factor to the odds you will be facing; to a great extent you pave your own way.

Odds Are Not the Same for Everyone

Everyone does *not* have an equal chance to win! Take "Alice" and "Jeffrey," for example. Each has the same amount of money to speculate with and both are subscribers to BLM lists and have access to other information sources. In August 1978 Alice sends $20 to a filing service company to play a longshot with projected odds at 4,000 to 1 for a Wyoming parcel valued at $50,000 plus overriding royalties. Jeffrey wants to play a similar high-stakes long-shot, but notices that, compared to past patterns, during the month of August the Wyoming BLM office is offering an unusually small number of parcels. He surmises that the overall number of applicants will probably remain about the same and therefore the average number of applications on each choice parcel will probably increase. So Jeffrey decides to wait for a better month. As it turns out, because of the shortage of parcels, Alice's odds were 9,000 to 1 against her. Jeffrey, who participated the following month when the number of parcels offered were back up to normal, had only about 4,000 to 1 odds against him. Jeffrey's strategy paid off in much better odds.

Alice and Jeffrey are fictional, but the situation is not. In August 1978 I received a report from a filing service which stated, "We put out close to 30 selections each month, depending on the size of the list released by the Bureau of Land Management. This month the BLM released the smallest list we have seen for the last ten years. The twelve parcels we've selected are the best of the list. There were four other parcels that we could have included, but they were not saleable in the near future." From this information we can assume that the number of entries per parcel was likely to increase. That is just what happened. The August 1978 winners list showed that the three parcels most actively filed for had entries of 9,373, 7,501, 5,934 cards respectively. The personalized note that I received from the filing service was much appreciated, and also points out that your choice of service agents can also affect your odds.

Alice and Jeffrey are taking another crack at it. Both are pursuing parcels that are valued at $25,000 each with projected odds of about 3,000 to 1 against them. They each decide to file two entries. Alice selects two parcels and files one entry on each, the maximum allowable per parcel per person. Unlike Alice, Jeffrey is married and therefore sends one entry for himself and one for his wife for the same parcel, taking advantage of the BLM policy which treats husbands and wives as separate persons for the purposes of filing. Hence, Jeffrey's odds of winning are 2 in 3,000 (reduces to 1 in 1,500). Jeffrey is in a better position to win the $25,000. Alice's odds are longer (2 in 6,000) but her potential gain doubled to $50,000; she has one chance going for her on each of two parcels valued at $25,000. To duplicate Jeffrey's odds Alice would need to file on two parcels valued at $12,500 each for which the estimated odds would be 1,500 to 1.

Taking this a step further, Alice, not wanting to be outdone by Jeffrey's multiple filing, decides to organize 10 of her friends. She forms a filing club whereby all club members file on the same parcel. Alice might pay all of the filing fees and lease fees and might act as the club's general manager, essentially renting the use of her friends' names for a kickback of a small percentage of the profits. Or, maybe all club members decide to share expenses and profits equally and give an extra 10 percent of the profits to Alice for her role as the general manager. True friendship will be tested since the lease will be issued in the winner's name. Is this type of filing strategy legal? More important, is it moral? In any event, it is a strategy that the BLM cannot do much about. How can the BLM determine who is filing as a club member? I am not suggesting the organizing of filing clubs. I am reporting on a filing practice that is being used by some persons in order to improve their chances of winning. Decide for yourself if you should do it.

Continuing the example, we see a further development of the "club" concept. Jeffrey gets wind of Alice's club and he decides to carry the club-filing strategy a step further. Jeffrey retains an oil consultant to select choice parcels for him. Then, Jeffrey either publishes the list of choice parcels for a subscription fee, or keeps the list confidential and offers to file applications with the BLM, on "hot" parcels, on behalf of all comers for a filing fee of course. Jeffrey establishes contacts with oil companies and charges his winning clients a commission for selling their leases. Jeffrey has minimized his risk and maximized his chances of winning—a filing service is born.

Alice, not wanting to be outdone, organizes her club into a partnership and also forms a filing service which caters to the general public. Alice and Jeffrey develop several thousand clients each, and then both begin to think how they can apply their force of numbers more competitively against the many other filing service companies. Alice and Jeffrey decide to form a pact; Alice will file her clients on the same parcel that Jeffrey files his clients on. Their collective chances of winning increase, although they have to split the profits. For a better chance at a $100,000 to $500,000 parcel it is worth their collaboration. See the picture? There are many levels of organized attempts to monopolize the winning of oil and gas leases. That is another reason why the odds are not the same for everybody.

Here is another example of how the odds vary between speculators. Alice does some research and finds that there are relatively few entries being filed for the lower-valued parcels in California. She notices that for the July 1978 offering of 10 parcels in California only an average of 65 entries were filed per parcel. This seems low compared with the filing activity in the Rocky Mountain states, especially in light of the fact that California is the nation's third largest oil producer and ranks second in its refinery capacity. In 1977, California had 43,361 producing oil wells in 234 active oil fields. California also is credited with having the greatest gusher of them all, the famed "Lakeview gusher," which blew in March 1910 and flowed out of control for 18 months, spewing 8.2 million barrels of oil before it stopped. Further, unlike those of the midwestern states, California's stringent securities laws restrict the operations of filing services. Also, the few parcels being offered keeps the filing agents away and in more lucrative fields. Alice makes the most of these circumstances by filing for one of the California parcels, while Jef-

The famed Lakeview gusher, March 1910.
AMERICAN PETROLEUM INSTITUTE

frey files on an equally valued parcel, but in Utah. Jeffrey does not realize that the oil and gas lottery is popular among the residents of Utah and that therefore his entry will meet with stiffer competition; several hundred to one odds against him.

Where you play, who you play against, when you play, and how you play all have an effect on your odds in relationship to others' odds. Since the odds can be altered by your playing strategy, I maintain that the odds of winning do not stack up the same for everyone. You might argue that two people who file for the same parcel would most certainly have the same chances of winning. I disagree. If both persons had the same chances of winning there would be the possibility of having two first-place winners, but there are not. There must be some deciding factor that chooses one person the winner as opposed to another. What decides a winner? Is it strictly a game of research, strategy and statistical odds? Is there an additional influencing factor that transcends the mathematics of speculation?

Lady Luck

I was on a skiing vacation at California's Squaw Valley when my friend David suggested we go try our hand at the gaming tables down at Lake Tahoe. I was reluctant to go at first since I wasn't much for gambling. Except for dabbling on Wall Street—the other Las Vegas—I have never played at the gambling casinos. But, rationalizations and the thoughts of the glamor of it all eased my resistance and I agreed to go. Next day we made the rounds of the casinos. My initial reaction was fascination, much like an out-of-towner's first visit to New York City's Times Square. That feeling quickly passed as my gambling impulses surfaced and began taking hold. We perambulated into Harrah's Club where I stopped to watch a roulette game for a while, then sat down to take care of some "personal business." Purchasing a couple of stacks of 25-cent chips, I decided to gamble on the show of color, black or red depending how I felt. I started my bet with one chip and doubled my bet each time I lost, keeping a wary eye on the "O" and "OO" when my losing streak mounted. Fortunately, I never got wiped out badly and, on balance, after a couple of hours, I had about $100 in winnings in front of me.

The board was being played actively with many people crowding around. As we played I noticed a well-dressed, heavy-set man, wearing thick glasses and a restrained obsessive look, edge in to the table. He observed the game for a while taking extensive notes after each play. I stretched a nonchalant look over his shoulder and caught a glimpse of some complicated formulas jotted in the upper border of his notebook. After notating a few plays he took out a slide rule, slipped through a half-dozen or so quick calculations, then impulsively proceeded to polka dot the board with chips, covering nearly every possible bet. He bet like this for five consecutive plays and lost every time. He had lots of style and action and most of the numbers going for him—yet, no win! In face of the conspicuous glances he received from his gaming peers, who looked at him as some kind of weirdo, he became flustered and made a hasty exit.

No sooner than the air had settled after his absence I was attracted to some boisterous commotion at the bar behind me. A casually dressed young man had just staggered off from his stool and was attempting to make his way towards our table. He was obviously smashed, as he was being half-carried by two "flashy numbers." He was laughing and babbling nonsensical sentences as he made a concerted effort not to spill the drink he carried. Reaching the roulette table, he teeter-tottered while fumbling through a bankroll to buy a couple of the red, five-dollar chips. The wheel of fortune was spun, and he plowed his clenched fist guarding one of the reds past a couple of players, and just in the nick of time slapped his bet on the green "OO" before the croupier tossed the ivory ball into the spin. The ball took a final bounce. A direct hit! His near "two-bill" win stirred a bit of excitement—mostly his own—and he bet again on the "OO" for the next spin. Another win! He gulped down some more of his drink exchanging some excitement-born exclamations with his lady friends. Again he bet, but with an increased ante. This time most of the other players figured this kid to be a natural, and they decided to ride with a winner. The "OO" was stacked high with chips. Another win! Three in a row! A fourth bet on "OO" by the winner drew a still heavier response of accompanying bets, but this time the number 9 won. The short-lived winning streak, which netted a fast cool grand or so to the lad, was over. Fumbling, the kid scraped up his winnings and with his two supporters, staggered back to the bar for a refueling.

Reflecting upon this sequence of events I began to look at games of chance more philosophically. What explains the long-shot winning streak and the equally unusual losing streak? Can it be understood in terms of one's frame of mind, karma, biorhythms, numerology, stellar or planetary influences? Are some people natural winners to whom winnings are attracted? Is it just luck? Does luck follow mathematically defined parameters, or is luck a principle unto itself? Is there a Lady Luck who rules the game of chance? Does she have the latitude, within the limitations of long-term statistical averages, to dole out different odds for each player? What explains the chronic losers and the winning streaks of the lucky winners? What games does Lady Luck play with us behind the scene? Who is she favoring, and why?

I was fascinated with my analysis of the monthly BLM winners lists. I noticed that there were a few family names which repeatedly won, and they were winning against very long odds. Either these people had to be filing numerous entry cards, or they were just plain lucky. Most likely, both are true; they file on many parcels each month and are lucky enough to win often. Thumb back a few pages to the abridged listing for the June 1978

Wyoming lease offerings. See how many multiple winners there are? I have recapped them below:

Winner's Name and Address	BLM No.	Acreage	No. of Entries	Estimated Value
(1) Greg Panos Salt Lake City, UT	WY-64	2,545.40	3,260	$92,000 plus $935,000 ORR
Geoff Panos Salt Lake City, UT	WY-159	627.59	1,212	$10,000
(2) Elizabeth Connell Denver, CO	WY-63	1,520	4,292	$73,000 plus $540,000 ORR
Robert L. Connell Denver, CO	WY-29	38.45	71	$ 500
Robert L. Connell Denver, CO	WY-184	320	762	$ 8,000
(3) John J. Puhl Portland, OR	WY-10	280	35	$ 750
John J. Puhl Portland, OR	WY-17	440	90	$ 1,500
(4) Marilyn J. Cone Lubbock, TX	WY-25	320	233	$ 3,000
Marilyn J. Cone Lubbock, TX	WY-87	40	87	$ 1,000
(5) Bruce A. Blakemore, Tr. Midland, TX	WY-81	200	82	$ 1,000
B. A. Blakemore, Tr.	WY-100	278.14	254	$ 6,000

Some of the people listed above won additional parcels in Wyoming as well as in other states. What are the odds of the Panoses both winning? What are the odds of the Connell's three wins? Perhaps these pros file cards on several hundred parcels each month in order to keep the statistical odds in their favor. How many thousands of applications by other speculators were in vain? How many big winners filed but one entry?

Can we improve our chances of winning? Can we lure Lady Luck through statistical strategic gaming? The odds of winning in the oil and gas lease lottery result from the combined interplay of statistics, strategy, and luck. In the next section I shall provide you with some additional guidelines which will help to statistically and strategically improve your odds of winning. But don't forget, *improving* the odds is the best we can do. Unpredictable chance holds the trump cards for all the games of chance. In the final analysis, even after you have studied this book, done your homework, developed your strategy, and improved your odds of winning, crossed your fingers, and filed your entry cards, when all is said and done, it is Lady Luck who turns the drum, churns the cards, and guides the hand that draws the winner.

Investment, Entertainment, or Gamble?

Is participating in the U.S. government's oil and gas lottery a gamble or a business investment? Personally, I do not see the lottery as an investment per se; it is a speculation at best, which could be a lot of fun if you approach it as a hobby. But, if played impulsively or carefree, shooting from the hip without much research, or, if played through a filing service company where the odds are stacked against you, then it is most certainly a gamble, and a long-shot one at that. In any event, the oil and gas lease lottery is not the type of gamble whereby the winners walk off with other peoples' money, less the house stakes. The $10 paid to the Bureau of Land Management is a filing fee for processing your entry. The filing fees are not pooled to pay off lottery winners. The winners win the right to lease parcels of land which, if potentially valuable, will be purchased by oil companies. Hence, winnings are payments made by the oil companies and not monies staked by other players, as is the case in state-run lotteries, race tracks, stock markets, or gambling casinos. This is an important distinction for moralists to consider.

The lottery system as used by the BLM was devised in order to provide all U.S. citizens equal access to our country's natural oil and gas resources. Traditionally, random lottery selection has been considered to be the fairest means of choosing among persons, as in the selection of persons for jury duty or the military draft. Nevertheless, under closer analysis the oil and gas lottery system has elements of gambling in it. There is a high degree of chance, money is being risked, and there is the ever-present temptation to participate in the lottery with increasing fever, and perhaps beyond one's financial means. If you feel that these elements of chance, risk, and temptation conflict with your personal convictions, then by all means don't compromise—don't participate. Also, if you are the type of person who would play the lottery impulsively like a scatter-brained gambler who sows his chips as if he were seeding a new lawn, then you should not be playing at all. This book was not written to give gamblers an alternative to the race tracks or casinos, but to reduce the emphasis on the gaming aspect of participating in the oil and gas lottery in order to bring participation into the realm of an investment, or at least down to a relatively low-risk speculation.

What the oil and gas lease lottery will be to you is what you make of it. It could be a speculative investment, an entertaining hobby, or an outright gamble. You can take a strategic business approach to this game or play it like a crapshoot. I trust that after you have studied this book you will lean towards using a prudent business approach when participating in the oil and gas lottery.

6
Oil and Gas Geology for Beginners

Your orientation to the Oil and Gas Leasing System would not be complete without an overview of where oil comes from and how it accumulates in subterranean pools. You should have a good general understanding of these topics, for which this thumbnail sketch will suffice. You do not have to become a geologist in order to effectively participate in the oil lottery. Frankly, anyone who can sign their name to the BLM entry card can participate. It's as simple as that. But, since our purpose is to improve the odds of winning I have included some basic information on petroleum geology which will broaden your perspective and help you to develop that subtle "feeling" for selecting parcels.

Oil and Gas Origin and Accumulation

The Earth's Crust. The outer zone of the earth, known as the earth's crust, is the zone on which we live and the part that we know best. Most of what we know about the earth we have learned from the materials of which the crust is composed. It is in the shallower depths of this outer zone (from the surface to about 30,000 feet) that oil and gas have been found.

The age of the earth, based on several methods, particularly the known rate of breakdown of radioactive materials found in the crust, is estimated to be almost five billion years. Throughout much of this vast span of time the earth's crust has been undergoing continual change. Forces within the earth have caused parts of the crust to be uplifted or lowered, and folded or buckled into high mountains and deep troughs. Always, the external forces of our planet, such as the wind, water, and extreme variances of temperature, are at work wearing away all land areas above the sea. While high mountains in one region were being eroded to flat plains, the lowlands in other areas were being elevated into highlands. Thus, portions of the earth's crust have repeatedly been raised to great heights, and then worn away. Many of our present-day mountains occur in areas that have been occupied by the sea innumerable times, accounting for the multitude of sea shells that may be found in the clays and sands on the tops of these high mountains. In time, these mountains also will be worn away through the slow process of erosion, and the eroded material transported back to the sea, forming new deposits. In this manner the surface of the earth has undergone continual change in the past, just as it is undergoing these same processes at the present time. Most of North America has been submerged many times beneath the waters of ancient seas—not all at once, but parts of it at one time and parts at another. Even the area now occupied by the great Rocky Mountains was once an ancient sea floor.

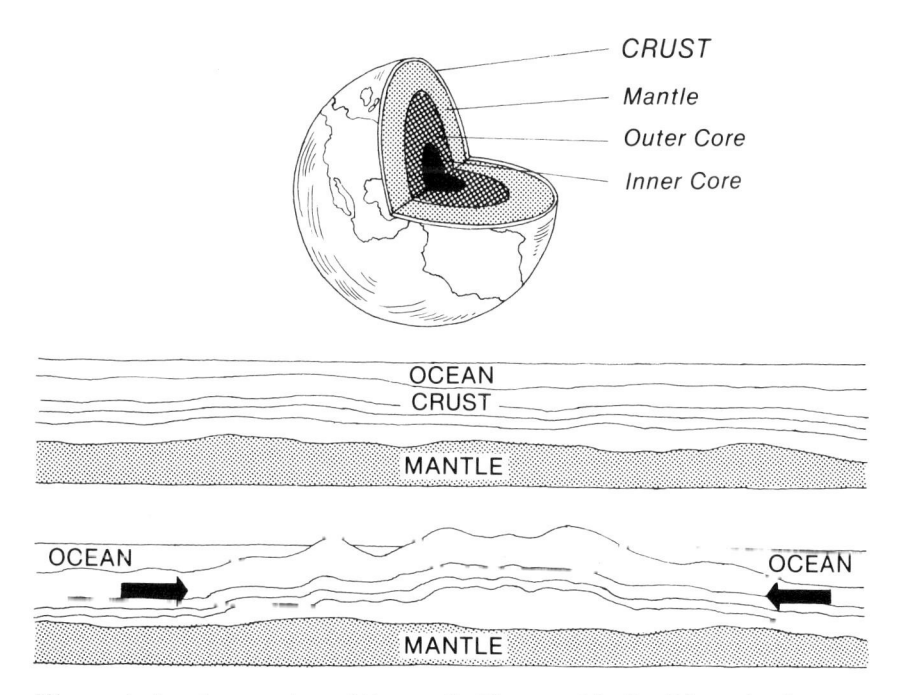

Figure 1. A cutaway view of the earth. The crust is the thin outer layer on which we live. The lower diagram shows how compressive forces (represented by arrows) cause folding and uplift of the crustal layer.
CALIFORNIA DIVISION OF OIL AND GAS

These changes in the earth's surface occur so slowly that they are scarcely noticeable during the lifetime of an individual. However, over a period of hundreds of millions of years, this cycle of uplift and leveling may be repeated over and over again.

Sources of Oil and Gas. During the time that parts of the continents are under the sea, not only are new sediments being deposited layer upon layer until they may reach thousands of feet in thickness, but the remains of the myriad plant and animal life that live in the sea are buried in the layers of mud and sand. These plant and animal remains, especially those of the tiny sea plants such as diatoms and algae, are thought to be the most probable source materials from which oil is formed. It is believed that some time after these remains collect in the muds, parts of them are converted into minute oil droplets. The exact process by which this organic material is converted into oil is not known, but it is believed that bacteria, heat, age, and pressure all play an important part.

Both oil and gas are naturally occurring mixtures of predominately hydrogen and carbon compounds. Oil in its primary state in the earth often contains a large volume of gas, thus at the same time the organic matter was converted into oil, natural gas may also have been formed; or, the gas may have been formed at a later date by chemical changes in the oil. However, natural gas can be formed from sources other than those from which oil is derived, as occurs when gas is formed in peat swamps or in coal fields. Therefore gas often occurs by itself, not associated with oil.

Migration and Accumulation. Owing to the steady addition of sediments to the sea floor, as the floor gradually sinks, the layers of mud and sand become deeply buried. With the continual increase in overlying weight, compaction gradually hardens the deeply buried layers of sediments. The mud or clay becomes shale upon hardening, and the sand becomes sandstone. Depending upon composition and degree of compaction many gradations of shale may result, such as sandy shales or silty shales, or claystones, all of which may be grouped under the general heading of shale. Sands and sandstones also may show many gradations; there may be shaly sands or silty sands, or sands so cemented that they are hard as concrete. Shales and sandstones are known as sedimentary rocks. The layers of shale or sandstone are called beds or strata.

Both shales and sandstones are composed of particles with

Figure 2. The beginning of the cycle of petroleum. Prehistoric seas flourished with plant and animal life in warm, shallow lagoons. CALIFORNIA DIVISION OF OIL AND GAS

Figure 3. With the passage of millions of years, the dead organic matter becomes buried under successive layers of mud which eventually hardens. CALIFORNIA DIVISION OF OIL AND GAS

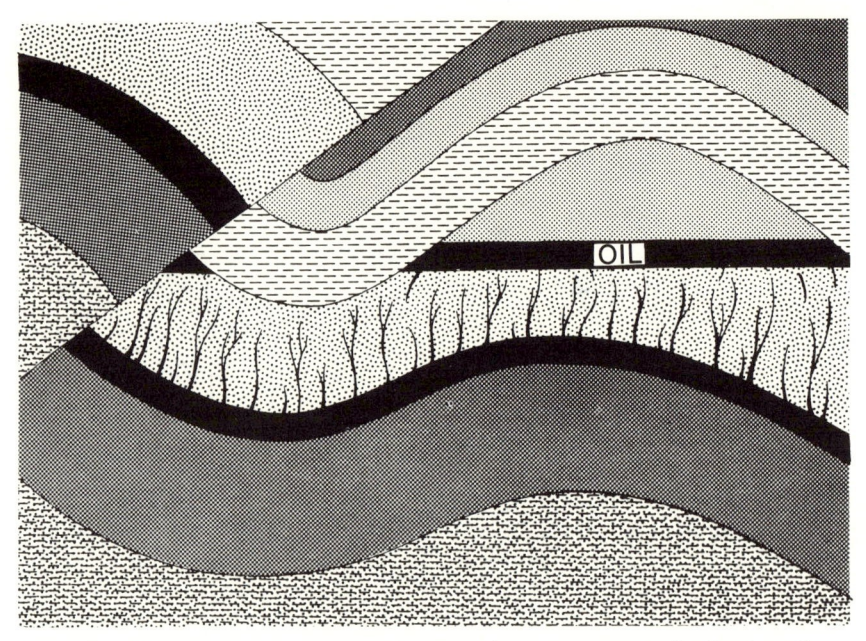

Figure 4. The formation of petroleum and gas occurs under heat and pressure as folding of the layers progresses. The hydrocarbons migrate upward into a sandstone layer where they become trapped by the overlying impervious rock. CALIFORNIA DIVISION OF OIL AND GAS

open spaces between the particles. In the sandstone or shale deep down in the earth, these openings, called pore spaces, are occupied by gas, oil, or water, or a combination of all three. Of course, water is much more common. In a sandstone the open spaces may account for 30 percent or more of the total volume, while in some types of sedimentary rocks the open spaces may be only a few percent of the total volume. Any rock with open spaces is porous and is said to have porosity.

When a mud has been compacted into shale, the pore spaces are not interconnected; therefore, the fluid in the rock is trapped in the individual pore spaces. In a sandstone these pore spaces are usually interconnected so that liquid or gas is free to move in any direction from one pore space to another. When the pore spaces are interconnected, the rock is said to be permeable, or to have permeability.

The compaction of the muds causes some of the fluid present—either water, or oil droplets that may have been formed in the muds—to be squeezed out into the sands where more pore spaces are available. Undoubtedly, other forces also play a part in moving the oil droplets from the muds into the sands, but compaction is considered the most important factor.

After the oil droplets have moved into the pore spaces in the sands or sandstone, they still do not constitute an oil accumulation because they are so widely dispersed in the water. To constitute an oil accumulation, the droplets must be quite concentrated so that oil occupies a significant portion of each pore space in the sand.

The movement of oil droplets through pore spaces is called migration, and is necessary if there is to be an accumulation. The exact manner in which these oil droplets become concentrated is not known, but it is believed that the accumulation is brought about by some combination of the following forces and actions:

(1) *Gravity.* Oil, being lighter than water, will rise through the water until some obstruction is encountered, prohibiting additional upward progress. The oil may move a considerable distance laterally at the same time it is moving upward.

(2) *Water currents.* Movement of the water in the sands may flush the oil along for considerable distances.

(3) *Crustal movements.* Bending and folding of the beds undoubtedly play an important part in the migration of oil. Tilting of strata that have been lying relatively flat accelerates the separation of oil and water, concentrating the oil in the highest accessible place.

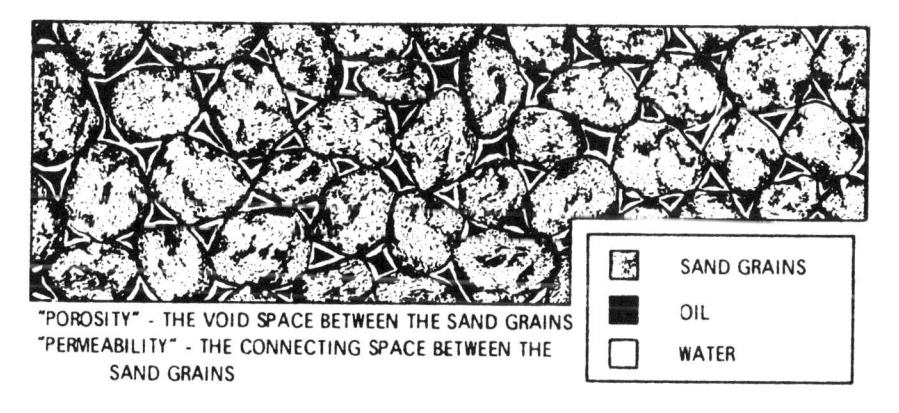

Figure 5. A sandstone containing oil and magnified about 20 times.
CALIFORNIA DIVISION OF OIL AND GAS

In summary, oil pools are formed when the proper combination of conditions is present. There must be *source beds* containing material from which oil can be formed. There must be a bed of *porous rock* with interconnecting pore spaces to serve as a reservoir rock. There must be an *impervious bed* above the reservoir rock to confine the oil to the reservoir rock. The beds must be formed into a *trap* so that oil can collect and be retained in the reservoir rock.

Oil and Gas Traps

When forces within the earth upraise segments of the earth's crust, they may uplift them either a small amount or sufficiently to form high mountains. Therefore, there are oil fields not only at the more moderate elevations but also in the shallow depths of the ocean and on high mountains.

At the same time these segments of the earth's crust are upraised, they may also be folded and buckled. Thus, the beds of sandstone and shale that were once the flat sea floor may become highlands of buckled and folded strata during these periods of crustal movement. As a result, these once-flat beds may now form long folds, called anticlines, or they may form any number of other features that could serve to trap oil.

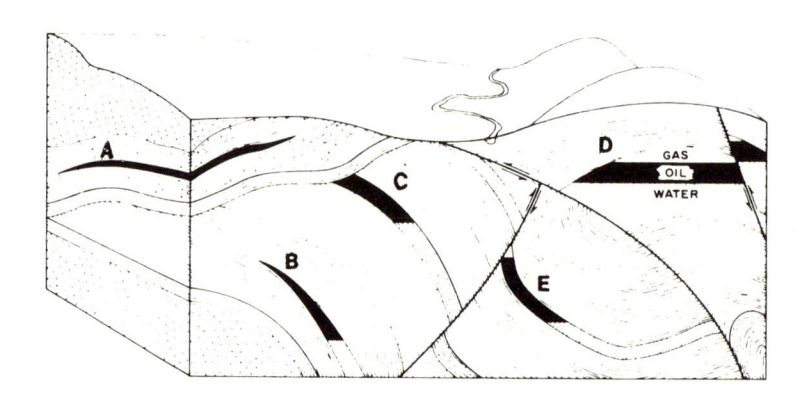

Figure 6. A cross section of the earth showing types of oil and gas traps. A, B, and C are structural-stratigraphic traps; D and E are structural traps. CALIFORNIA DIVISION OF OIL AND GAS

OIL AND GAS GEOLOGY FOR BEGINNERS 73

Anticlines. Of the many types of structural features present in the upper layers of the earth's crust that serve to trap oil, the most important is the anticline—the type of structure from which the greater part of the world's oil has been produced.

Anticlines are long, relatively narrow upfolds of beds in the earth's crust; and, when the proper conditions are present, oil accumulates within the closure of these folds.

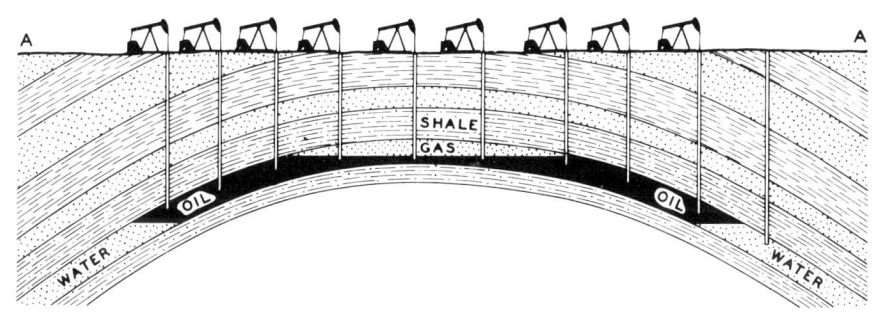

Figure 7. Longitudinal view of a typical anticline. The oil cannot escape upward because of the impervious shale bed above the oil sand; neither can it travel downward because of the water which is always associated with an accumulation of this type. CALIFORNIA DIVISION OF OIL AND GAS

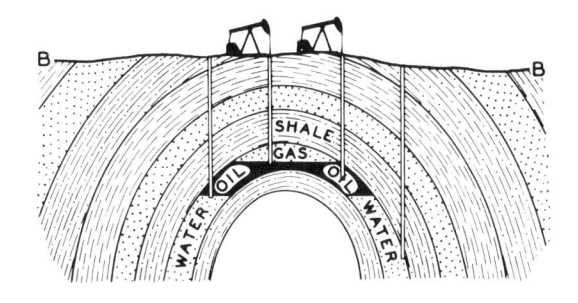

Figure 8. Left: *Lateral or end view of a typical anticline.* CALIFORNIA DIVISION OF OIL AND GAS

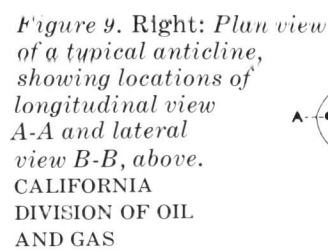

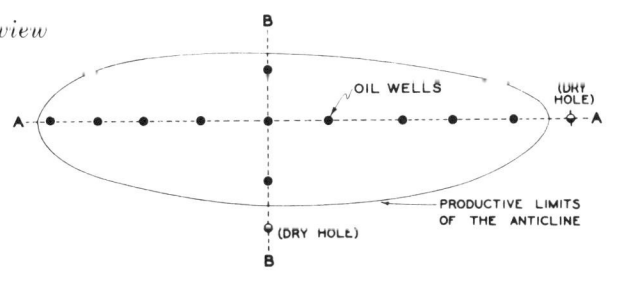

Figure 9. Right: *Plan view of a typical anticline, showing locations of longitudinal view A-A and lateral view B-B, above.* CALIFORNIA DIVISION OF OIL AND GAS

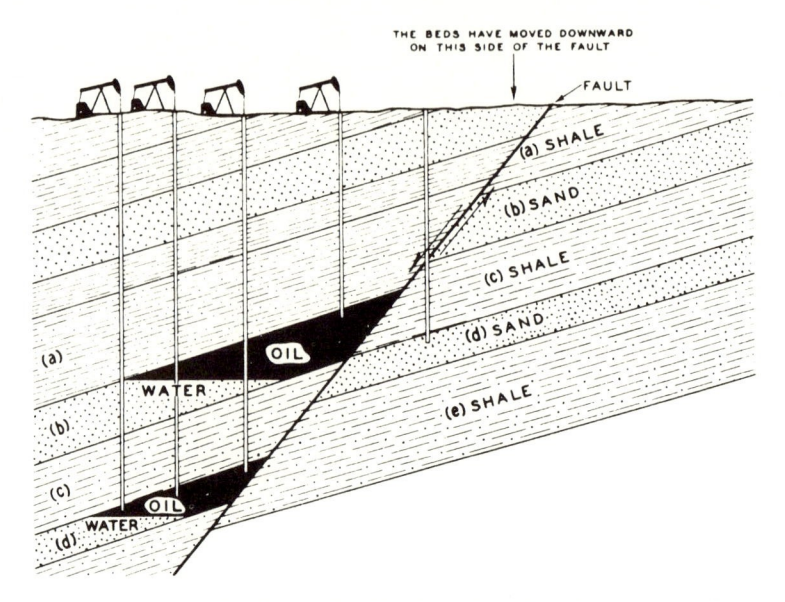

Figure 10. An example of an oil field where faulting has caused the entrapment of oil. Note that the beds opposite the oil zones are impervious. CALIFORNIA DIVISION OF OIL AND GAS

Faults. A break resulting in a displacement in the crust of the earth is called a fault. Often the movement along a fault places a shale bed opposite a sandstone bed, sealing off the sandstone bed. At other times the gouge in the fault zone forms a seal. (Gouge is the broken, crushed materials formed by the movement of the rocks against one another along the fault.) In such instances oil may travel up the sandstone bed until it reaches the fault and then can go no farther. This type of structural feature which serves to trap oil is called a fault trap.

Stratigraphic Traps. Sediments are deposited under such widely diverse conditions that many of the resulting beds vary greatly in thickness, texture, and pore space. These variations of deposition often result in beds that are suitable for trapping oil. In instances where this occurs, the beds are said to form a stratigraphic trap.

For example, a sand bed that was laid down as a beach or nearshore deposit may pinch out between converging shale beds. When these beds are inclined, the sandstone bed provides a suitable oil reservoir.

Changes in sedimentation may cause part of a sandstone bed to become very silty or tightly cemented, sealing the connected

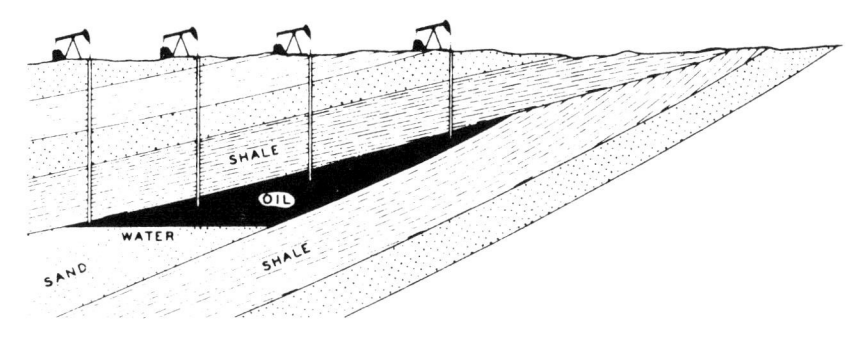

Figure 11. An example of a stratigraphic trap in which the oil zone pinches out. CALIFORNIA DIVISION OF OIL AND GAS

pore spaces and thereby reducing the permeability in that part of the bed. When such a bed is inclined, the oil is trapped by the impermeable part of the bed and is thus prevented from migrating farther up the incline. This type of stratigraphic seal is often referred to as a permeability barrier.

A third type of stratigraphic trap occurs when sand is deposited as an extensive lenslike shape surrounded by clay. In this type of trap there often is very little, if any, water present with the oil and gas in the sand.

Another important type of stratigraphic trap is formed as the result of the angular unconformity which occurs when beds dip-

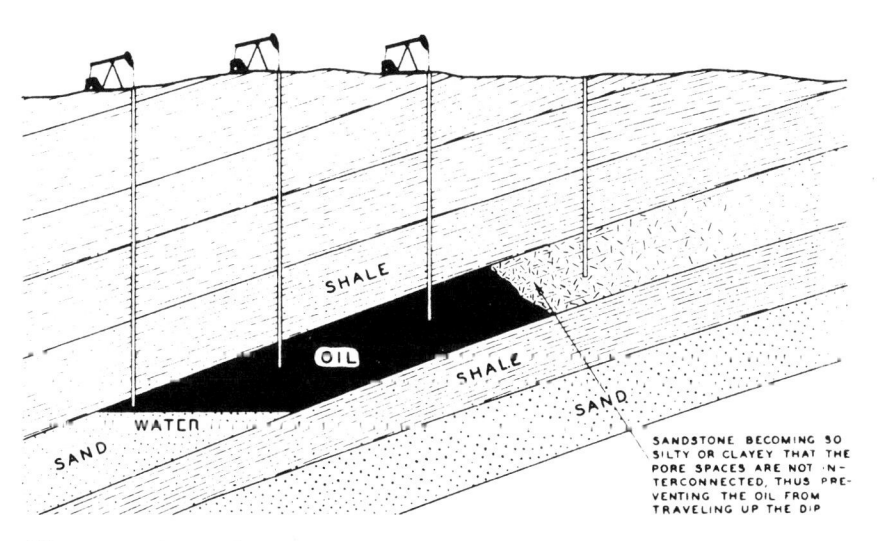

Figure 12. A stratigraphic trap where changes in sedimentation act as a permeability barrier. CALIFORNIA DIVISION OF OIL AND GAS

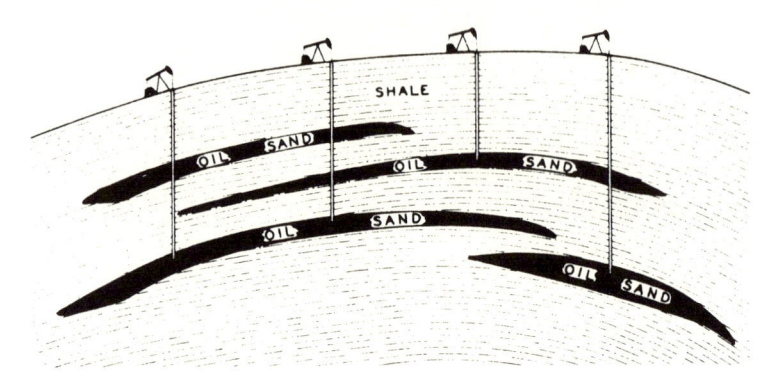

Figure 13. A stratigraphic trap where sand lenses are interspersed in a shale bed. The shale acts as a permeability barrier. CALIFORNIA DIVISION OF OIL AND GAS

ping at one angle are overlain by beds dipping at a different angle. As an example, beds that dip steeply may be overlain by flat lying beds. The horizontal beds thus effectively form a seal for the oil or gas present in the steeply dipping beds. This kind of unconformity forms the trap for many oil accumulations.

Many of the oil fields in the United States consist of not one but several individual oil pools. For example, the Midway-Sunset

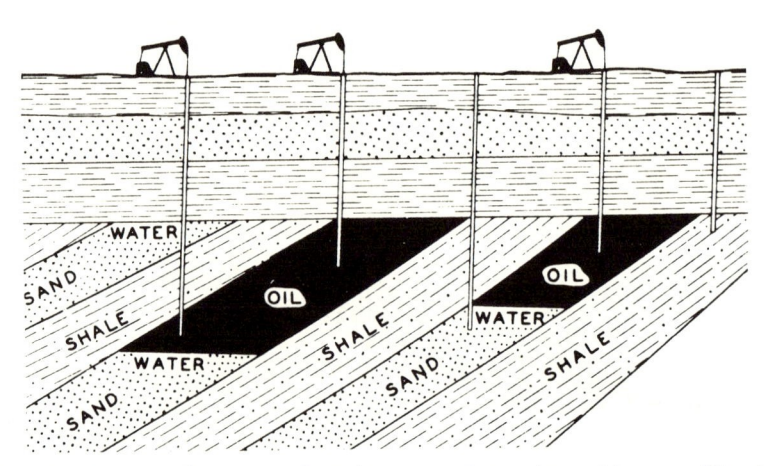

Figure 14. An angular unconformity *type of stratigraphic trap. The flat-lying shale bed above the oil zones acts as a permeability barrier.* CALIFORNIA DIVISION OF OIL AND GAS

field in Kern County, California, is made up of a large number of individual oil accumulations collected in each type of trap described.

More detailed information is contained in a 67-page book, *An Introduction to the Energy Resources of California*, published by the California Division of Oil and Gas, (1416 9th Street, Room 1316, Sacramento, California 95814). For a more comprehensive perspective of the oil industry, to include information on exploration, drilling, production, refining, transportation, environmental factors, and so on, I suggest you order a copy of this reference; it is free for the asking, and the order reference number is TR03. For the more serious oil lease speculator there is an additional reference worth having, *Manual No. AM09—Principles of Stratigraphic Nomenclature*, also free and available from the California Division of Oil and Gas. Although these references focus on the California oil industry, they nevertheless cover oil industry basics common to any locale and I recommend that you include them in your reference library.

By now you should have a thorough understanding of the U.S. government simultaneous oil and gas leasing system. Let us proceed to the most exciting part of this enterprise: choosing a parcel.

Part II
Choosing a Parcel

7
Where's the Action?

Well Begun Is Half Done

The most difficult task confronting the oil and gas lease speculator is choosing a parcel. Considering that we are attempting to locate a few acres of potentially oil-valuable (and marketable) land out of the 755.4 million acres that are in federal ownership, our task seems formidable. And the more we personally get involved with the search, the more formidable it is. To accomplish our task we can proceed in one of two ways; we can do the research ourselves or we can hire a professional to select the parcels for us. Choosing to do the research yourself will involve many hours of study and there will be cost outlays for maps, lists, reports, geological surveys, etc. However, being self-sufficient has decisive advantages we should not overlook. Hiring someone else for advice on parcel selections will save the time and energy of doing research, but there will be the additional cost of paying the professional for his services. Further, relying on someone else's recommendations has disadvantages which we will soon discover.

This section analyzes the two methods of selecting parcels, the advantages and disadvantages of each method and the pitfalls to avoid. By the time you finish this section you will have the knowledge to participate confidently in the oil and gas lottery game. Also, whichever method you use, you will learn some strategies that will improve your odds of winning. However, before we zero in on a parcel we will first take a general perspective by identifying the broad areas of the United States, under Bureau of Land Management administration, where oil and gas is known to exist and where future oil and gas provinces are likely to be found. Our study effort will formulate where, and to a great extent how well, we will play the lottery. A good broad foundation will pay off in dividends for you later when you select parcels. "Well begun is half done."

Identifying Prospective Areas

Look at the "All Lands" columns in Appendix B. Can you identify the principle oil- and gas-producing states? These are the provinces of the known geological structures. States with no oil or gas production were excluded from the list. The rule of thumb for parcel selection is its proximity to producing fields. You would have a better chance of marketing a lease adjacent to a major oil field in Wyoming than if you had a lease on, say, a parcel in Idaho. The fact that a state is high in oil or gas production does not really help us much since the only lands that become available to us under the lottery system are lands under federal ownership classified as public domain. So let's look at the oil and gas production from the public lands.

Carefully peruse the production figures in the "Public Land Only" columns of Appendix B and compare them with the production figures for each of the respective states in the "All Lands" columns. Notice how Texas, which ranks as the nation's top producer of oil and gas, has no production from public lands. Within what other states is public land unproductive? From our analysis thus far, we can see that only the following 18 states have public lands with proven oil and gas production:

Alabama	Alaska	Arizona	Arkansas
California	Colorado	Kansas	Louisiana
Mississippi	Montana	Nebraska	Nevada
New Mexico	North Dakota	Oklahoma	South Dakota
Utah	Wyoming		

The producing states without oil or gas production on the public lands should not be totally discounted from our consideration. That there has been no recent production on these public lands does not preclude there being production in the future. The 14 oil and gas producing states where there is no oil or gas production on the public lands are:

Florida	Illinois	Indiana	Kentucky
Maryland	Michigan	Missouri	New York
Ohio	Pennsylvania	Tennessee	Texas
Virginia	West Virginia		

Thus far we have identified two preliminary lists of public lands from which to prospect. But, we must analyze further. We should consider under what jurisdiction the public lands are; i.e., is the land under the jurisdiction of the Bureau of Indian Affairs, National Park Service, Bureau of Land Management, etc.? Only those public lands that are under the administration of the Bureau of Land Management can be offered by the BLM in its lottery. Hence, as a general rule, we can eliminate from our lists those states where there is no public land under BLM administration. To determine which states have public lands under the administration of the BLM please turn to Appendix C. Review this table thoroughly. States with federal ownership of land but no oil or gas production were not included in the table. For each state take note of the acreage and respective percentage which is under BLM administration. Which states on our lists can we eliminate? Illinois, Indiana, Kentucky, Maryland, Missouri, New York, Ohio, Pennsylvania, Tennessee, Texas, Virginia, and West Virginia currently have no acreage under BLM administration. Unless some acreage is offered by the BLM on behalf of other agencies, it is reasonable to assume that there will not be any lands offered in these states. On occasion the BLM does administer oil and gas leases for other agencies. The frequency and the amount of acreage offered, however, is too minimal to warrant much consideration. Hence, for current consideration our second list is reduced to two prospective states: Florida and Michigan.

Now, still referring to Appendix C, notice which states have so few acres under BLM administration that offerings of land, if any, would be incidental. The states are Alabama, Arkansas, Florida, Kansas, Louisiana, Michigan, Mississippi, Nebraska, and Oklahoma. On occasion I have noticed lucrative parcels offered in these states. But such offerings are few and far between, and when they are made, they usually attract a lot of lease applications. Further, the large research base that would need to be maintained to establish a state of readiness to evaluate and file for the few and infrequent offerings of leases in these states makes it impractical for the novice speculator to consider. Therefore, I have also excluded these states from further consideration.

States in which there is a large production of oil and gas on public lands and where there is a large number of acres under BLM management are the most likely areas where relatively many offerings of leases can be expected. Can you identify these states? There are several exceptions. I wrote to each BLM Office of Supervisory Jurisdiction to get a better handle on where the action is. The Alaska BLM office replied that it has been some time since monthly simultaneous oil and gas filings have been accepted by their office, and that due to the unsettled condition of land status in Alaska, no lease offerings are scheduled in the future. Land status is still pending and under study by the government pursuant to the Alaska Statehood Act of 1958, and the Alaska Native Claims Settlement Act of 1971. Therefore, we can delete Alaska from our list.

The BLM office in Oregon, which has jurisdiction over public lands in Oregon and Washington, stated that some interest has been shown in oil and gas exploration, particularly in the western, central, and southeastern areas of Oregon. The state of Washington, encompassing 42,693,760 acres, has 12,570,384 acres under federal ownership, of which 273,505 acres are administered by the BLM. Oregon, with 61,598,720 acres, has 32,179,932 acres under federal ownership, of which 15,669,216 are administered by the BLM.

The BLM office in Idaho indicated that their office has received a "substantial increase" in wildcat filings for new lease applications since 1971. Idaho, with a total land area of 52,933,120 acres, has 33,848,735 acres under federal ownership, of which 12,132,718 acres are administered by the BLM. Although none of these states has produced any commercial oil or gas, the increased exploration interest in these states and the large number of acres that are under BLM administration prompts me to add Oregon, Washington, and Idaho to our prospective list.

To recapitulate: From our analysis we derive two lists of states as most likely areas of oil and gas lease speculation under the simultaneous filing system. First, the states in which public lands have proven oil and/or gas production: Arizona, California, Colorado, Montana, Nevada, New Mexico, North Dakota, South Dakota, Utah, and Wyoming (Arizona and South Dakota have relatively little oil/gas production on public land). Next, the states without oil or gas production on public lands: Idaho, Oregon, and Washington.

Narrowing the Search

There is one reference that every oil-lease speculator should read: *Future Petroleum Provinces of the United States*, prepared by the National Petroleum Council's Committee on Possible Future Petroleum Provinces of the United States. Although this 138-page summary report is 10 years old, it is still the most comprehensive summarized assessment of the possibilities for further crude oil and natural gas discoveries throughout the United States available to date. One hundred and forty-one geologists participated in the study which included both land areas believed to have negligible or no potential and areas known or generally believed to have definite potential. The report language is technical yet easily read and understood by the layman. Numerous tables and geological maps are used throughout the work. It is available from the National Petroleum Council, 1625 K Street N.W., Washington, D.C. 20006, for $5. Address your order to the director of information.

I have taken the liberty of summarizing and, on occasion, of reproducing verbatim some of the salient findings of the study, including remarks for only those states which appear on our two prospective lists.

Look at figure 15. Get an idea of where the current oil and gas fields are. Locate the 13 states from our two select lists on this map. Notice the distribution of the producing areas across these states. Now study figure 16. What are the most favorable prospective oil and gas areas? Locate the 13 states on this map. Notice which states have the most favorable prospective areas and the location of these prospective areas in each state. The NPCC's summary report stated that the "basinal" areas are and are likely to continue to be the sites of the major oil- and gas-producing areas. The prospective onshore basinal areas of the United States cover approximately 1.8 million square miles.

In addition, the report stated that bordering parts of the basinal areas are large structurally complex areas of thick sedimentary rocks which are also considered to be prospective oil- and gas-producing areas but are of secondary importance. The report concluded that most of the United States remains largely unexplored. Extensions to old fields and discovery of new fields at both conventional and greater depths are forecast for all regions. The giant oil fields of Fairway in East Texas and the Black Lake in northern Louisiana (where there was an ultimate recovery of more than 100 million barrels) were found in recent years in intensively explored areas. They serve as reminders of the extent to which the productive area has not been depleted. Moreover, the report stated that many high-potential areas are indicated by the geology and extent of exploration in parts of California,

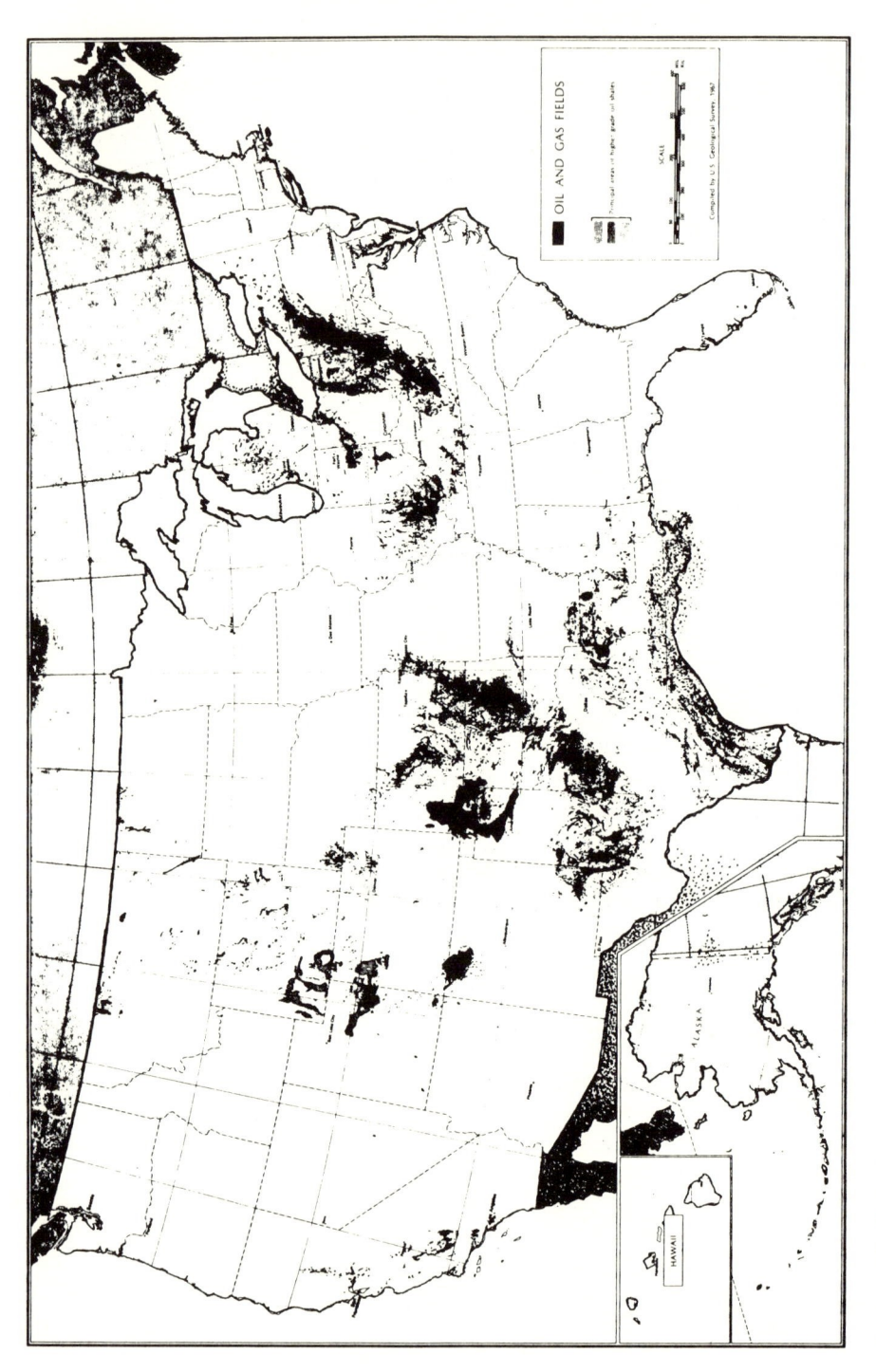

Figure 15. Petroleum producing areas of conterminous United States. U.S. GEOLOGICAL SURVEY

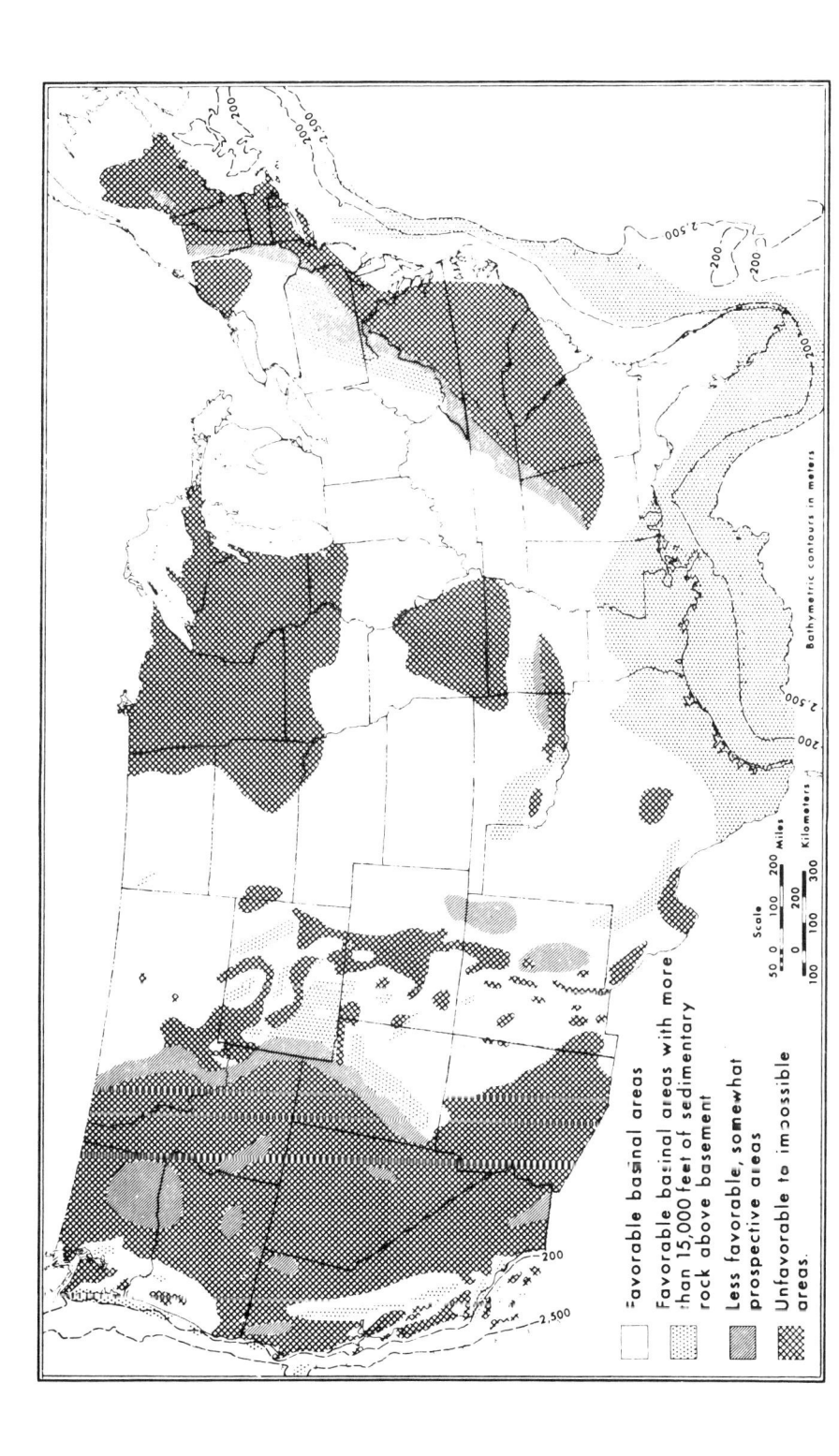

Figure 16. Prospective areas of conterminous United States. U.S. GEOLOGICAL SURVEY

Colorado, Montana, New Mexico, North Dakota, Utah, and Wyoming. A high percentage of the new petroleum confidently foreseen will be found in stratigraphic, combination stratigraphic and structural, and complex structural traps. This does not preempt companies from finding crude oil and natural gas fields in unusual and surprising geological environments. Their efforts continue to uncover geological formations hardly imagined in advance of drilling.

What follows is an abridgement of NPCC's analysis of the petroleum potential for the 13 states of interest. The summary makes reference to geologic terms which may be new to you, e.g., *Tertiary* and *Pennsylvanian.* To acquaint yourself with the terms that are used to identify various strata, refer to figure 17.

Arizona. There are two principle areas of Arizona that have speculative potential for possible future discoveries: the northeast region and the southern region.

Northeast region. This area has moderate-to-poor overall potential for future discovery of petroleum reserves. Development has been retarded largely because inert gases bearing helium have completely filled several likely petroleum traps. The presence of helium increases the predrilling prospective risk, adversely offsetting the economics. Further, parts of the prospective area are composed of Indian and national park and monument lands, where leasing is prohibited. Past drilling has tested only a small percentage of the prospective area and volume. This low drilling density makes geological appraisal difficult. The surprise discovery of the Dineh-bi Keyah oil field, Arizona's largest, in unlikely geology—a volcanic Tertiary rock intruded into Pennsylvanian rocks—should have the effect of making geologists less wary of similar structures elsewhere.

Southern region. Large quantities of open-access land are available for future exploration where lower Mesozoic and Paleozoic rocks offer favorable source and reservoir characteristics. Prospects for discovery, however, are conclusively secondary to basin areas to the east (Permian basin) and the north (Paradox basin). (Do not confuse Permian *basin,* a map location, with Permian *system,* an identification of strata.) Unfavorable factors include lack of established production, complicated geology, the possibility of flushing of the prospective reservoirs by the abundant fresh water, and the presence of several military and other government reservations.

California. The onshore basins offer the most promising source

ERA	SYSTEM	SERIES
CENOZOIC	QUATERNARY	Recent Pleistocene
	TERTIARY	Pliocene Miocene Oligocene Eocene Paleocene
MESOZOIC	CRETACEOUS	Upper Lower
	JURASSIC	Upper Middle Lower
	TRIASSIC	Upper Middle Lower
PALEOZOIC	PERMIAN	Upper Lower
	PENNSYLVANIAN	Upper Middle Lower
	MISSISSIPPIAN	Upper Lower
	DEVONIAN	Upper Middle Lower
	SILURIAN	Upper Middle Lower
	ORDOVICIAN	Upper Middle Lower
	CAMBRIAN	Upper Middle Lower
PRECAMBRIAN		

Figure 17. Relative Positions of Strata. U.S. GEOLOGICAL SURVEY

for future petroleum reserves. An estimated 24,729 billion barrels of petroleum are present in this area. Experience suggests that large oil fields may be found which are completely hidden by the complexity of the subsurface, as well as the outcrop. Many lesser accumulations may be present in small or deep traps, and economics will greatly affect exploration for such accumulations. Seven areas hold the most promise in this state:

San Joaquin Valley. Several sparsely drilled, prospective areas remain in this extensively explored basin, which include areas where seismic data has been poor and, hence, little drilling has taken place, areas of favorable terrain where the possibility of stratigraphic traps definitely is indicated, and areas underlain by thick, largely untested sedimentary rocks. Crude oil fields are anticipated in the southern part of the valley and additional natural gas fields are expected in the northern, sparsely explored Cretaceous strata which could contain the gas equivalent of as much as 3.3 billion barrels of oil-in-place. Most of the estimated reserve of 12,666 billion barrels of oil-in-place for this valley, however, is expected to come from the central valley and the Bakersfield arch areas. ("Oil-in-place" is the total amount of oil located in underground reservoirs, of which only about one-third can be ultimately recovered using present *enhanced recovery* technology.) The San Joaquin Valley, which has produced more petroleum than any other California onshore basin, probably holds the greatest potential for undiscovered reserves. Miocene, Eocene, and Cretaceous strata offer the most promise.

Ventura basin. Although extensively explored, this basin unquestionably has accumulations of crude oil remaining to be discovered which could total 4.95 billion barrels—nearly triple the ultimate recovery potential of its existing fields. The area has numerous complex structures and stratigraphic traps, many of them unpredictable and undefinable except by drilling many exploratory wells. Several objectives are at untested depths in the Tertiary and Cretaceous strata. Natural gas fields, rather than oil fields may exist below 15,000 or 20,000 feet.

Los Angeles basin. Exploration of this, the richest of U.S. oil basins has been, and will continue to be hampered not by geological conditions by by urban and suburban growth. Important accumulations of crude oil doubtlessly remain undiscovered in lower Pliocene and upper Miocene strata in the deeper part of the basin (maximum depth approximately 25,000 feet), in the San Gabriel Valley in the northeastern part of the basin, and in complex traps along the known producing trends.

Central coast ranges. This area, which includes the Half Moon basin, the Pajaro embayment, the Salinas Valley trough, and the Cuyama basin has three major oil fields accounting for 90 percent of the estimated 2.5 billion barrels of known oil-in-place. An estimated additional 2.5 billion barrels of undiscovered oil remain, probably in Miocene sandstone, at moderate depths in the Salinas Valley or the Cuyama basin. However, the area is obscured with a complex geology of thrust faults which will require intensive and imaginative geologic study along with a liberal program of exploratory drilling to uncover any new reserves that may be there.

Santa Maria basin. This relatively small area of 1,700 square miles is perhaps the most thoroughly explored basin in California. Fifteen commercial fields were discovered between 1902 and 1952. No significant fields have been discovered since. Additional exploration, which could yield from 100 to 600 million barrels of oil-in-place, depends on crude oil price increases in order to make exploration for the exceptionally low-gravity oil (heavy crude) profitable. (Heavy crude, which looks and feels like tar, is difficult to extract from a well, hard to produce and refine, and has a low yield of gasoline and other desirable by-products.)

Sacramento Valley. This area has been the most important producer of nonassociated (dry) gas in California, and important discoveries of dry gas (but probably not oil), mainly in stratigraphic traps in Eocene and Cretaceous strata, are confidently expected with an ultimate potential estimated at 5.822 trillion cubic feet of gas. Important accumulations in deeper strata are considered less likely, but the great volume of untested lower Cretaceous strata on the west side of the valley presents a challenge to the future.

Northern coast ranges. These areas consist mostly of outcropping Cretaceous and Jurassic rocks. Two small basins, the Humboldt basin and the Sonoma-Orinda-Livermore basin, offer the possibility of additional small reserves in the Tertiary structure.

In contradistinction to these seven prospective areas the following areas have been, and continue to be, considered unfavorable for prospecting for oil or gas: the Modoc lava plateau in the northeastern section of the state, the Eastern Desert–Sierra Nevada province, southern coastal California, and the Imperial Valley.

Colorado. Favorable prospective basinal areas could produce significant future petroleum discoveries. The areas with the highest potential are the Piceance basin in the northwest and the Paradox basin in the southwest area. Less attractive is eastern Colorado, especially the crests of the Sierra Grande arch and the Apishapa uplift in the southeastern area, which are not considered attractive for further exploratory drilling.

Piceance basin. The potential for the development of significant future petroleum reserves in this area is very good to excellent. The comments for this basin parallel those made for the Uinta basin in Utah. Therefore, please see the references for Utah and the Uinta basin for further information.

Paradox basin. This area has very good potential for future development of petroleum reserves. The basin overlaps into Utah, and therefore I have given more detailed commentary on it under reference for that state.

Eastern Colorado. One of the lesser prospective areas within the eastern Rocky Mountain region is eastern Colorado. Nevertheless, the Raton basinal area is worthy of speculative consideration.

San Juan basin. This basin is primarily situated in New Mexico, overlapping into the southwest region of Colorado. The subsurface geology is almost unknown in many areas because of the relatively small amount of drilling outside the productive limits of the basin. The possibility of finding additional fields in this area is attractive.

Idaho. With no known production to date, this state provides the speculator with a high risk potential. Most of the state is considered unfavorable to impossible for future oil and gas discovery. The geologically complicated Idaho-Wyoming Overthrust Belt is the most likely prospect for future discovery; nevertheless, it is still considered to be highly speculative. Within the structurally complex overthrust belt favorable source and reservoir rocks are present, but the major barrier to successful exploration involves the location of the wells necessary to test the mountainous terrain. Improved seismic techniques may assist in overcoming this barrier. The average well density is scarcely sufficient to enable adequate evaluation of the area or the sedimentary rock volume. (The Idaho-Wyoming Overthrust Belt is part of a huge disturbed zone characterized by complex geology, favorable to the accumulation of oil and gas, that extends from Canada to Utah, and possibly into southern Arizona.)

Montana. Generally, the basinal areas covering most of the eastern portion of the state provide some potential for further discoveries. The more prospective area is in the northern region of the state with the Williston Basin in the northeast being the most lucrative. The western region of the state is generally felt to be unfavorable for future discoveries, except for the small basins and thrust faults of the Disturbed Belt there which provides some speculative potential. Although there is oil production in the Crazy Mountain–Bull Mountain trough in Montana (and in South Dakota) neither area appears to have high potential for significant additional discoveries.

Nevada. Most of the state is considered to be an unlikely prospect for future petroleum discoveries. The eastern region of the state, which is in the Great Basin area, has some speculative appeal. The Great Basin area is essentially unexplored, having an average of one exploratory well per 500 square miles of prospective area. Large quantities of open-access land are readily available for future exploration. However, this area may not contain large reserves of petroleum, even though several of the necessary geological parameters are present. There is a high probability that any large petroleum accumulations present have been destroyed by the repeated severe structural deformation which characterizes this area. Encouraging future exploration is the Eagle Spring oil field (perhaps 10 million barrels of ultimate recovery) which was discovered in an unusual geological environment. Nevertheless, the area is hardly expected to contain large resources of petroleum.

New Mexico. This state has favorable basinal areas with the geologic potential for future petroleum discoveries. The presence of one or more giant accumulations is possible; however, history would indicate that much of the potential reserves will be contained in numerous small-to-medium-size accumulations. The most prospective areas are the San Juan basin in the northwest region, the Raton basin in the northern area, and the extreme eastern part of the state which borders along Texas. The geologically complex southwestern region of the state contains several basins which have been explored to a limited extent by drilling and which hold relatively poor prospects for discovery. The general central portion of the state is considered to be unfavorable, although not "impossible." The unattractive geology revealed by drilling suggests the prospects of the Sierra Grande arch and of a large area south of the Pedernal Hills in New Mexico to be doubtful.

San Juan basin. Cretaceous sandstone fields in this basin have produced approximately one-third of the crude oil and most of the natural gas. Ultimate recoverable reserves of the natural gas fields of the San Juan basin are estimated to total more than 15 trillion cubic feet. Although the San Juan basin has been intensively drilled, the deeper parts of the basin are essentially unknown.

Eastern region. Shallow beds of Permian age in eastern New Mexico (Eddy County) have been commercially productive since 1909. Southeast New Mexico is also a well established producing area. These producing provinces are good prospects for new discoveries. In fact, it is thought that all provinces east of the Sierra Grande–Pedernal structures eventually will be proved productive of oil or gas, with the exception of those areas in which the Precambrian basement lacks the sedimentary rock essential for the accumulation of oil and gas.

Southwest region. Geological information is scattered in this area and will require further exploration before the full potential can be assessed properly. Based on the information available the lower Mesozoic and Paleozoic rocks show favorable characteristics. Also, large open-access land areas are available for future exploration. However, exploration for future production will be hindered because of: (1) the presence of extensive surface and subsurface volcanic strata, which complicate normal geological and geophysical exploratory techniques; (2) the obscuring of the oil and gas trap geology by structural deformation and erosion; and (3) the possibility of flushing of the prospective reservoirs by the abundant fresh water.

North Dakota. Discoveries of accumulations in combination structural-stratigraphic traps encourage the prospects that additional similar accumulations remain to be found. The nonproductive Cretaceous strata is considered to be more speculative. The most lucrative prospect is the possibility for further discoveries in the huge Williston basin which overlaps into Montana. It is estimated that this basin's discoverable oil-in-place will at least equal the amount already discovered.

Oregon. The Pacific Northwest has a marine Tertiary section along its entirety with sufficient area, thickness, and volume (100 cubic miles) to be attractive for exploration. However, the more favorable basin area is offshore. The approximately 150 onshore test wells, all drilled in geologically favorable areas, were dry. Much more speculative is the low potential region in the eastern part of the state where there are some potential source and reservoir beds. What little exploratory drilling has been undertaken has provided only traces of gas and oil, however, and no commercial production has been found to date. Although not an attractive area, this extensive volcanic province is so little known that prospects for commercial production cannot be eliminated.

South Dakota. This state ranks the lowest as a potential site for future discoveries when compared to its eastern Rocky Mountain neighbors. The estimated undiscovered oil-in-place for the entire state is less than one one-hundredth of the estimated undiscovered oil-in-place for the Montana–North Dakota Williston basin; and about one four-hundredth of the possible undiscovered potential reserves of Wyoming's Powder River basin. One large potential for the state may be the muddy sandstone reservoirs in the Cretaceous strata, but thus far, no oil has been found, and even traces have been few.

Utah. Most of the eastern and southern regions of the state offer very good potential for future petroleum discoveries. The most promising areas are the Uinta basin in the northeast and the Paradox basin in the southeast; more speculative is the Great Basin in the east.

Uintah basin. Every geological system (strata) from Pennsylvanian through Tertiary produces crude oil and natural gas in this area. Most of the larger fields are stratigraphic traps. And most of the future oil and gas accumulations are expected to be found in sandstone reservoirs in stratigraphic or structural-stratigraphic traps in strata now productive. Pennsylvanian and Mississippian carbonate rocks may contribute to a limited extent. The average depth of exploratory wells is less than 5,000 feet, which indicates that much of the attractive sedimentary section remains untested. Continued exploration, especially in the deeper and untested parts of the basin, probably will result in the discovery of several small-to-medium-size fields and at least one additional giant field.

Paradox basin. This area has a very good potential for future development of significant oil and gas reserves from Paleozoic rocks. Stratigraphic and combination structural-stratigraphic traps probably will continue to be most important in the future discoveries. Past drilling has tested less than 0.2 percent of the prospective sedimentary rock volume in this area. Exploration costs and risks generally are high for most of the area. However, the possibility of finding one or more giant fields is attractive and should compensate for the exploration costs and risks.

Great Basin. This basin includes the western portion of the state, overlapping into Nevada. Future petroleum prospects in this area are much more speculative in comparison to those areas of Utah discussed above. (For further information on this basin, refer back to the comments under the heading for Nevada.)

Washington. Please see comments under "Oregon."

Wyoming. Of all the states in the Rocky Mountain region, this state holds the greatest potential for future petroleum discoveries. Every geological system—from Cambrian to Tertiary—produces crude oil and natural gas. Upper Cretaceous and Tertiary sandstones yield most of the natural gas fields. Most of the crude oil and the natural gas found to date is contained in structural traps. Most of these are large surface anticlines, but most future discoveries are expected to be in stratigraphic traps and, to an extent, in structural-stratigraphic traps. The discoveries of important stratigraphic accumulations of crude oil in Permian carbonate rock (such as the Cottonwood Creek in the Big Horn basin) and in upper Cretaceous sandstones (Patrick Draw in the Green River basin and several fields in the Powder River basin), encourage the belief that more such accumulations remain to be found in large sparsely drilled areas. Stratigraphic traps may exist at any depth, but it is likely that additional exploratory wells in the deeper parts of the basins will be on traps discovered by geophysical surveys.

The more prospective areas, and in order of decreasing estimated potential, are: Powder River basin in the northwest, Green River basin in the west and southern region, Big Horn basin in the northcentral area, and the Wind River basin in central Wyoming. The petroleum potential of these regions is assuredly high. But, because of the large expanses of prospective land it will be many decades before the full potential of the area could be fully explored and realized. If the number of years it has taken to explore and establish the present oil- and gas-in-place are considered, the task of discovering the future postulated oil and gas would require more than 60,000 wells per year for the next 30 years—a ridiculous figure!

Exploration

We have just seen where the future postulated petroleum provinces are for our 13 select states, which should give you some idea about where you might like to prospect. But, before deciding what state or states to zero your speculative efforts in on you should also become aware of each state's current exploration and development trends. A non-oil- or gas-producing state can experience an overnight boom. On the other hand, petroleum company shifts in exploration policies and priorities, changes in state regulations, etc., can hamper exploration and wane speculative fever in other areas. To keep current on the general trends of exploration and production in each state I recommend that you subscribe to the semi-annual and annual reports of the Interstate Oil Compact Commission (IOCC). The IOCC is made up of 36 states working together for the sole purpose of promoting and encouraging the conservation of oil and gas. To this end the IOCC provides a forum for the discussion of any relevant subjects. Part of the forum is a report, by each state's official, on the state's exploration, drilling, and production activities. The state reports are most useful in keeping you informed of the general trends. The forum also includes committee reports on such issues as legalities, regulatory practices, environmental protection, enhanced recovery, etc. Whether you do your own research or not, reviewing the reports will make you a more astute speculator. The IOCC has its annual meetings in December and its semi-annual meetings in June. Reports of the meetings are published shortly afterwards and are available free to any individual upon request. For your copy write to the Interstate Oil Compact Commission, Headquarters Office, 900 Northeast 23rd Street, P.O. Box 53127, Oklahoma City, Oklahoma 73152. Ask for "The Oil and Gas Compact Bulletin" covering the meeting dates you desire.

What follows is a summary of the oil and gas activity reports portion of the IOCC's bulletin featuring their 1978 midyear meeting. In some instances I have intentionally not condensed segments of the report in order to provide some additional insight into the problems faced by the petroleum industry with respect to drilling, production, environment, etc. So let's run through each of our select list of 13 states again, this time spotting the current exploration, development, drilling and production trends of each area. Utah has not been included since no report was made by this state to the IOCC.

Arizona. It could be that Arizona's time to really enter the realm of oil producing states is near. If leasing activity is any criterion, the time is certainly near. Anschutz Corporation has acquired more than 5 million acres of oil and gas leases in 11 of Arizona's 14 counties. Other companies, both major and independent, are leasing. With the vast amount of acreage under lease, it would seem only logical that there will be considerable exploration activity within the state in the near future.

Pyramid Oil Company, Santa Fe Springs, California, has drilled two wells in the north-central portion of Mohave County. One of these wells has been plugged and abandoned. Operations on the second hole were suspended during the winter months. Several shows (traces) of oil and gas were reported from about 2,260 feet to 3,100 feet. Pyramid reports that these zones will be tested.

Energy Reserves Group has added two producing wells to its leases in the Teec-Nos-Pos Field in Apache County. Two more wells drilled by this operator have been temporarily abandoned. A third has been plugged and abandoned.

Kerr-McGee Corporation, at a public hearing, was granted permission for closer well spacing in the Dineh-bi-Keyah Field in Apache County. This operator has been issued drilling permits for three additional wells in this field and plans are to drill a total of seven wells in the field. This field has produced 14.6 million barrels of oil since its discovery in 1967.

California. In 1977, six gas fields were discovered in northern California: Greenwood, Walker Creek, Florin, Catlett, Peace Valley, and Cache Creek fields. In addition, seven new gas pools were found in six established gas fields, one new area was located, and the productive limits of six fields were extended.

In central and southern California, two oil fields were discovered, Cal Canal and Careaga Canyon. 13 new oil pools were discovered in 12 established fields, one new area was found, and the productive limits of nine fields were extended.

The California Division of Oil and Gas approved 2,831 notices to drill oil and gas wells in 1977. The 1977 figure represents a 10 percent decrease from the 3,138 notices approved in 1976.

Total footage drilled for new wells in 1977 was 6,314,097 feet, a seven percent decrease from the 6,771,761 feet drilled in 1976.

In 1977, California's oil production increased by eight percent, rising from 855,548 barrels per day in 1976 to 926,027 barrels per day in 1977.

Colorado. During 1977, the Oil and Gas Conservation Commission of the State of Colorado approved 1,390 drilling permits. This compares with 1,352 permits issued in 1976. Drilling activity has been high during the past few years and is expected to remain at a high level in the near future. There were 56 new discoveries

A wildcatting rig in central California.
STANDARD OIL COMPANY OF CALIFORNIA

during the year, 38 gas wells and 18 oil wells, none of these has yet resulted in a significant field and most of them are in the Denver-Julesburg Basin.

Production for 1977 amounted to 39,459,630 barrels of oil and 190,685,916 thousand cubic feet (mcf) of gas, of which 3,781,550 mcf was carbon dioxide. These figures represent an increase of 426,135 barrels of oil or one percent and 4,144,711 mcf of gas or 2 percent over the production figures for 1976. Production continues at a relatively high level due primarily to the continuation of development in the Spindle and Wattenberg fields.

During the year, there were 64 hearings held before the Conservation Commission. This is a gain of 21 over the year 1976 for a 49 percent increase. In general, activity of the industry has been high in Colorado and could have been higher had it not been for delays and restrictions due to federal government requirements. The annual statistical and activity report of the commission will be published in a few weeks. The report will cover this subject matter in greater detail and give much more information on the oil and gas industry in this state.

Idaho. During the calendar year 1977, five drilling permits were applied for and issued. Of this number, three operations were in progress at year end. The remaining 1977 permits commenced operations during the first quarter of 1978. Only one well, permitted in 1975, was completed during the year.

In February 1977, a 14,330-foot wildcat was completed and abandoned in the overthrust belt of eastern Bonneville County. This represents the deepest well of record to be drilled in Idaho through 1977.

Primary drilling interest remains focused in that portion of the overthrust belt in eastern Idaho. Permits issued were for a targeted 13,200-foot test in Caribou County near the Wyoming line, a 10,500-foot test south of Montpelier and a 13,200-foot test east of Bear Lake, both in Bear Lake County, a 17,500-foot wildcat 30 miles southeast of Idaho Falls in Bingham County, and a 10,500-foot venture west of Driggs in Teton County. The operations near Driggs and Montpelier culminated in early 1978 as failures.

While success has thus far eluded Idaho operators, new discoveries adjacent to the state boundaries and a large expanse of relatively undeveloped area assists in maintaining a high level of interest in the area. Interest also is continuing in southwestern Idaho counties. A commercial discovery remains to be made in this state.

Montana. Gas production in Montana continues to increase. Total for 1977 was 47,234,941 mcf, up by 3.02 billion cubic feet over last year's gas withdrawals of 44,212,874 mcf. The bulk of the increase is due to both new well production and the continued process of returning abandoned wells to production as upgraded facilities become available. Marketed associated gas (gas produced with oil) in 1977, which is included in the total shown above, also increased over last year's associated gas production by 271,071 mcf. This is mainly the result of a concerted effort to conserve all gas produced with oil where economically feasible.

Montana's oil production for 1977 was 32,680,054 barrels, down by 134,206 barrels as compared to the total for 1976. Although 1977 overall production decreased, two specific areas had substantial increases.

Oil output from the Powder River basin area has steadily increased since 1975 and was up by 302,598 barrels over 1976. Successful enhanced recovery programs at Bell Creek, a major field in the basin, are the primary factors in this increased production.

The high success rate of active exploratory (wildcat) drilling and development drilling (on existing fields) in the Williston basin portion of eastern Montana has also increased the total production from this area over the past two years. Oil is from the deeper Paleozoic reservoirs. As compared to the total 1976 output, oil production was up by 125,255 barrels in 1977.

There were 678 wells drilled in Montana in 1977, 109 fewer wells than in 1976. The number of exploratory and development wells drilled were down by 76 and 33 wells respectively. Weather and rig availability were responsible for a portion of the drilling decline. The 172 wildcats drilled included 11 oil and 7 gas new field discoveries and 17 new significant field extensions. A total of 506 development wells resulted in 220 gas and 98 oil completions.

The outlook for future oil and gas development in Montana is good. Emphasis will primarily be on the overthrust belt area as well as the shallow Cretaceous sand gas reservoirs of northcentral and northwest Montana. The high success rate of active exploratory drilling in the Williston basin portion of eastern Montana is also expected to continue to generate more drilling along this flank of the basin with similar success.

Nevada. The 1977 Nevada oil activity is tabulated below (there are no gas producing wells in Nevada at the present time):

State drilling permits issued: 36
Wells started: 23
Wells completed: 20
Wells completed for production: 8
Footage drilled: 132,093

Production (bbls)

	1977	1954—1977 to Date
Eagle Spring Field	112,312	3,209,942
Trap Spring Field	548,226	567,281
Totals	660,538	3,777,223

Total producing wells: 20

New Mexico. Oil production declined by 5.32 percent in New Mexico during 1977 to a level of 87,222,646 barrels. Gas production was down only 1.35 percent to 1.198 trillion cubic feet, apparently more in response to restricted demand by certain pipelines rather than to a decrease in producing capacity.

New locations were up 30 percent in the southeast and 61 percent in the northwest standing at 1,893 for the state as a whole. Oil well completions declined by 5 to 477 while gas well completions hit their all-time high of 830—up from 518 in 1976 and 703 in 1956, the previous high year. Blanco-Mesaverde Pool development wells accounted for 235 gas wells out of the total. Completions totalled 1,538 with 7,194,000 feet of hole being drilled.

In response to development of a small very low pressure gas pool near the community of Wagon Mound in Mora County and carbon dioxide gas potential, 50 new drilling locations were filed in Division District IV during 1977.

North Dakota. During the period January 1, 1977–December 31, 1977, 240 wells were drilled compared with 277 for the previous year. On January 1, 1978, there were 32 wells drilling, up 9 from the previous year. A total of 254 wells were completed during the period and 351 permits were issued. The number of permits issued was up 105 from that of the previous year.

In 1977, 13 new pools were discovered.

Of the 254 wells completed, 120 were oil producers, but 20 producing wells were abandoned, bringing to 2,154 the number of wells capable of producing. Stripper wells (wells extracting the last of the extractable oil) made up 687 of the producers on the basis of 10 barrels per day.

Crude oil production for the year ending on January 1, 1978, was 23,272,804 barrels for an average of 63,761 barrels per calendar day. This was an increase from the 61,303 barrels per day for the previous year. On the basis of actual producing days, the wells in North Dakota averaged 44.5 barrels per day per well.

Oregon. No new drilling permits have been issued for oil and gas drilling in the first six months of 1978. Four permits are currently active: Reichhold Energy, two permits in Columbia County; John Rex, one permit in Jefferson County; and Mobil holding the forth permit (area not designated).

Mobil continued "filling in" on its 900,000 acre lease block in western Oregon. This is one of the largest exploration ploys in the state's history except for offshore exploration in 1961–67. Mobil is planning to start on a 14,000-foot well in June. Floyd Cardinal of Billings, Montana, has acquired 500,000 acres of oil and gas leases in northwestern Oregon and southwestern Washington. The leases include approximately 70,000 acres of state submerged lands.

Texaco, Standard and Gulf hold nearly 500,000 acres of leases in central Oregon. None of these companies has announced drilling plans for 1978.

The department has issued three permits for drilling 500-foot-deep wildcats; a fourth was applied for thus far in 1978. No deep wells have been applied for as yet this year.

Northwest Natural Gas Company has applied to deepen its 2,000-foot hole on the west side of the Mt. Hood volcano to 4,000 feet. Depending on results of this test, the company may begin an extensive shallow-hole program.

South Dakota. Exploration for oil and gas was at the third highest level in the state's history during 1977. A total of 53 holes were drilled to a record total footage of 403,054 feet. There was an average of 4.5 drilling rigs in operation per day each month, with a maximum of 9 rigs during September. This increased activity resulted in the completion of 32 oil wells and 2 gas wells, the largest number of completions in one year. Of the 32 oil well completions, 6 are classified as new discoveries and the remaining 26 as field development wells (wells in producing fields). Not all of the indicated producers were on the pump at year's end. Most of South Dakota's oil wells produce from the Red River dolomite of Ordovician Age, and most are in Harding County.

Washington. The Washington state legislature passed no legislation pertaining to oil and gas matters in 1977. During the year, the oil and gas supervisor continued with routine administration of the Washington Oil and Gas Conservation Act. Oil and gas drilling accounted for a total of 2,815 feet drilled by three exploratory wells in two counties.

Wyoming. From January 1, 1977, through December 31, 1977, there were 1,881 drilling permits issued by the state oil and gas supervisor's office, reflecting a 14.8 percent increase over the 1,638 permits issued during 1976. This drilling activity has kept 135 to 140 drilling rigs operating constantly through the entire year and resulted in the discovery of 40 new oil and gas fields.

During 1976, production was 134,148,510 barrels of oil and 330,220,509 mcf of gas. During 1977, production increased to 136,471,589 barrels of oil, or 1.73 percent, and 338,260,404 mcf of gas, or 2.43 percent above 1976.

The year has been frustrating to oil and gas operators in the state because of the position the federal government, particularly, the Forest Service, has taken with respect to RARE II (Roadless Area Review Evaluation). Access to drill viable prospects in portions of the overthrust belt has been delayed temporarily, and perhaps permanently, in order to protect the wilderness. The overthrust belt of western Wyoming is believed to have greater potential than any other area onshore in the continental United States. The Wyoming oil and gas statistics for 1977 are available to anyone interested in obtaining a copy of that compilation.

To Conclude

The NCC and IOCC reports are only general indications. By the time this book goes to press many changes undoubtedly will have occurred. New oil and gas fields will have been discovered and new theories postulated regarding future petroleum provinces. Also, changes in company plans for exploration, development, and drilling will have occurred. Nevertheless, the information provided thus far should be sufficient to narrow your search down to the state level. If you desire additional information, check your local library for copies of the *Oil and Gas Journal*, published weekly by the Petroleum Publishing Co., 1421 S. Sheridan Rd., Box 1260, Tulsa, Oklahoma 74101. This magazine provides the latest information on exploration, drilling, production, and includes trade related articles. An annual subscription is $65. Another good source of information is *Annual Reviews of Oil and Gas Activity*, a two-volume report published by Petroleum Information, Box 2612, Denver, Colorado 80201. Volume one is statistical, including information on leasing activities, estimated expenditures for drilling and exploration, etc. Volume two focuses on the geological, engineering, and cartographic aspects of discoveries and important extensions completed during the year. The price is $25 a copy. If you wish to obtain the comprehensive document, two volumes totaling 1,492 pages, from which the abridged NCC summary report was compiled, ask for "Memoir 15." Although out of print, it is available from Books on Demand. Refer to Appendix E for the address and for additional geologic references of interest to the more serious speculator.

Now, to make a decision.

8
Your First Decision

In order to choose a state to speculate in you will need to formulate your strategy, and that will depend on your personal style. Keeping in mind all the material you have covered thus far, take an inventory of your personal resources and preferences. Ask yourself a few questions. Do you prefer the prospects of more frequent but smaller wins or do you prefer a chance at a bonanza but at long-shot odds? Do you require a lot of stimulating monthly action or do you have the patience to wait for several months or even a year for the "right" gamble to be offered, at perhaps better odds? Do you have the time to do a lot of research? Money to make a lot of filings? Are you able to hire professional expertise to assist you with parcel selections?

As an example, self-sufficiency is important to me, and I have the time and happy-interest to get personally involved in the selection of parcels. I chose California as my "stompin" grounds because of its fairly good potential and its low profile with the filing agents. There aren't many parcels offered in California and most of the parcels that are offered are not lucrative enough to attract much touting by professionals. Hence, there is virtually no publicity about the simultaneous offerings in this state. Most professionals play and advertise the leases in the Rocky Mountain states. Also, the strict laws in California further discourage filing agents from operating there. California is a proven petroleum province with excellent future potential. It has a sufficient number of acres under BLM management to assure an adequate supply of parcel offerings—at least adequate for the one or two filings per month, or so, that I like to make. Maps and information, at a reasonable cost, are readily available from the California Division of Oil and Gas. The BLM office in Sacramento provides its filing and results lists at modest cost. Because of the voluminous research data available I could deal directly with the government agencies without depending on a middle-man. The California lease offerings and wildcat drilling activity are not so numerous that I would require more than a few hours each month to participate; an essential factor for me since demands on my time are great. California also appeals to me because I reside in Los Angeles, and the local public libraries and university libraries abound with technical support materials. Also, the mail service between Los Angeles and the BLM office in Sacramento is faster than the service between Los Angeles and the BLM offices in other states. I receive the California filing list at least one to two days earlier than the lists I receive from other states. This gives me more time to research and select my parcels. For me, all these advantages outweigh the disadvantages of relatively lower valued parcels.

As appealing as California is to me it does not satisfy all of my speculating requirements: it is unlikely that I could win a million-dollar oil deal there. Since I have a hankering for winning a bonanza to fulfill my dream of becoming an oil tycoon, I decided also to play the lottery in the vicinity of the new oil-rush, namely the Rocky Mountain region.

Among the Rocky Mountain states Wyoming is the most lucrative by far. In my earlier years, while an engineering student at Utah State University, I took weekend prospecting trips into the Green River basin. I was excavating in the weathered Eocene shale beds searching for rare fossil fish specimens. One morning while hiking deeper into the desert I came across a congenial old timer who was in search of similar booty. We got to talking and he told me of a legend about an early settler who built a cabin from slabs of the local shale. Within the cabin was a grand fireplace, also made from the shale. When the settler lit his first fire he was surprised to see his masonry go up in flames. The shale was so impregnated with oil. My fellow prospector concluded the story by telling me to pick up a piece of the darker, nearly black, shale. "Put a match to it son," he urged in a confident manner. I struck a few wooden matches attempting to ignite the shale. The shale smoldered. The heat drew out some droplets of oil which caught fire. "That's oil shale. The hills are full of this stuff," he said. And so they were. (Technically, oil shale contains a bituminous material called kerogen, which yields oil when heated.) Hidden deep beneath the shale beds, in more easily extractable form, are many fields of oil pools waiting to be discovered. Venturesome wildcatters have responded in increasing numbers to the prospects of tapping some of Wyoming's liquid gold.

I would have joined the Wyoming bandwagon except that the

amount of publicity and touting that the lottery gets from the filing agents, so eager to cash in on the oil there, creates odds too high for my liking. Therefore, I have chosen New Mexico as the second best location for *me*. The BLM in New Mexico occasionally offers leases estimated to be valued in the hundreds of thousands of dollars, yet the odds of winning leases in this state have been showing up several times better than the odds for parcels of equal value in Wyoming. There are fewer agents touting the New Mexico parcels. New Mexico is also attractive because supportive information is readily available and because New Mexico is a proven petroleum producer and has plenty of oil-potential land under BLM jurisdiction, an active ongoing exploration program, and excellent potential for future discoveries.

Since I do not have time to personally research the geology, exploration trends and drilling activity in states other than California, I use consulting firms for my parcel recommendations for New Mexico and other states. For a nominal charge, or even for free, consulting firms provide listings of the most lucrative parcels. Use of consulting service agents is covered in the following chapters, and a summary of the services provided by a number of such firms appears in Appendix F.

If I do not see a New Mexico parcel offering of my liking, or I notice that the parcel is being touted by too many firms, I may file for lower-valued parcels in Colorado, Montana, North Dakota, or Utah, provided that the parcels are not receiving too much attention by the filing firms. I stay away from Idaho, Oregon, and Washington because these states are unproven as petroleum provinces, sufficient geological data is not available to assist me, it's too speculative and the parcel offerings are too infrequent to warrant my attention. Arizona, Nevada, and South Dakota are also too far-fetched for *me*. I emphasize "me" because they might be an excellent speculation for someone else. Arizona is receiving a lot of attention lately with millions of acres being leased for their petroleum potential. The pros leasing in this state either have a lot of goats to graze or they have caught scent of something big. A few years' time will tell. Oil is where you find it, and the continued discoveries of new fields in unlikely geology proves that finding oil can be anybody's guess. For the patient speculator who can wait, perhaps several months, for a good potential lease to become available and who has the time and money to hold on to a lease for perhaps several years, Arizona should not be discounted. Exploration, drilling information, and maps are readily available. The small number of parcels offered each month and the relatively low immediate value and marketability of the leases keep most of the hungry filing agents away, leaving almost odds-on for most parcels. Likewise, Idaho, Oregon and Washington might appeal to some speculators. Leases in Oregon totalled 447,558 in 1978, up from 176,000 last year, and Washington had 80,000 new leases issued in September alone compared to fewer than 1,500 during the same month in 1976. Since it was not until recently that wildcat leasing activity increased in these three states there will not be too many expiring leases that become available for the simultaneous filing. Nevertheless, for some of the more speculatively minded who have the financial resources and lots of patience these three states offer a ground floor opportunity with little initial competition.

These comments give you an insight into my train of thought and the factors that influenced me to select the states where I file. Because California and New Mexico are of primary interest to me does not mean that they are the best locales for you. Selection of a state or states is a personal consideration. The factors to consider in making your decision are similar to those I needed to consider in making my decision, but the value judgment that you place on each factor is a weighted personal matter which only you can make. Don't simply choose California or New Mexico because I found these states right for me. Be creative. Personalize your strategy. This is the beginning of the development of your approach to playing the lottery. You may wish to read the book in its entirety before deciding on a state. If you choose the same states that I have, I will welcome the competition. There is plenty of action in the oil-lease lottery to accommodate many more participants. Another one- or two-hundred thousand entries per year is not going to appreciably affect the odds, especially for those who play the lottery strategically, to improve their odds, as indicated in this book.

Now, let's zero in on a parcel.

9
Using a Filing Service

By now you should have a good idea where you wish to speculate for an oil lease. Is it in Arizona? Montana? North Dakota? Let's assume that you have decided to play the oil and gas lottery in Wyoming and California. You chose Wyoming because you like a lot of action and want to get right into the heat and glory of it all, and the prospect of landing a million-dollar oil deal appeals to you, in spite of the longer odds. To hedge your position, you also chose California, with its much better odds, although relatively smaller deals. Having chosen the states where you will speculate you will need to select a potentially valuable tract from among those being offered by each respective State BLM office. Perhaps you are an attorney, or, just as busy a housewife. You do not have a lot of time to spend doing the research necessary to select a parcel, or maybe you are just not interested in personally getting too involved. Then, consider using a filing service.

Recently, many firms have sprung up which, charging nothing to $100 and more per application, plus the $10 BLM entry fee, will assist you in selecting the most lucrative parcels from the many being offered each month by the Land Offices. You might have noticed their ads in your local newspaper or in one of the many specialty magazines. A typical ad reads:

GAMBLE $10
WIN $1,000,000
U.S. GOV'T OIL & GAS LOTTERY
For free information write to:
XYZ Oil Inc.
9999 Bungalow Road
Anyplace, AZ 85000
Or call collect 1-800-123-4567

Over the years I have answered every such ad that I have come across. I found that the services provided vary widely between the companies. Some service agents provide a comprehensive service package including parcel evaluations and recommendations, preliminary lists, research on previous lessees, analysis of current drilling activity, analysis of open lease filings and lease assignments, filing assistance, maps, winners lists, marketing assistance in selling your lease, and loaning the first year's lease rental amount to you. Most service agents do not provide such comprehensive services, preferring to specialize in one or two primary activities. Of the 200-some-odd filing service firms in operation I optimistically believe that most are reputable and truly concerned with serving their clients' needs. Unfortunately there are some sleezy operators whose unscrupulous tactics taint the filing-service industry. Their only concern is profit and they will go to most any means to justify their end. They prey upon that little bit of greed within each of us which can so easily overshadow our rationale and lead us astray. At least one currently operating service is purported to have links with organized crime. Then, there are the "grey area operators" who charge exorbitant fees for otherwise legitimate services, hoping to cash in on the naivety of the rank oil scout. They charge thousands of dollars for filing assistance, some even insisting that their clients sign an agreement to share their winnings, just for the simple service of completing and mailing an entry card. Let us examine how services could fleece you, the advantages and disadvantages of using a service, how to choose a filing service, and, finally, some strategies to employ when using a filing service.

Myriad Ways to Fleece You

You can be sure that if there is a way to take advantage of you, somebody out there has set up a scheme to do it. W. C. Fields' well-known "And remember dearie, never give a sucker an even break" sums it up. Some service agents make their livelihood by this motto. Here are just a few of the schemes, gimmicks, and angles used by the con artists:

(1) A service sends you a supply of the official BLM entry cards, all preprinted with the service's address. This locks the filing service in as a middleman between you and the BLM, and between you and the oil company interested in buying your lease. The use of the service's address and their strategy to act as a middleman is not in itself any indication of wrongdoing. The Board of Land Appeals has ruled that cards bearing a common

address are acceptable for filing in the simultaneous oil and gas leasing program. What determines a filing service's reputability is what they do with their middleman vantage point. They can act as your agent lining up deals and conducting negotiations on your behalf. They keep you informed of all communications with oil companies and all offers made; you make the decisions. They collect a commission for their brokerage services. But you cannot really be sure that your best interests are being served if you have someone else receiving your mail and offers.

Suppose you win a parcel worth $100,000 plus a 5 percent overriding royalty. Through his contacts at the major oil companies the agent finds an interested buyer, but he neither tells you about the prospect nor tells the oil company your address. Instead, he calls you to tell you that he has located a company we will call Slippery Oil Company, which is interested in your lease. He tells you that they are looking for a quick deal since they are planning their next fiscal year's wildcat activity and could possibly include your parcel into their drilling schedule, if you act now. You are further lured by the potential of immediate profits from the ORR. The agent tells you that Slippery Oil will pay you, say, $58,000 plus a 3.5 percent ORR. What the agent does not tell you is that Slippery Oil is owned and operated by his brother-in-law, whose only function is to rip-off suckers. You fall for the fast talk and assign your rights to the lease over to Slippery. You make a quick 58 grand, plus override, less the 10 percent sales commission you pay to your agent.

Meanwhile, the agent calls back the major oil company to tell them that his client, Slippery, has just acquired the rights to the lease and is interested in consummating the deal at $100,000 plus 5 percent ORR. Slippery Oil retains 1.5 percent of the ORR and a 42 percent profit on the deal, which is split with the agent who all along led you to believe that he was working to get you the best deal. After all, he did tell you that since he is receiving a commission for his services it is to his advantage to get you the highest price possible for your lease. He might also be collecting a finder's fee from the major oil company for directing the sale of the lease to them. If you are gullible enough the insidious agent will talk you into signing the assignment of your lease over to Slippery Oil before you get paid, literally stealing the lease from you. Slippery, being the new lease owner, sells the lease and doesn't send you a dime. You call the agent and he tells you that he is sorry but cannot do anything for you. Meanwhile, if you press too hard, Slippery Oil folds, changes its name and location, and pops up elsewhere to continue its sham under a new guise.

(2) Employees of some filing services file on the same parcels that their employer is recommending to its clients, thereby directly competing with the clients. This is a conflict of interest. A filing service could enter every family member, relative, and friend on a parcel. All those filing fees paid to them by their clients provide them funds to do it. If one of those "borrowed names" is drawn as a second-place winner, and you won using your agent's address, how conscientious an effort do you think the agent will make to market your lease? When you win, the agent could call you to tell you that he will gladly advance the lease rental to the BLM on your behalf, no interest payment due and no repayment of principal until you have sold your lease. It sounds like a good deal so you let the agent take care of everything for you. There are only fifteen days to act; the lease rental payment must be made within that time. Meanwhile, as the middleman the agent can act to block you in any number of ways in order to make you default on your rental payment so that the second-place winner receives the lease. For example, the agent makes you lose time by telling you he will send you a loan service agreement for you to sign, but he never sends it. When you telephone him asking about the agreement form he was to send you, he tells you that it might be held up in the mails and that you should give it a couple more days. You are led to believe that the BLM is flexible with the fifteen day deadline while one stall after another takes you past the point of no return.

Another tactic: when the BLM sends you notification of your win, addressed to the agent, the agent writes on the envelope, "addressee unknown," or "refused." You have no way of knowing what is going on. The BLM, not having your real address, cannot contact you. Not hearing from you within the fifteen day rental due date, the BLM disqualifies you and the second place winner gets the lease. If the lease is worth, say, $50,000 plus ORR, the agent could get a $5,000 commission by selling it for you, or by cunningly maneuvering you into a default he can split the $50,000 with the second-place winner. If you later complain, he can always lie his way around you, saying that he sent you the loan service agreement but never heard from you and so he thought that you were not interested in his services. Even if he sent you a loan service agreement and you returned it, he could toss it away claiming that he never received it—unless you were smart enough to send it certified. But even then, he could "accidentally" refuse delivery. Or, the agent could send you a loan service agreement with such ridiculous terms or with such nebulous wording that you would have to be foolish to sign it. He could also send it to you late in order to put pressure on you to sign it. If you sign the agreement, he gets the lease. If you delay signing the agreement in order to negotiate better terms you may fall into a default with the BLM.

When you play the lottery you do not know who the second place winner is or what affiliation the second place winner may have with the agent. It is likely that the type of person who would use a filing agent's address is one who does not want to get involved with all the details. He is also likely to be the type of person who would not take the time to follow-up on his entry.

(3) The temptation of filing a lot of "borrowed names" on a parcel is great indeed. A variation of this theme, which is slightly more involved, would be for the filing service to file a score of fictitious names on a badly wanted and valuable parcel. All of the filing cards would, of course, bear the common address of the service. This would give the filing service much greater odds of winning. The service would concentrate on a very active state such as Wyoming. Let's say that the filing service enters 100 bogus names along with 1,000 legitimate entries from their clientele. With thousands of entries being submitted on some parcels and a total influx of filings running at about 2.5 million, how is the BLM to know which cards are bogus? The BLM does not verify the addresses, social security numbers, or the signatures on entry cards. Even if the BLM were looking for similarities among signatures they would be difficult to spot. The same person using different pens, different size and length of strokes, plus the different names, adds enough variety to make the bogus cards go unnoticed in the lottery. Also, rubber stamped signatures are allowed and it is permissible to machine print the address and other data on the entry cards, thereby affording the mass production of bogus entries. If one of the bogus cards wins, the service agent is notified of the win by the BLM as if it were one of his real clients. The agent then generates a bogus power of attorney giving himself or his associate full authority to act on behalf of the phantom client who is said to be out of town on business, should anyone ask. The agent pays the rental, assigns all rights in the lease to his buddy at Slippery Oil Company who

in turn markets the lease. The bogus name fades out of the picture. A hundred bogus cards filed in a 3,000 card filing reduces the odds to 1 in 30 for the agent to win. Not bad if the agent is chasing after a $50,000 deal plus ORR.

A variation of this fraud is for the agent to use real names and social security numbers from his inactive client files. The agent signs the clients' names and enters his service's address on all of the cards. Forging the necessary documents, the agent gains power of attorney. The chances are that the client would not find out that his name was used, unless the client was actively watching the winner's lists. There was one case where the agent entered a client's name for a parcel without the client's authorization. Coincidentally, the client filed his own card on the same parcel and won the drawing. The BLM noticed the duplicate entry and disqualified the winner. The filing agent, if questioned, could stonewall claiming that he never filed the card, that it must have been the client who tried to pull a fast one by filing duplicate entries.

(4) Some service agents attempt to get their clients to sign a limited power of attorney giving the service discretionary power to choose the parcels, complete the entry cards, and to make filings on behalf of their clients. This is a valid and moral service which may serve the needs of some clients. However, a filing agent who is more concerned with his own gains could use the discretionary powers to file all of his clients on the same parcel, thereby maximizing the chances of having one of his clients win at the expense of lengthening the odds for each of his clients. The agent does not care as long as he is able to collect a brokerage commission for marketing the lease for somebody. Whether or not that somebody is you or someone else will not change the agent's profit one iota.

(5) A variation of the foregoing can be used by a service without the need of a power of attorney simply by limiting the number of parcels that the agent recommends to his clients. As was explained in chapter five, some filing service companies play the odds to their favor by getting as large a base of clients as they can find to file on one or two choice parcels. The services would have little chance of getting a crack at a piece of the action without their clients' collective help. The filing service companies who provide their clients with a long list of recommended parcels and who encourage their clients to select their own parcels from the list are most closely living up to being "service" agents.

(6) An expansion of this maneuver is for filing services to agree among themselves to recommend the same one or two parcels and share the resulting profits. Three coordinated services commanding around 1,500 clients each could gain an excellent advantage by narrowing their clients in on the same parcel. In a 5,000-card, big-deal filing, 4,500 entries give the services a 90 percent collective chance that one of their clients will win. Incidentally, several services' recommending the same parcel does not necessarily mean that they are in cahoots with one another. Sometimes there are not that many exceptional parcels offered by the BLM, so coincidentally the services are recommending the same parcels.

Since you cannot prove conspiracy, you can expect the practice to continue. There are ways to work around it, as we will discuss below. Coordinated filings by services can work to the advantage of the prudent lottery player.

In all fairness to the reputable services I must interject that I do not feel that there is anything morally wrong with a filing service placing all of its clients on one or two parcels in order to maximize its own opportunity for gain, provided that the agent acts within the intent of the rules and regulations governing the lottery and provided that the agent complies with the intent of other applicable laws; securities, mail, consumer, etc. Where the wrong is being done is in the lack of "full and fair disclosure" to the potential clients. It is the concealment, misrepresentation of facts, deceit, and the immoral intent of a business which makes it wrong. Prospective clients should be fully apprised in writing of the gaming strategies to be used by service agents when filing their clients' cards, the resulting anticipated odds, affiliations with other agents, and so on. In that way clients can prudently evaluate their risks. If a client decides that he wants to participate in spite of the circumstances and the odds, who could fault the service agent? Is there anything wrong with a used car dealer selling a "lemon" if he levels with you and tells you that the car is a piece of junk, and suggests that it be purchased only to strip for parts?

(7) Some agents, in order to get more of their clients to win, will file their clients on rank wildcat leases for which there is virtually no competition. This keeps the clients enticed to continue playing, and provides the agent with a good track record for use in his sales literature.

There are a lot of sincere and trusting people who play the oil and gas lottery, many who are uneducated in business affairs and who know less about the potential pitfalls of participating in the lottery through a filing service. They believe everything that they are told by a perfect (or rather, imperfect) stranger to whom they trust hundreds, even thousands of dollars.

(8) Some filing services operate fly-by-night, boiler-room bucket shops. They will open an office staffed with fifty highly trained telephone hucksters who use purchased lists of prospective client names. Prospects are telephoned and presented with a psychologically prepared written pitch which is dramatically read to them. The presentation is in block diagram form which shows the promoter what counterresponse he should use for every type of objection that could be raised by the "fish." With a little practice, the most novice operators can effectively reel in an impressive list of clientele within a matter of days. Then, any number of tactics may be used to separate winning clients from their leases. The service skips town as quickly as it came, changes its name, and sets up a new operation elsewhere for a repeat performance.

(9) In addition to the above schemes, filing service agents could bribe or otherwise influence BLM officials to provide inside assistance for winning the lottery. I have not heard of this being done, but it should not be ruled out as a possibility. Some of the Rocky Mountain states are known havens for racketeers, and it is anybody's guess how widespread their influence peddling might be.

The most active of the simultaneous oil leasing states, Wyoming, now has its lottery system computerized. Sophisticated white-collar criminals could access the computer and tamper with the programming so that the computer will favor certain names, social security numbers, or addresses. Tampering could be done remotely in the computer's telecommunications lines, and because of the technical complexity involved the tampering could go unnoticed.

These are some of the possible ways you could be taken in the oil-lease lottery. There are many variations to the schemes I have outlined. Whatever possible sham you can conceive you can figure that it is being implemented somewhere by at least one conman.

In order to curtail filing service abuses in the lease lottery, the

Bureau of Land Management proposes to amend its oil and gas leasing rules. Some of the more important changes likely to be implemented in 1980 are:

(1) Only two types of filings would be proper, those signed and fully completed by the applicant and those signed and fully completed by an agent on the applicant's behalf. All cards must be signed within the filing period. These requirements would prevent agents from receiving presigned cards from their clients. The BLM's position is that presigning entry cards reduces the value of the statements of qualifications contained on the card and fosters illegality. In at least one case a presigned card was filed after the purported entrant had died.

(2) The return address used on an entry card would be required to be the applicant's personal or business address. A filing service's address could no longer be used. Winners of leases would be required to personally sign the lease form. The first year's rental payment would have to be made directly by the applicant. No lease could be assigned before it is issued, nor could any agreement to assign a lease be made before the lease is issued or before 60 days from the time the applicant is notified of winning the lease, whichever is sooner. In light of the schemes discussed earlier in this chapter the purposes of these provisions should be obvious. Delaying the assignment of leases provides a "cooling off" period for the winner, minimizes undue influence over clients by agents, and allows all parties interested in obtaining the lease an equal opportunity to approach the lessee within a specified period.

(3) No agent could have assignment agreements with oil companies or middlemen. This rule would outlaw "kickback" arrangements between filing services and oil companies and brokers.

Do not get the idea that the entire filing service industry is corrupt. There are excellent services operating. Those not toeing the line will eventually have to pay the piper. They cannot victimize their fellow man without reaping the consequences. No one truly gets away with anything, although it may appear for a while like they do. Sooner or later everyone must pass the gatekeeper whose price is merit, not insidious deeds and dirty money. Knowing the potential hazards of using filing services, you can now play the lottery defensively. Make sure that when you do participate you play fairly. Don't compromise your integrity.

Some Advantages and Disadvantages of Using Filing Services

As we have just seen, the primary disadvantage of using the services of filing agents is that you could get short changed should you choose an irreputable one. To minimize your potential exposure there are procedural safeguards which you could take. These will be discussed a little later in "Choosing a Filing Service." Some other disadvantages of using service agents are:

(1) You are limited to play the lottery in the locations where the agents evaluate and recommend parcels. Because of the relatively large number of lease offerings of exceptional value in Wyoming most agents favor this state for their recommendations. Parcel evaluations for the less active areas such as California are more difficult to come by and more costly.

(2) Your filing interests are in opposition to the filing interests of the service agents. It is to the agent's advantage to limit his list of recommendations to a few choice parcels in order to increase the number of filings per parcel. This narrows the agent's odds of landing a handsome commission while widening the odds of winning a lease for each of his clients. In this respect, agents are biased towards serving their self-interest. Assuming a sufficient supply of lease offerings exists and all other factors being equal, the greater an agent's self-interest the smaller will be the list of parcels recommended.

(3) You are subject to the influence of the agent's salesmanship. You might be encouraged to sell your lease too soon, or for too little.

(4) You may be incurring unnecessary costs for having the agent file your cards with the BLM, a service you could easily do for yourself.

(5) There is no industry standard of performance, regulatory body, or license required for lease-lottery service agents. Therefore, it is difficult to ascertain the competency of the agent. Perhaps the leases that the agent recommends are not as good as they were figured to be. Also, the agent could make errors.

In spite of the disadvantages there are a number of advantages to utilizing the services of a professional filing agency, assuming, of course, that you are associating with a reputable and dependable firm. Some of the more substantial advantages are:

(1) You are able to get a free broad perspective of the lease offerings and the marketplace by getting on the mailing list of many service agents. Most services send out free preliminary lists which provide the township/range-location of the hottest parcels being offered, including the estimated market value and comments about ambient exploration and drilling activity.

(2) Service agents can give you more personalized attention than can the BLM. They can provide you with a variety of flexible options tailored to meet your needs. For example, if you expected to be traveling at the time the official filing numbers were to be released you could obtain the agent's recommendations dictated to you over the telephone. Service agents provide geological evaluations, the BLM does not. Service agents also research lease ownership and generate preliminary lists. The BLM does not provide this information except for inquiries made in person. If you do not want to hassle about reviewing monthly lists, making filings, etc., there are some agents who will accept a power of attorney permitting them to enter the lottery on your behalf. Further, because of the competition among the service agents for your business you should be able to obtain your desired services at competitive prices.

(3) Filing services save you time. Trying to analyze all of the BLM offerings for all of the states by yourself is impractical. Service agents can also save you time in marketing your lease. Through their long-established contacts within the oil industry they know where to sell your lease.

(4) Filing services can also save you money. Agents spend hundreds of dollars on trade publications, research, lists, and consultant reports in order to keep current of exploration and development trends, drilling activities, etc. The cost of this overhead is proportioned among their many clients enabling each client to obtain a lot of valuable information at a reduced cost. Further, through their contacts and information sources, agents know the market prices of leases and therefore can negotiate the best deal for you.

(5) Some services guarantee to buy your lease from you at a minimum price. By being assured a minimum price for your lease before you participate you are able to weigh the payoffs against the anticipated odds to determine if it is worthwhile for you to file for the parcel.

(6) Most filing agents will lend you the money to pay your first

year's lease rental, should you win. Hence, you can participate in the oil and gas lease lottery on a limited budget. This also enables you to go after the larger tracts which you might otherwise not be able to afford. Most agents guarantee that if they do not sell your lease you do not have to repay the loan. By having the agent's money at risk you can be sure that the agent will only recommend parcels that he believes could be sold.

The pros and cons considered, I believe that the advantages of dealing with filing services outweigh the disadvantages. Whether you are a novice or a pro you can gain benefit from the services of a professional agent.

Choosing a Filing Service

According to an information specialist at the Bureau of Land Management's Wyoming office, "there is no prohibition in the mineral leasing statutes against using the services of an agent to obtain an oil and gas lease. A number of filing service companies, throughout the United States, offer to assist the public in participating in the drawing for federal oil and gas leases. Some of the companies only offer filing services, whereas others also offer geologic information on the tracts available for leasing. These leasing service companies are not required or licensed by the federal government and we regulate them only so far as to assure compliance with the federal oil and gas leasing regulations." In other words, you have the right to have somebody else complete your filing cards for you. You have the right to give full power of attorney to another individual to act on your behalf. You also have the right to assign part or all of your profits from the sale of your lease to another party.

Whether you would be acting prudently in exercising these rights is questionable, especially in light of the fact that filing service companies are virtually unregulated and are not required by any private or government agency to meet minimum professional codes or standards of performance. There are a few states, however, who consider oil and gas leases to be "investment contracts" and therefore subject to compliance with securities laws. Generally, this means that the loan of rentals and the offer and sale of leases by service agents for their clients is prohibited unless the service company qualifies its securities under the state's "blue sky" statutes. Such qualification does not represent endorsement of the service firms, their activities, or their staffs.

"Qualification" means that the service firm has paid a registration fee and has filed its sales literature with the state. The service company, and not the state, has the responsibility to assure that its sales literature contains "full and fair disclosure." Hence, the securities statutes serve more as a means of providing the state with the ammunition to prosecute individuals, rather than serving a prophylactic function. The fact that qualification of a filing service under a state's blue sky laws is required does not guarantee that a service will take the initiative to register. The service agent may not even be aware that his activities fall within the jurisdiction of some state's securities law. The agent will be able to set up his business and operate until his activities come to the attention of the state's securities commission, or other similar regulatory body, who most likely will issue a desist and refrain order until qualifying registration by the service firm is met. It is evident, then, that it is left up to the consumer to judge the reputability of the service agent with whom he does business.

Filing service companies are easy to set up. Anybody can do it, and very little starting capital is required. An 18-year old kid with a few hundred bucks and an entrepreneurial spirit can be in business overnight. All it takes is a few geology-minded contacts who will evaluate the BLM lease offerings and select the top ten. The geologists telephone or wire their recommendations to the budding agent, who transmits the list under his own name by telephone, wire, or mail to his clients, who pay him for the information. The lad can also provide filing assistance for clients at an additional fee. To develop a clientele he can advertise his services in classified sections of various trade magazines. To help clients sell their leases he can refer them to lease brokers, who give him a finder's fee for the referrals, and he's in business. You can see how easy it is to begin a filing service.

Many operate in this mode, which is all right; but maybe you want more stability behind the service you choose. You may want a larger service with a more comprehensive service plan. After all, the service helping you to select leases and, hopefully, subsequently helping you to sell your lease, could be handling up to a million dollars of your estate. With so much at stake it is best to associate yourself with a service firm upon whom you can depend. A one-man set-up operating out of a post office box might be sufficient to meet your needs. His expertise might be better than a firm boasting fifty employees who in reality are nothing more than telephone solicitors at a bucket shop.

Finding a filing service company suitable to your needs will take some time and research effort. To help you get started in this pursuit I have included in Appendix F a list of some filing service organizations with a description of their services. Additional names of individuals or organizations that specialize in providing oil-lease filing services may be located in the yellow pages of telephone directories, listed under "Oil and Land Lease," or "Federal Leasing Services," or "Leasing Service." Filing services may also be located through business or professional associations, such as local bar associations; through oil and gas trade publications, chambers of commerce, state industry development agencies; and through their advertisements in business and sports magazines and in the business pages of newspapers. The chances are that you will not find many services operating in states with stringent securities laws, such as California and some of the southeastern states.

Write to as many filing services as you can. Review their sales literature. You will notice a wide variety of services and options available to you. Beware of any service that has flashy sales jargon, or which leads you to believe that you can get the inside track on a get-rich-quick scheme. The sales literature should clearly point out the risks involved. A reputable service will disclose the anticipated odds you will face for each of the parcels it recommends. The estimated cash value and overriding royalty should also be indicated. There is no reason for you to pay exorbitant fees or percentages of your winnings just to receive a list of parcel recommendations. Avoid any service with ridiculous fees. Lists should generally run from no charge to around forty dollars per state for the more comprehensive reports, and there should be no strings attached. The ideal service will provide a long listing of parcel recommendations covering several states and for which it charges a nominal fee. You select the parcels and file entries directly with the BLM.

Make sure that the lists are dated. One service mailed me a preliminary "teaser list" which stated, "The leases described herein are recommended for filing *this month*" (emphasis mine). I checked the legal descriptions of the parcels being recommended against the legal descriptions of the parcels on the current BLM list of offerings. There was no correlation. "This month" as used by the filing service was nebulous. It was only after I made a specific request for a listing for the next possible filing month that I received a rundown that correlated with the upcoming BLM offerings.

There are filing service brochures which guarantee that, should you win, you will be able to sell your lease for a minimum amount. At first glance this makes you feel secure knowing that you can make a minimum amount. But, how good is the guarantee? I have noticed at least one guarantee that stated that if the lease could not be sold for the minimum indicated amount the service would refund the amount their client paid the service as a filing fee. The guarantee was so loosely worded that conceivably all the service had to do would be to refund to the client the fee paid for one filing. What if the client filed many times before winning the unmarketable parcel? Another service's guarantee stipulated that you would get your fee back if the agent could not sell the lease within *five* years. Read the sales literature carefully. If you do not understand something, write to the company for clarification. You should get direct, clear answers. If their answers are vague or evasive, take your business elsewhere.

Before using a filing service contact the Better Business Bureau in the city where the filing service is located. Also call the local state consumer office, usually located in the state capital. Local offices are in the telephone directory in the city or county government listings. Remember (it is worth repeating), many filing services maximize their opportunity for gain while lessening yours. There is an old maxim, "Be wary of the man who urges an action in which he himself incurs no risk."

Strategies When Using a Filing Service

When dealing with a filing service you will need to use both defensive and offensive strategies in order to improve your position in the oil and gas lease-lottery game. First we'll look at some defensive measures you should take.

You have a lot of potential money at stake and you really do not know who you are dealing with when you use a filing service. Probably your only contact with a service agent will be through the mails or by telephone. Therefore, as a general precautionary policy give as little freedom to a filing service as you possibly can. Establishing self-sufficiency will decrease your chances of being ripped-off while also improving your odds of winning.

Never, never, use the address of a filing service. This is a sure way to invite a bad deal or even the loss of your parcel. You want *your* address to appear on the BLM entry cards so that the BLM can communicate directly with you and so that your address appears on the BLM winners list, thereby enabling oil companies interested in buying your lease to contact you directly. Placing a middleman at this stage of the game accomplishes little, if anything, for you. It gives the agent the opportunity to purchase the lease from you cheap while he holds off competition. If you happen to be overseas and have no friends or relatives in the United States whose address you can use and it comes down to a choice between not being able to enter the lottery or using the address of a filing service, it would be best if you did not participate. Your $15 to $25 would be better spent in another venture. If you insist on using the address of a service agent, just make sure he's a saint. Even then, you are still exposed. If you use an agent's address the second or third place winner could run interference to block you from obtaining your lease. To campaign against the use of filing service addresses on BLM entry cards, one trade newspaper suggested the following guerrilla tactics for runners-up. The second or third place winner—or anyone else who wants to play havoc with the lottery—sends a letter to the first-place winner at the service's address. (I am assuming that the troublemaker recognized the address to be that of a filing agent.) The letter is sent certified, restricted delivery, and requesting return receipt showing to whom delivered and date and address of delivery. The Postal Service must deliver the letter only to the addressee or to the service agent *if* the addressee has given written notice to the Postal Service that the agent is authorized to sign and receive mail on his behalf. The chances are that the service agent did not get an authorization from all of his clients to accept mail for them, and therefore the letter would be returned to the sender. It would also be returned to the sender if it was refused or not picked up. The reason for nondelivery is designated on the letter by the postal clerk. The sender can mail a copy of the nondelivered envelope to the BLM to show that the service agent is not properly authorized as an agent or that the addressee does not exist at the address. This ploy can put a monkey wrench into the works for a year or more, forcing the BLM to postpone issuing the lease until the matter can be resolved. With this potential exposure, why take a chance using a stranger's address? If a filing service does not permit you to use your address on the entry cards, do not do business with them.

If, in spite of my recommendations to the contrary, you use a filing service address, you should know that the BLM will mail your losing entry cards to the filing service. Make sure that the filing service forwards the cards to you. This will be your proof that your agent entered your card on the parcel you selected. Sometimes the filing cards are stamped by the BLM. However, date-stamping is not a requirement and is not always done. Therefore, when sending your payments to the filing service who is doing the filing for you, always insist on making one check payable to the agent for his fees, and another check in the amount of $10 payable to the BLM for their filing fees. Your cancelled check from the BLM is your proof that the service agent sent your payment to the BLM office. For convenience, some filing services request that only one payment, covering both their fee and the BLM fee, be made payable to the service company. Services handle many entries and it is easier for them to make one check payable to the BLM for all of their clients' cards. But, this procedure leaves you without an easy way to verify that your entry was received. You could order microfilm records of all of the entries the BLM received and check to see if yours was included, but this is costly and impractical. I hope that I have been able to convince you to use your own address and to file your own cards directly with the BLM.

Another defensive precaution is not to sign any contracts to sell your lease through a filing service until after you win a parcel. Why should you have to sign an agreement for selling your lease in order to buy a list of parcel recommendations? If a service agent insists on a sales agreement before providing recommendations, do not do business with the firm. The contract should be entered into only after you have won a lease and when you want to contract the agent's services to market the lease for you. Some agents try to get you to sign the agreement before you win in order to lock you into using their lease-brokerage services. They state that they will only make loans for lease payments to clients who have signed agreements before filing their entries. Not so. If you win a valuable lease you can be certain that you will immediately receive contacts from several brokers who want to lend you the lease amount and sell your lease. Any agreement that you do sign at that time should be reviewed by your attorney.

A reminder: Proposed rule changes require that no agreement to assign a lease be made before the lease is issued or before 60 days from the time the applicant is notified that his filing has priority, whichever is sooner. If an agent asks you to sign a postdated agreement, I advise staying away from the deal and the agent. It might get you the loan you need to pay the lease rental, but it may also disqualify you as a leaseholder. It is also likely that the terms of the agreement coming from an agent who promotes postdating will be stiff, shady, or otherwise to your detriment, and that the agent is counting on getting you to sign under duress, after you have won and there is limited time in which to pay the rental fees. Whether or not the proposed rule is effected by the BLM it would be a good one for you to incorporate as part of your personal policy.

I recall a news story of a client who won a valuable lease through a filing service, but who was subsequently rejected by the BLM due to a technicality. The client had signed a service agreement with the agent prior to filing his entry card and winning the lease. The BLM ruled that the language of the agreement implied that the service agent had an enforceable right to share in the profits of any sublease, assignment, or sale of the lease. Therefore, the BLM concluded that the agreement created an "interest" in the lease as that term is defined in 43 CFR 3100.0-5(b). The client did not indicate to the BLM that there was an "other party in interest." Hence, the disqualification. Just because a filing agent sends you a legal form to sign does not mean all is in order. It is best that you first get the lease in your name, then negotiate instruments for selling the lease.

Many filing services require you to presign the entry cards and mail them to the service, which then completes your entries by dating the cards and writing in the official parcel numbers for you. This procedure has worked and the BLM has been issuing leases to the winners. But what is to prevent a second-place winner—or anyone else—from examining the microfilm records of entry cards and determining that the date and parcel number are not in the same hand as the signature? The inference would be strong that you must have presigned the card and had your agent complete it for you. This is just the ammunition a not-so-friendly "place" or "show" entrant may need to challenge your winning entry. In light of the BLM's recent position that presigning reduces the value of the statements of qualifications contained on the card and fosters illegality, why expose yourself to the risk of having your entry challenged for presigning? If you want your agent to file entries for you, give the agent a power of attorney to manually sign, date, and to otherwise complete the entry cards on your behalf. This procedure is acceptable to the BLM as long as the cards signed by an agent reveal your name, the agent's name, and the relationship the agent holds with you.

Keep in mind, however, that giving the agent such discretionary power enables the agent to improve his odds of winning at the expense of minimizing yours. Only the most rank amateur would send $25 to a filing service and leave it all up to the service to speculate for him. If your personal circumstances require that you give discretionary power to a filing service, make sure that you carefully check the reputability of the filing service, and have a lawyer review the power of attorney. To give the least control to the agent and the best odds to you, your power of attorney should specify exactly how you want the agent to act on your behalf; the states in which to file, parcel sizes, parcel values, number of entries, frequency and time of filings, etc. You should also specify alternate courses of action the agent should take if your desired options are not available.

Another procedure that you should use to protect yourself is to pay the first year's lease rental yourself. The greater your self-sufficiency, the less you can be influenced and controlled by an unscrupulous agent. An agent is not making you an interest-free loan to pay your lease-rental because he is being a nice guy. He is doing it to lock you into his brokerage services. What if the loan you anticipate falls through? If you do not have the money to make the rental payment, borrow it from your family or friends. If you win a valuable lease it should not be too difficult to get their help. If you do not want to risk alienating family or friends, in the event the lease will not sell—or will not sell for a long time—try to obtain a personal loan from your bank or credit union to cover the rental fee. If these options do not appeal to you, then only file on parcels for which you can afford the rental payment. There are a sufficient number of small but valuable leases, 40 to 350 acres, to enable the low-budgeted speculator to participate. If you enter on the more valuable leases, around $50 to $100 per acre, you will still be playing for relatively high stakes with a low ante. Should you win, pay the rental directly to the BLM, get the lease issued in your name, then negotiate with an agent for their marketing services. This places you in the driver's seat and the agent on the defensive since he will be under pressure to give you a better deal because he knows that other interested parties may soon be contacting you with their offers.

Now let's look at some offensive strategies to use in order to zero in on a lease. We were going to play the lottery in California and Wyoming. By now you have probably realized that almost none of the services recommend parcels in California—I know of only one—and therefore you are highly limited in playing with the aid of filing services in this state. Because of the wildcat activity in Wyoming, most filing services make lease filing recommendations for this state. Their heavy touting places you at a disadvantage when using their recommendations because it increases the number of entries, lengthening your odds. By playing a few strategies you can stay in the action while greatly improving your odds.

First get on the mailing list to receive the advanced listings of recommendations from at least a dozen or so filing services so that you will know for what parcels *not* to file. Services provide free subscriptions to these lists upon request. Most lists are published before the official BLM posting and therefore the lists do not have the official BLM filing numbers. The lists do, however, provide the legal description of parcels, acreage, and estimated values. Compare all the lists you have received against one another. How many services are recommending the same parcel? If there are several services touting the same parcel, you can expect your odds to be lengthened on that parcel. Is there a valuable parcel that is being recommended by only one or two services? That is the one for which you should file. Your odds of winning are better, assuming that all other factors—the number of clients available to each service, the number of clients entered on each parcel by the services, value of leases, acreage, etc.—will average out equally. (Review Appendix A.) The more services you can get to send you their advanced lists, the more accurate will be your estimation of odds for each parcel. The trick is to keep your name on the services' mailing lists. If you do not occasionally use their services you will eventually be dropped from their list.

Perhaps you noticed several parcels that were being recommended by only one or two services. Which one should you choose? Generally speaking the lower-valued and the smaller sized parcels will attract fewer entries. It's up to you. Do you want higher stakes at longer odds, or, will you settle for a smaller fortune at more favorable odds? Note that a smaller sized parcel might be more valuable than a larger sized parcel. It is the price per acre that counts.

Usually the filing service companies will charge a fee for providing you with their final list of recommendations which includes the official BLM filing numbers. One service sends the final list out free and with no obligation. They hope that you will return their favor by selling your lease through them. If your ethics allow it, you can determine all the official filing numbers for all of the parcels listed on the advanced list of recommendations of any filing service. Order the "Notice of Lands Available for Simultaneous Filing" from the BLM office. The cost is $5 for the Wyoming monthly list, less in other states. This listing will show the legal description and the official filing number for each parcel. Compare the legal description of each parcel on the filing services' advanced listing of recommendations with the legal descriptions on the BLM list. When you have a match, note the corresponding BLM filing numbers. This enables you to file your cards directly with the BLM, circumventing the filing services and their fees. Publishing this procedure is not going to rest easy with the filing services. If it is used by too many people the services may change their style of operating in order to close this loophole. Until then, have yourself a field day if you are so inclined.

Do you want to get away from all touted parcels and still file for valuable tracts? It will take you more time, but the lower odds are worth it. You will need to order maps showing structures, subsurface contours, fields, and drilling activity. (Sources for maps are given in Appendix E.) It would help if you studied some geology. You will also need a wide collection of filing services' recommendations and the corresponding monthly BLM notice of available lands. Plot the filing services' recommendations on your maps, noting the value of each lease. Now, perusing the legal descriptions on the BLM listing, find parcels that are adjacent to those parcels recommended by the filing services. Due to the large number of parcels offered by the BLM in Wyoming, you should be able to find a few "adjacent parcels." Check the map to make sure that the adjacent parcels are located in the same geological formation in which the filing services' parcels are located. Check distance to current fields and make sure that there are no dry holes on the adjacent tracts. The chances are that you will be able to locate equally attractive parcels, but for which there is no touting, and therefore relatively few entries. Many filing services do not recommend all of the choice parcels. Remember, they want to minimize the choice in order to maximize the number of entries per parcel. Therefore, you should be able to find parcels that are good candidates for profit and which are not being touted. After several months you will be an expert in selecting valuable parcels for which there is little competition. If your time is limited consider focusing your research efforts on one primary area.

By using all of these procedures and strategies you will be able to bring your odds of winning down to around one in one or two hundred instead of the one in five to ten thousand most novices experience. You also protect yourself against potential rip-offs by the "blue-suede-shoe boys."

10
Zeroing In on Your Own

By far, self-sufficiency is the best strategy. It provides the flexibility to work an area independently from the influences of the filing services. By staying out of their range you provide yourself with the best possible odds. You will often have to forego filing on the prime parcels where many of the services concentrate their firepower. But the next best opportunities are still lucrative and the lower odds on these parcels give your speculation a better payout potential per dollar risked.

Self-sufficiency has its price. You will need to develop a resource library and you will need to spend plenty of time doing tedious research before you can select your tracts. This is the same problem that credentialed oil scouts in major oil companies face. The majors use such sophisticated techniques as topographical surveys via satellite, computer-produced multisurface mapping, and computerized risk analysis. In spite of their level of expertise, all the pros, measured as a group, averaged only a 26.9 percent success ratio on wildcat drillings during 1977. According to the American Petroleum Institute's report of drilling statistics for 1977 there were 9,961 wildcat wells drilled in the United States. Of these wells, API reported that 1,209 were oil wells, 1,477 were gas wells, and 7,275 were dry holes. In 1978 the success ratio for wildcats tests in the U.S. dropped to 17 percent. You might be wondering, in light of the track record of the pros, can you as a layman locate fruitful parcels? The answer is, yes! There are some nontechnical procedures, strategies, and inferences that you can use which will put you right in the ballpark with the pros regardless of your geologic aptitude. It is not necessary for you to pinpoint drill sites. It is enough to locate a few hundred acres of land in a potentially lucrative area. Whether or not oil or gas is found is a secondary consideration. We are primarily interested in the cash we receive up front for our lease, an amount we get regardless of any petroleum finds. The ORR is frosting on the cake. Our job is easier than that of the pros since we can deal in more general terms and at low risk. The oil companies need to commit hundreds of thousands of dollars on a precisely calculated drilling program.

Although you will be working in relatively general terms you will still need to consider a lot of variables. To this end you will need plenty of information. The more informed you are the better decisions you will be able to make. The remainder of this chapter considers the various resources that are available to you and how you can utilize them to help you in selecting parcels. For purposes of illustration I will be referring to California. The concepts apply equally to any state in which you would be scouting. However, the availability of information, the sources of the information and the costs will vary from state to state.

BLM Drawing Lists

The Notice of Lands Available for Oil and Gas Filing (Drawing List) is the most basic information source the do-it-yourself speculator requires. The drawing list tells you what tracts are being offered, where they are located, what special stipulations apply to the lease, acreage of the parcels, and the serial numbers of the prior lease holders. The drawing list is published on the third Monday of each month, and can be obtained for one dollar per month from the California BLM office. (Drawing lists for other states are available from the corresponding BLM state offices.)

Before attempting to select parcels, take several months time to watch the game in order to orient yourself. Analyze the drawing list. You will probably notice a pattern developing. One of the first things you will realize is that only a dozen or so parcels are being offered each month and that they are not being offered throughout the 44 million acres of federally owned land. Parcel offerings are localized in a few counties. In 1978, the California counties where most of the parcels were offered were: Monterey, Fresno, Kern, San Luis Obispo, Kings, San Bernardino, and Imperial. Our earlier investigation in chapter seven disclosed that the San Joaquin Valley, California's most productive onshore area, holds the greatest potential for future oil discoveries. Hence, I am prone to concentrate my attention on those above counties that are located in this basinal area, i.e., Fresno, Kern, and Kings. Further, analysis of the 1978 drawing lists indicated that of these three, Kern County had the greatest representation in the number of parcels offered. Having more parcels offered provides greater opportunity for selectivity and therefore Kern County becomes an excellent candidate for our scouting efforts.

In order to help confirm my suspicions that Kern County was a potentially lucrative area I wrote to the Western Exploration Division of Getty Oil Company to ask if their company would be interested in acquiring leases that I would win in this area. They replied affirmatively, "Yes, we are interested in the San Joaquin Valley and Sacramento Valley of California on a selective evaluative basis." Their letter also stated that they could not define specific areas of interest because their company also simultaneously files on federal leases. The reply was assuring. I did not want to file for leases that might be technically sound but for which there was no interest.

Based on my analysis thus far I decided to focus my further research efforts on Kern County. This is generally the approach you will need to take to narrow your efforts down to a small, more manageable geographic area. It is not difficult. Common sense, resourcefulness, and patience will lead you to the right areas.

To continue with the drawing lists. You probably noticed that lease offerings sometimes carry "special stipulations." The special stipulations are additional to the "general stipulations" that embrace all leases. Be particularly mindful of the special stipulations. They could render an otherwise valuable lease worthless. Special stipulations can cover almost any conceivable issue. The following are typical examples of special stipulations which have been made part of some of the leases that have been issued by the BLM.

> No occupancy or other surface disturbance will be allowed on slopes in excess of 50 percent without written permission from the District Engineer, Geological Survey, with the concurrence of the District Manager, Bureau of Land Management.

> The leased lands are in an area where an endangered species is known to occur. All viable habitats of this species will be identified for the lessee by the Bureau of Land Management during the preliminary environmental review of the lessee's proposed surface disturbing activity. This analysis shall also include, on Bureau of Land Management initiative, formal consultation with the U.S. Fish and Wildlife Service to determine whether or not the proposed activity would jeopardize the continued existence of the species (see Section

While referring to the monthly BLM drawing list, the author's 14-year-old daughter, Dawn, marks the locations of lease offerings on an oil map.

7 of the Endangered Species Act of 1973 [16 U.S.C. 1536]). This process may result in some restrictions to the lessee's plan of development, or even disallow surface disturbance. To assist in this process, the lessee may be required to provide a report from a wildlife biologist, acceptable to the District Manager, Bureau of Land Management, identifying the anticipated impacts of the proposed plan of development on the endangered species habitat.

Portions of this lease lie within the viewshed of a state designated scenic corridor. No facilities will be allowed on ridgetops or other areas visible from Highway 166 unless specifically authorized by the District Manager. Dirt roads used by the lessee for other than normal maintenance may require sprinkling with water to keep dust to a minimum.

The leased lands are in or near an area where sand dunes are used for recreational purposes; no location of drilling or other exploratory or developmental operations on the sand dunes is permitted under the authority of this lease.

The leased area has been utilized by the Department of the Navy as a bombing range. That Department has completed explosive contamination surveys of the area. The United States, however, cannot and does not give any assurance that contamination does not exist in any part of the area. Accordingly, the United States neither warrants nor represents that the lands are safe or suitable for oil and gas leasing activities. In view thereof, the lessee absolves and releases the United States from any and all liability of whatever nature for damages for personal injury, death, or damage to property arising out of operations under this lease which may be suffered by the lessee, his successors and assignees, and the agents, servants, and all employees of either.

As a rule I avoid leases clouded with special stipulations that pertain to environmental protection. Not knowing the environmental politics involved, why take unnecessary risks? I also avoid parcels with special stipulations, the impact of which I cannot ascertain. There are many parcels that are being offered that do not have special stipulations imposed. To be on the safe side stick to the "clean" deals.

I usually stay away from leases in urban and suburban growth areas. There will be less chance of confrontation with special interest groups. Any potential obstacle to develoing your lease is a potential obstacle to marketing your lease. Occidental Petroleum Corporation is learning this lesson the hard way. They spent about $4 million acquiring leases and fighting city hall over the last eight years for rights to drill on a small strip of the Pacific Palisades area estimated to contain $2 billion in oil and gas reserves. Although the Los Angeles city treasury would gain $50 million from badly needed royalty payments, the city refused to budge, claiming that the proposed drilling would be incompatible with the residential and public recreational uses now in existence on adjacent properties. Occidental is going to court to fight it out, and it may be several more years before a final determination is reached.

What about the size of the parcel you should select? This is based on your pocketbook and the amount of confidence you have in your research. Generally, if you choose small acreage parcels your lease-payment risk will be low, but so might be your potential gain, and the odds of winning the parcel considered in light of your time and cost to win it may not be worthwhile. Generally, the larger acreage parcels increase your lease-payment risk but also increase your potential profit. When deciding on acreage size, remember that it is the value per acre that counts. Whenever in doubt, wait it out. Do not take the risk. You do not have to file each month. Wait another month or so until a parcel is offered of which you are more confident.

Another item on the drawing list that might be helpful is the serial number of the expired lease. Through this number you can track down the lease-ownership history and find out when it was acquired and how long it was held before being dropped. What ultimate value this information serves is often uncertain. If we find that lease XYZ was owned by Miss Q and held one year, then dropped, we might assume that Miss Q could not find a buyer for her lease and, deciding not to throw good money after bad, dropped the lease. This might not be the case. Maybe she received many offers for her lease but held out for a ridiculous amount. Perhaps she relinquished the lease due to a lack of funds, or maybe she passed away or simply forgot to make the next year's rental payment.

If you notice that a major oil company owned the lease and then dropped it, you might assume that the lease must be worthless. Perhaps. Maybe nearby exploration proved fruitless. Or, maybe the lease is potentially valuable but the oil company dropped it in order to buy another lease. If you recall, there is a limit to the number of acres that can be held under lease. Also, it is virtually impossible to adequately test drill all of a major oil company's lease holdings within a 10-year limitation. There are not sufficient rigs available to do all of the drilling that would be required. It becomes evident then, that knowing who the prior owner was and how long the lease was held before being dropped does not provide us with a conclusive input. It could be misleading. This information, at best, can help to confirm our analysis. For example, if you notice that the lease was dropped by a major oil company after two years, just after several of their test drillings came up with dry holes, you should be wary of the lease. But if the lease expired after ten years and just after a single test drilling turned up dry, you might still consider filing for the lease if all other factors are favorable, if, for instance, it is within current exploration trends, if you feel that more than one test well would be necessary to prove out the lease, etc.

Some speculators research lease ownership records to look for leases that are in their eleventh, twenty-third, or thirty-fifth month of holding. They hope to find a lessee who may be considering dropping his lease. Occasionally valuable leases are dropped because lessees do not know how to market them. They may not be aggressive enough and panic if they do not sell their lease in the first, second, or third year. They assume that the lease is worthless and are afraid to risk additional funds for continuing their lease. Also, a hitherto unmarketable lease might suddenly become valuable if an oil company decides to test drill nearby or if an oil strike is made in the vicinity of the lease. The lessee might not have been keeping abreast of latest developments and his dropped lease becomes somebody else's gain. This is a valid strategy for obtaining leases. It eliminates simultaneous filing competition since it enables you to acquire leases before they are reoffered in the lottery. You will need to pay the lessee a premium to acquire his lease. The premium amount will depend upon how good you are at negotiating and what the lessee's circumstances are like. With a little salesmanship you should be able to acquire such leases by only offering a fractional interest in the overriding royalty. The lessee should be happy with this arrangement since he would get nothing when he discontinues his lease.

You can obtain information about lease ownership, addresses of lessees, and a brief history of each lease by visiting the public room at the BLM office, which for California, is located in Sacramento. This information is generally not available from the

BLM state offices by telephone or mail. If you are fortunate to live near the BLM office, then take advantage and research this additional information.

BLM Results List

Equally important as the drawing list is the results list. The result list shows the names and addresses of the first-, second-, and third-place winners. It shows the number of offers that were filed and also gives the lease serial number. The drawing date is also shown. The results lists for California are available from the state BLM office for $1 per month. For your convenience you may open a copy-work deposit account to provide you with an annual subscription to the lists.

Analyze the results lists. How many entries are being filed on each parcel? Is the pattern consistent? Do some parcels get a disproportionate number of entries? Maybe these parcels have been touted. Where are these parcels located? What are the usual number of entries for the parcels in your chosen area? In Kern County I have noticed anywhere from around 25 to over 400 entries made per parcel. If there was a consistent pattern of only a few entries for parcels in a given area I would be suspicious of the area. There are too many people scouting for deals for a good area to go unnoticed. It happens on occasion, but not that often. Suspect touting if you notice that one or two parcels have considerably more entries filed on them than other parcels have had that are in the same area. This is a favorable sign since it implies that leases in the area have potential. You will seldom find filing companies touting for known goat pastures, because it's a waste of their resources. Nevertheless, a higher number of filings in an area is not in itself conclusive of anything. Filing companies make mistakes, and as indicated earlier, may have alternative motives to their filing patterns.

Who are the winners? Look their names up in the telephone book and call them. Most winners are excited and happy to share their excitement, even with a stranger. You will be surprised how much you can learn in this way. Ask winners if they used an agent, and who the agent was. Once you know who the filing agents are that are working the area write to them for free information. Call winners six months and one year after they have won their leases and ask them if their leases are still for sale.

What are they asking for the leases? Do they know of any other leases in the same area that have sold for the price they are asking? This will give you an idea of an area's marketability. Chit chat about how long they have been playing the lottery before they won. You will be encouraged when you hear a winner tell you how they just got a check for ten grand after only his third try in the lottery. You will also hear the hard luck stories. Perhaps some sobbing widow will tell you how she threw away several thousand dollars in filing fees over the last ten years before she finally won a lease for which she paid a rental of $2,300 and after nine months hasn't received one inquiry—yours was the first call.

The Interstate Map Co., P.O. Box 896, Scottsdale, Arizona 85252, compiles a monthly "BLM Lottery Winners Report," which it sells on a subscription basis for $12 per year. This report indicates the BLM simultaneous winners and their addresses for leases in Colorado, Montana, New Mexico, Nevada, Utah, North and South Dakota, and Wyoming. Their advertising does not indicate if the second- and third-place winners are included in the report nor if the number of entries filed and respective BLM parcel numbers were shown. Inquire before ordering.

The results list is the score sheet. It tells you the winning action in the lottery. Make full use of it. If you want to delve more deeply into the action then consider obtaining the BLM microfilm records of all those parties who have filed entries.

BLM Microfilm Filing Records

Each BLM office makes a monthly microfilm record of all the eligible entry cards that it has received. These records are available for inspection at the BLM state offices by the general public. Additionally, the microfilm is available for purchase at $15 per roll. In states where the filing activity is low the entire filing records might fit on one roll, whereas in other states where there is a high filing interest the filing records on even one parcel might require several rolls of microfilm. A study of filing records is too costly a proposition for most persons to undertake. There is also the problem of locating a compatible microfilm reader in order to be able to retrieve the data. After you have located the reader (maybe one is available at your local library) you will need to spend a lot of time to scan all of the entries to determine who filed and for what parcels they filed. Knowing which companies are filing and where they are filing is valuable input. Equally valuable is being able to spot the use of common addresses by many entrants, a sure sign that the entries were placed by filing services. The circumstances of cost and time considered, however, having the complete filing records is a luxury item, nice if you can have them, but not crippling to your analysis if you are without them. See "Computerized Drawings," in chapter thirteen for information on the microfische records available for filings made to the Wyoming land office.

Some consulting firms provide a listing of "significant" filings for each parcel. The $40 to $50 you will spend for this abridged listing is worth the saving in time. Do not confuse this abridged listing with the Winner's List some companies provide.

Open Land Filings

Another source of information which can assist you to select a lease is the BLM records of open land filings. As you will recall, open land filings are noncompetitive filings for wildcat lands. Leases are issued to the first filer. Records of open leases that have been issued are maintained by the BLM and are available for inspection by the public. If you cannot abstract this information from the public room at the BLM office you might try obtaining the information from a consulting firm. Knowing the open land filings of the independent and majors is useful input, but not crucial to your analysis. If you can easily obtain this added input, fine, otherwise do not worry about it.

Assignments

Every time a lease changes ownership, in part or full, the change is recorded with the BLM. This information is a matter of public record and can be useful to the oil-lease scout. It provides you with a means of follow-up on the results list to see the turnover of leases. It will tell you who has bought the lease and also how fast the leases are being sold. As far as I am concerned this information is another luxury item. I do not mean to down play its usefulness; I just think that you can learn as much by telephoning the winners. You cannot conduct a probing dialogue with a listing of assignments. With telephone rates as low as they are you will get a lot of information for the few dollars in calls that you make.

Maps, Bulletins, and Reports

A primary consideration in our analysis of parcels is location. As a general rule there will be greater speculative interest—higher demand and easier marketability—in parcels that are located in the proximity of proven, currently productive oil or gas fields. Plenty of unexplored acreage exists around proven fields, and therefore oil companies will generally favor these areas as opposed to testing "frontier areas" at remote distances from existing pipelines and roads, and where no immediate market is available. The large and long-term investment that is required to develop boondock areas is not economically justified under current oil and gas prices. Within the defined producing areas, the demand will be greater for parcels that offset the higher production areas. Parcels adjacent to low-production areas where wells may produce slowly or require expensive special recovery procedures, will not attract as great a percentage of investment dollars.

When considering the location of a parcel we must also consider its vertical geologic profile in relationship to the nearby producing geologic structures. Is the parcel correlated stratigraphically with the strike line? The parcel may be located on the flank of a major producing fault trap with no dry holes between the producer and the parcel. It looks like a good prospect. However, the parcel might be located on the opposite, nonproductive side of the fault trap. Equally important is the depth of the oil-producing strata under your parcel. Your parcel might be located a couple of miles from a major producing field where production is from shallow depths—a few thousand feet. However, the same producing strata could dip steeply where your parcel is located, perhaps to 15,000 feet. The cost of drilling increases exponentially with the depth drilled. All other factors being equal, an oil company will favor shallower test drilling. Also, a company would prefer to test drill where the subsurface geology is known or can be inferred with reasonable accuracy, as opposed to test drilling a subsurface too complex for charting. So you can see why subsurface contours and structures are essential factors to consider when analyzing a parcel.

Another major factor to consider is the history of drilling activity on, and nearby, the parcel. How deep were the test wells, how many were drilled, where were they drilled, what did the core samples show, which wells were productive and how productive were they, and what wells have been plugged and abandoned? You should answer these questions for any parcel you are investigating. An aggressive drilling program, although having proved fruitless, does not necessarily discount a parcel. On the contrary. It may prove that the area is highly suspected of being productive. On the other hand, the test drilling could have been intensive and sufficient data gathered to prove its futility for further exploratory drilling.

At first, attempting to analyze all of these variables may seem unwieldy, and it is. With time, as you delve deeper into your research, you will become more comfortable as a self-sufficient oil scout. Fortunately, there is a lot of supportive information available to help you in your research. I have provided a list of references in Appendix E. For California the primary resource is the California Division of Oil and Gas, which provides a lot of information, most free of charge.

Most basic to your research are maps. You will want to locate your prospective parcels on an oil map. How to understand township/range map designations and how to locate a parcel on a map is discussed below. The Division of Oil and Gas provides regional wildcat maps showing all of the wildcat oil and gas activity. These maps also outline the limits of oil and gas fields enabling you to readily check the location of your parcel in relationship to existing production. In addition to wildcat maps, the California Division of Oil and Gas provides field maps which show all of the drilling activity within each field. Both maps indicate the drilling operator, the depth of the well, and the results of the drilling. Maps are wall-sized, scaled one inch to a mile, and updated annually. A weekly Map Revision Bulletin is provided. Maps do not show surface contours or subsurface geologic structures. Instead, to complement the maps, the division publishes a two-volume text of 1,325 pages which details the subsurface geology for oil and gas fields. Also included in this reference are cross-section geologic charts of the basinal areas where the oil and gas fields are located.

An additional reference you will need is the Weekly Summary of Notices to Drill, Rework, and Abandon. This tells you of all the current and proposed drilling activity, designating the operators' names, names of the wells, type of wells—wildcat, service, or dry hole—and indicates the locations of the wells. Each year the state oil and gas supervisor recaps all of the weekly summaries into one statistical report of wildcat activity. Additionally, a history of all wildcat activity for the state, through 1963, is published in a book called *Exploratory Wells Drilled Outside of Oil and Gas Fields in California*. Numerous other supportive publications, bulletins, and reports are provided which can assist you to analyze your parcel.

The resources discussed in this chapter should be considered in conjunction with one another when analyzing a parcel. No one piece of information will be conclusive to your decision-making. You will need to process all of the information with your mental computer and come up with a "go," or "no-go," decision. Sometimes you will be forced to make decisions in spite of missing data. You will need to extrapolate from the known data to infer the unknown. Each circumstance of evaluation will be different, and so the weight of each variable will differ. A hard and fast rule by which you will be able to select profitable parcels with certainty cannot be developed. How good your parcel selections are will be based upon how well you have done your homework and how talented you are at being able to intuitively evaluate several variables to come up with the right decision. After a few months of analyzing parcels you will develop a good judgement for evaluating leases.

Once you have selected your parcel, develop some filing strategies. File all eligible family members on one parcel to improve your odds. Consider forming a company, or a partnership. In so doing, make sure that you comply with the multiple filing provisions of the Oil and Gas Leasing Regulations. Also consider the superstrategies discussed later in this chapter.

The U.S. Land Survey System

To provide an orderly plan for the survey of government lands the Second Land Ordinance (1785) established the Public Land Rectangular System. Under this system reference points of known latitude and longitude were identified. Through each of the reference points a true north and south line called a principal meridian was run and marked on the ground. Next, a base line was run east and west from each reference point and also marked on the ground. Currently there are 36 such reference points with marked principal meridians and base lines located in different parts of the United States. On either side of the principal meridians square units of land called townships, measuring six miles on a side, were laid out. A tier of townships running north and south was designated a range. Any township can be described in terms of this axis system: so-and-so townships north or south of a named base line and so-and-so ranges east or west of a named principal meridian. The terms *township* and *range* are abbreviated T and R respectively.

Each township is divided into 36 sections, each one mile square and containing 640 acres. The 36 sections are numbered 1 to 36, starting in the northeast corner and running alternately right to left and then left to right, as illustrated in figure 18. Each section can be located by its number, township, and range.

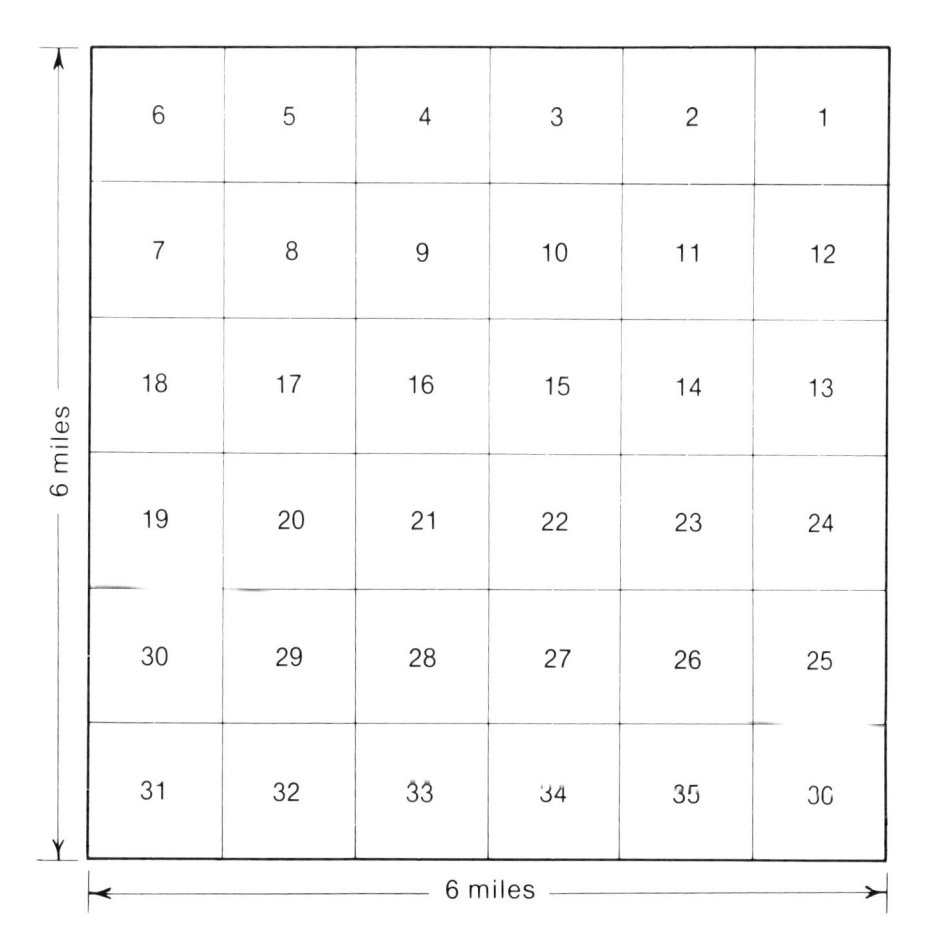

6	5	4	3	2	1
7	8	9	10	11	12
18	17	16	15	14	13
19	20	21	22	23	24
30	29	28	27	26	25
31	32	33	34	35	36

6 miles (vertical) × 6 miles (horizontal)

Figure 18. Township

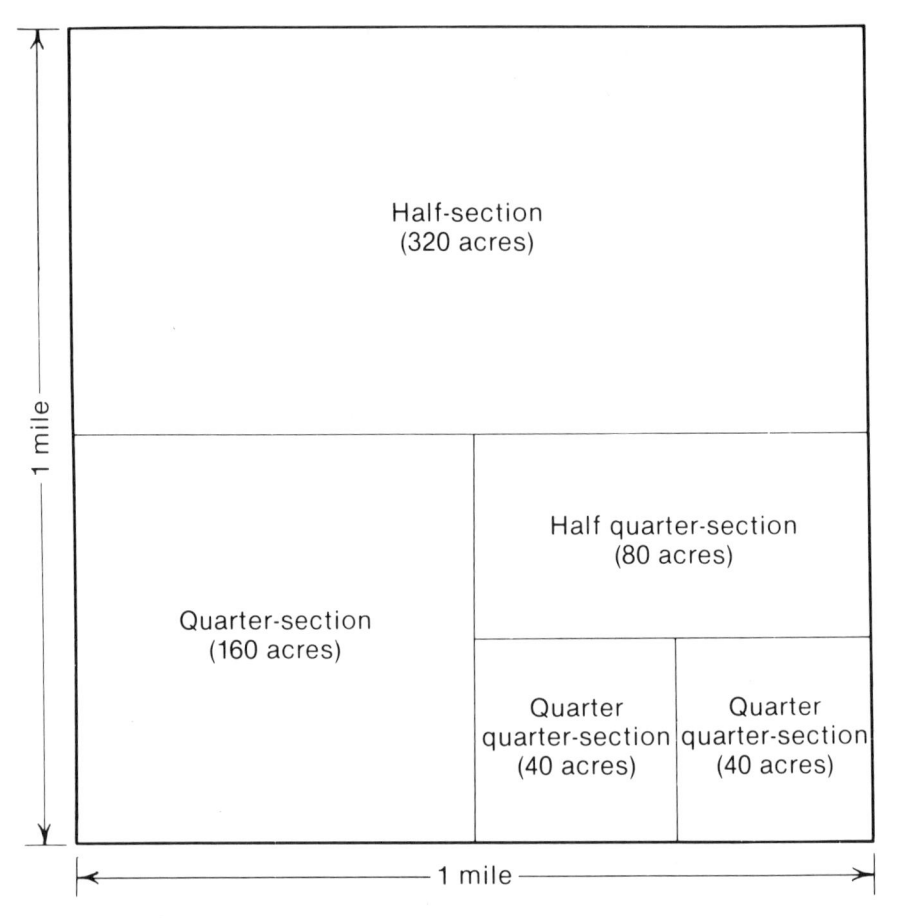

Figure 19. Section

Each section may be subdivided into half-sections (320 acres) and quarter-sections (160 acres) which may be further subdivided into half-quarter-sections (80 acres) and quarter-quarter-sections (40 acres). Figure 19 illustrates the subdivision scheme of a section. As an interesting side note, the acre came into use as a standard of measure on account of the amount of land one man could plow in a day. On that basis it would take 25 men about 30 days to plow New York's Central Park, which should give you some idea how big an acre is.

Under the rectangular survey system it is very easy to describe and locate any one parcel of land. There cannot be another parcel of land with the same identification. The following legal description of a lease parcel appeared in the September 18, 1978,

"Notice of Lands Available for Oil and Gas Filings" for California. It is typical of the legal descriptions used by all State BLM offices and filing services. Notice the use of compass-point designations in the description. Subdivisions of a section of land are always described in relation to the four points of the compass.

T. 11 N., R. 24 W., Kern County
Sec. 21, S½SW¼ and W½SE¼;
Sec. 28, NW¼NW¼;
Sec. 29, E½, N½SW¼, and SE¼SW¼.
640 Acres

The key provided in figure 20 will help you understand the compass-point designations used in the legal description. The

NW¼NW¼	NE¼NW¼	Northeast quarter (NE¼)	
SW¼NW¼	SE¼NW¼		
N½SW¼		West Half of Southeast quarter	E½SE¼
Lot 1 / Lake	Lot 2		

Figure 20. Key to Subdivisions of a Section

trick is to insert the word *of* between compass-point designations. Thus, NW¼ of NW¼, NE¼ of NW¼, N½ of SW¼, etc.

Now, referring to figure 21 locate the legal description of the California parcel on the township. The configuration of the parcel is shown as the shaded portion.

You will often notice that a legal description of a parcel makes reference to "lots." Lots are used to indicate irregularities, compensations, or corrections in acreage. Sometimes the township or section is irregular due to lakes or mountainous terrain. Mountains may increase the acreage of a section beyond 640 acres which would require lots to compensate the acreage change. Also, errors in surveys are corrected by the use of lots.

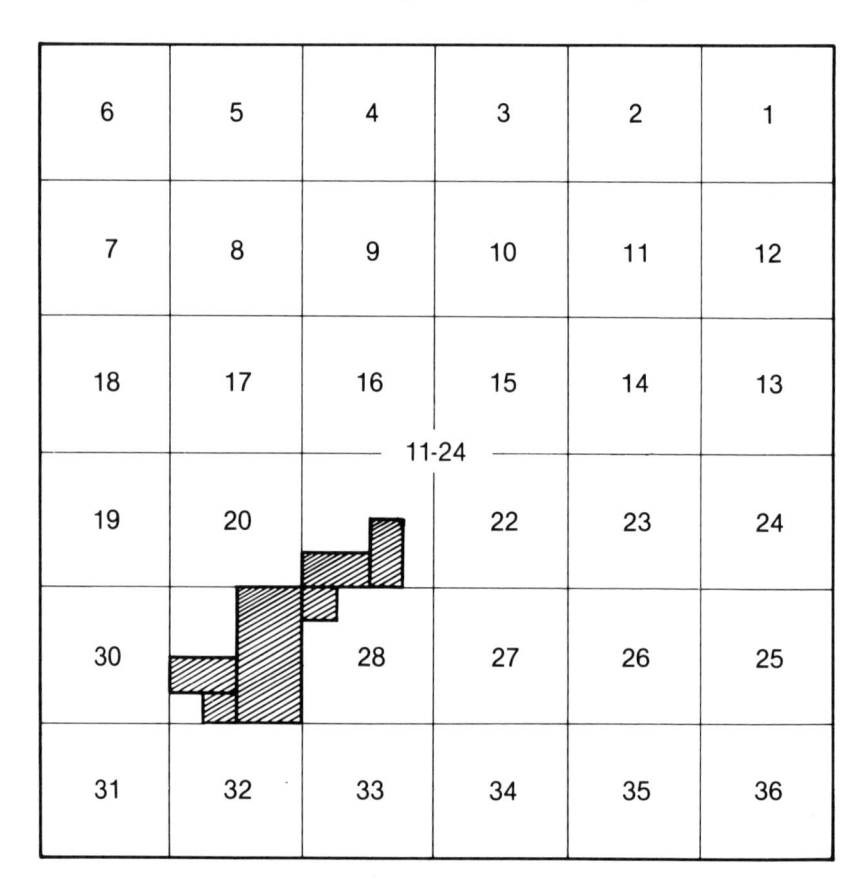

6	5	4	3	2	1
7	8	9	10	11	12
18	17	16	15	14	13
19	20		22	23	24
30		28	27	26	25
31	32	33	34	35	36

Figure 21. Township 11 North, Range 24 West

Lots do not have a specified number of acres and can be of any shape.

Only about 74 percent of the total area of the public domain lands has been surveyed. Unsurveyed land is also offered for lease and is described by measurements and boundary markers, usually called metes and bounds descriptions. A metes-and-bounds description begins at a certain well-defined point and then follows the exterior boundaries by courses (directions) and distances. For example, here is a metes-and-bounds description for an Idaho parcel:

> Beginning at the southeast corner of township 7 south, range 5 east, of the Boise Meridian, Idaho, proceed 6 miles east, thence 5 miles north to the point of beginning, a pile of rocks 105 feet southeast of a fork in the creek, thence west 20 chains, thence north 20 chains, thence east 20 chains, thence south 20 chains to the point of beginning.

Now let us consider some strategies for choosing parcels, strategies apropos to the Aquarian Age.

Superstrategies

Are your biorhythms at a "triple-low"? Is Saturn in your house? Are the phonetics of your name balanced mathematically with your date of birth? How are you influenced by sunspot activity? How does the moon affect your decisions and actions? Do you have lucky days and lucky numbers? Are you jinxed? If so, can amulets or potions be used as antidotes to ward off the bad influences? Can prayer rugs and lucky symbols work for you? Can you be hypnotized into success? As we move further into the Aquarian Age we are growing in our awareness about the hidden forces at work around us. It was not too many years ago when mention of astrology, numerology, biorhythms, and the like, would furrow brows. Today, such topics are commonplace even among the conservatively minded. How often have you been asked what sign you were born under, or heard someone mention biorhythms? Attitudes about the role numbers play in our lives are also changing. The number 7 is considered to be lucky, 13, unlucky, especially if it is the date of a Friday. So strong has this influence of numbers grown that the number 13 is now skipped when labeling the floors of many skyscrapers since property managers have found that so-called conservative businessmen will not rent office suites that are located on the thirteenth floor.

How valid are these concepts? Are we growing more superstitious, or are we becoming aware of forces that we can learn to utilize or work in harmony with for our benefit, as, for instance, in winning the oil and gas lease lottery? Personal testimonies and some preliminary scientific inquiries indicate that there are subtle principles and forces at work which influence us. We do not live apart from the cosmos. We act and react in a cause and effect universe where everything is effecting everything else to one extent or another. Even the faintest twinkle of a star, millions of light-years distant from us, affects our physiology. It creates chemical changes within our eyes which trigger a whole set of electrical impulses in our nervous system. These faint twinkles have moved people to write poetry, songs, and even to spend their lives in research of the stars.

It is reasonable then, to assume that the much closer planetary bodies must also exert their influence on us as they dance in orbit through the sky. And, certainly, the moon and sun affect us. But the extent to which we are influenced on subtle levels by these celestial orbs is still speculative. It is interesting to note that in 1978, when record trading volume was registered on the New York Stock Exchange, the largest solar flare on record was reported. Whether or not solar flare activity influences emotions is yet to be proven scientifically. However, in researching the influences of the sun on our planet scientists have found that a positive correlation exists between the cyclical appearances of solar spots and our long-term cyclic weather patterns. And weather effects our behavior.

The study of cycles is a growing science. Research findings show that all aspects of nature work in cycles, and cycles within cycles. We can postulate that there must be cycles during the year when people would be more prone to speculate in a lottery than at other times. Professional fund raisers and mail order houses find that their incomes are directly linked to cycles. Perhaps the link is due to a general economic tide which provides people with more spendable money at certain times of the year. Or, the link could be due to the effects of summer vacations and religious holidays when people change their priorities for spending. Whatever the case, cycles do exist and their study might assist you to find the months of the year when participation in the oil-lease lottery would be less, thereby providing you with better odds.

The main problem in getting involved in the study of cycles, which if it is to be comprehensive would need to include astrology and numerology, is the lack of information. And, for the most part, the information that is available is clouded with so much misinformation that attempts to find one's way through these fields is frustrating and could in fact be detrimental. In fact, the entire field of subtle causes and effects is so confused with misinformation that, as tantalizing as it may be, you might be better served by staying away from it.

Over the last several years, I have noticed a flood of advertisements for occult methods to win lotteries. Don't fall prey to these techniques. Séances, magic spells, divination, witchcraft, and the like should definitely be avoided. You never get something for nothing in this cause-and-effect world. You might win a lottery with the "aid" of some of these techniques, but the trade-off will undoubtedly be to your detriment.

Relying on psychic prophecies is another technique being employed by some speculators. Can a psychic tell you where the next major oil field will be discovered? Can a psychic "read" you to determine what subtle forces are blocking you from winning the lottery and then prescribe a course of action for you to take that will remedy your bad luck? Perhaps some can. You should know that psychics see *potential* situations based on current and past circumstances. How clearly they see, and their interpretations of what they see, will determine what they tell you. Circumstances are continually changing, every second. What the psychic predicted may not happen due to the changes in circumstances that have occurred since the reading. Also, psychics cannot pinpoint the time an event will occur. A psychic told a friend of mine that he would soon come into a lot of money, so he went out and bought a new car, which he could not afford, and overextended himself on his credit cards. He never did realize the prophecized windfall and consequently fell into acute depression when he could not meet his bill payments. In the spring of 1978, a leading California psychic predicted that huge oil reserves would be discovered in Nevada before the year ended. The year ended with no such discovery made. Another notorious California psychic made his prediction in early 1979, stating that before the year ended vast deposits of oil will be discovered in Arizona and New Mexico. At this writing, the prophecy remains to be proven. Regardless, geologists have long felt that Arizona and New Mexico are strong candidates for oil and gas discoveries. With stepped-up drilling activity in these areas it is only a question of time when significant discoveries will be made. With the number of psychics making predictions about oil discoveries in known petroleum providences it is likely that someone will be right some time. Because of the uncertainties involved in psychic readings I do not advocate using psychic services as a strategy for your oil lease speculations.

About the best superstrategy that I can think of that will help you win the lottery is to develop a positive mental attitude. A positive mental attitude is certainly better than a negative one. Thought is the basis for action. Therefore, it can be said that thoughts are your most valuable asset. Think positive and you will act and be positive. As you think, so you are. If you maintain a high self-image then you will project that high image as your reality. Whatever you dwell upon you perpetuate within yourself. In this respect you make your own odds and create your own success. You do not need to file dozens of applications in order to win a lease. You should be able to file one well-placed application backed by a strong positive disposition, and win.

You might ask, then why do some people with a positive mental attitude lose? Maybe winners win because they earned it. At least that is the explanation according to the ancient Asian lore which states that the "science of treasures" teaches that mineral wealth is alive and moves from place to place under the sovereignty of the chief of the genii, the divinity of wealth. It is he who brings out the treasures or hides them based on the merits of individuals. According to this philosophy, having a strong mental disposition is not enough. If you are on a losing streak it is probably due to the need to shift your life energies into more constructive channels of expression. In any event, if you find yourself never able to win the lottery do not try to plow through your misfortunes with sheer numbers of entries. On the contrary, stop playing for a while, analyze your situation, improve your mental attitude, then get back to participating in the lottery when you are radiating with positivity. To help you develop a more positive attitude I recommend reading Napoleon Hill's *Think and Grow Rich* (Fawcett) and *Success Through a Positive Mental Attitude* (Picket), coauthored by Hill and W. Clement. Also helpful for developing a positive mental attitude is the practice of meditation. You might give it a try.

This chapter has covered some of the more common strategies that are increasingly being used by speculators. I truly hope that you avoid the pitfalls that I have mentioned and that you find the time to follow the recommendations made on mental development. I believe that mental development is the superstrategy par excellence for playing the oil lease lottery, as it is for any endeavor you undertake.

Now, I suggest you reflect for a while upon the material covered in parts one and two. Let it digest. Review any chapters and items that you are not clear about. Then we will consider the technicalities involved in filing for parcels.

Part III
Filing for Your Parcel

11
How to File

This part of the book deals with the mechanics of filing your entry cards directly with the Bureau of Land Management. It does not deal with filing strategies, as these were dealt with in Part Two. Nor does it tell you how to file for a parcel through a filing service; filing procedures vary from agent to agent and are discussed in detail in Appendix F. Again, I urge you not to have a filing service handle your entries for you. Do your own filing. It is more fun to complete the entry card yourself, and if you are like most lottery players, you will want to mail your own entry so that you can give it your final blessings before dropping it into the mail box.

The mechanics of filing are the easiest aspect of the simultaneous oil and gas lottery system. Nevertheless, do not treat this topic lightly. There are certain procedures required by the Bureau of Land Management which you will need to follow. It is very disheartening to be eagerly waiting for the drawing results only to find that your entry was rejected due to a technicality, and that all of your research efforts and costs have been for naught. Study this section carefully. A little extra care on your part will assure that you will not be one of the thousands of people each year whose entries are rejected by the BLM.

All offers to lease federal oil and gas lands available for simultaneous filing must comply with the regulations in 43 CFR, Part 3100, which provide for the following:

(1) All filings must be submitted on the official entry form, the Simultaneous Oil and Gas Drawing Entry Card, Bureau Form 3112-1, dated February 1976 or later. A limited quantity of these cards can be obtained free from any BLM state office. Larger quantities (more than 50) of this form can be obtained, also free of charge, from The Denver Service Center, Bureau of Land Management, Federal Center, Building 50, Denver, Colorado 80225. Reproduced copies of the franked postal entry card will

157

not be accepted for inclusion in the drawing. (Reproduction of the card for use in the mails is considered a violation of the postal regulations promulgated under Title 18, U.S. Code, Section 501.)

(2) A $10 filing fee must accompany the entry card. The filing fee may be paid in cash or by money order, bank cashier's check, or bank certified check. If you are submitting more than one card to the same BLM land office you can submit one remittance for the total filing fees.

The BLM has been accepting personal checks but plans to eliminate this practice. During 1979, at any given time, the BLM had over $100,000 in dishonored filing-fee checks, an average of 10,000 bum entries per month! Once word got out that drawings were conducted before checks cleared banks, an increasing number of people stopped payment on their filing fees upon learning that they did not win. I believe that a large amount of the dishonored funds came from shady filing services each of which cashed their clients' checks and submitted one check drawn on a foreign bank to the BLM to cover the filing fees. When none of the entries won, the services telephone-transferred funds out of their banks before their payment to the BLM cleared, smoothly taking the government for thousands. To counter this, the BLM is now depositing checks sooner, not accepting checks drawn on foreign banks, and considers the amount of an uncollectable remittance a debt due to the United States that must be paid before the applicant is permitted to participate in any future drawings.

(3) Only one complete leasing unit, identified by parcel number, may be included in one entry card. Lands not on the posted list may not be included. An applicant is permitted to file only one offer to lease (entry card) for each numbered parcel on the posted list. Submissions of more than one entry card by or on behalf of the applicant for any parcel on the posted list will result in the disqualification of all the offers submitted by that applicant for that particular parcel.

(4) Entries and filing fees must be submitted to the appropriate BLM office having jurisdiction over the parcels for which you file. In other words, offers to lease Wyoming parcels must be submitted to the Wyoming BLM office; to lease Colorado parcels offers must be submitted to the Colorado BLM office; to lease North Dakota parcels offers must be submitted to the Montana BLM office, etc. Entries filed in the wrong office will be rejected.

(5) An applicant is permitted to file on as many parcels as he or she wishes.

(6) Filing of the offer to lease will be considered as acceptance by the applicant of any lease terms, conditions, or special stipulations embraced in the lease.

(7) Advanced rental payments should not accompany the entry card. Advanced rental will be called for after the first priority card has been determined and examined for compliance with the regulations.

The completion of the drawing entry card is simple. If you are the sole filer, only your name, address, and social security number appear on the front of the card. These you enter into the appropriate blocks provided on the card. As a general rule I line through the name and social security number blocks not used. In the blocks on the lower right of the card enter the parcel number. The parcel number must include the "state prefix" as shown on the drawing list, such as WY, CA, NM, etc. The state prefix is not necessarily the state in which the parcel is located. Rather, the state prefix designates the state in which the BLM office is located which has jurisdiction over the parcels for which you file. To cite an example, North Dakota parcels have the state prefix MT in the parcel numbers. The state prefix is part of the parcel number and therefore its use in describing the tract applied for is mandatory. If leading zeroes are part of the assigned parcel number, their use in describing the tract applied for is also mandatory. On the back of the entry card enter your signature in the space provided. Your signature should correspond to your printed name, exactly as you have entered it on the front of the card. To be on the safe side, since procedures may change, do not use a rubber stamped signature or otherwise mechanically imprint your signature. Next to your signature enter the date in the space provided. This date must be a date within the specified filing period. See chapter twelve under "Filing Deadlines" to determine the correct dates. Line through all of the unused blank portions of the card. See the sample in figures 22 and 23, which illustrate a simultaneous oil and gas drawing entry card as it should be completed. Make sure to make your entries on the card legibly. Your entry card must be read without ambiguity by the BLM office clerks. Your name and address on the entry card also serves as your mailing address in the event your card is not drawn. The postal clerks will need to read your address to assure return mailing of your entry card.

When two persons are jointly filing for a lease it is necessary for both people to enter their names and respective social secu-

Form 3112-1
(April 1978)

UNITED STATES
DEPARTMENT OF THE INTERIOR
BUREAU OF LAND MANAGEMENT
WASHINGTON, D.C. 20240

POSTAGE AND FEES PAID
U. S. DEPARTMENT OF THE INTERIOR
INT 415

U.S. MAIL

SIMULTANEOUS OIL AND GAS DRAWING ENTRY CARD

Print or type

WELLS   WILDCAT   O
Last name   First name   Middle initial

Last name   First name   Middle initial

10349 MAIN ST APT 3
Street Address

GUSHER   WYOMING   82001
City   State   Zip code

123-45-6789
Social Security
or Taxpayer Number

Parcel number WY0071
applied for

The return of this card indicates that you were *not* successful in the drawing and your offer is rejected.

Figure 22. Drawing Entry Card—Front

NONCOMPETITIVE OFFER TO LEASE FOR OIL & GAS

Undersigned offers to lease for oil and gas all or any portion of the identified parcel of land which may be available for noncompetitive leasing, and certifies: (1) applicant is a citizen of the United States, an association of such citizens, a partnership, a corporation, or a municipality organized under the laws of the United States or any State thereof; (2) applicant's interests in oil and gas offers to lease, leases, and options do not exceed the limitation provided by 43 CFR 3101.1-5; (3) applicant has not filed any other entry card for the parcel involved; and (4) applicant is the sole party in interest in this offer and the lease if issued, or if not the sole party in interest, that he names and addresses of all other interested parties are set forth below. The undersigned agrees that the successful drawing of this card will bind him to a lease, on Forms 3110-2 or 3110-3, and the appropriate stipulations as provided in 43 CFR 3109.4-2 and the posted notice.

INSTRUCTIONS

This card must be fully completed, signed, and sent to the appropriate Office of the Bureau of Land Management. It *must* be accompanied by a $10 filing fee. Compliance *must* also be made with the provisions of 43 CFR 3102. If qualifications of association or corporation have been filed previously, identify serial record involved _____.

If you are successful in the drawing, you will be required to pay the first year's rental of $1.00 per acre or fraction thereof prior to issuance of lease. No copies or facsimiles of this form will be accepted.

Other parties in interest — All interested parties named below must furnish evidence of their qualifications to hold such lease interest. See 43 CFR 3102.7.

Signature of Applicant	Date
Wildcat O Well	4/17/79
Signature of Applicant	Date

Other parties in interest

Title 18 U.S.C., Section 1001, makes it a crime for any person knowingly and willfully to make to any department or agency of the United States any false, fictitious or fraudulent statements or representations as to any matter within its jurisdiction.
IF YOU FILE MORE THAN ONE CARD FOR THE SAME PARCEL, YOU ARE AUTOMATICALLY DISQUALIFIED

☆ GPO 778-770

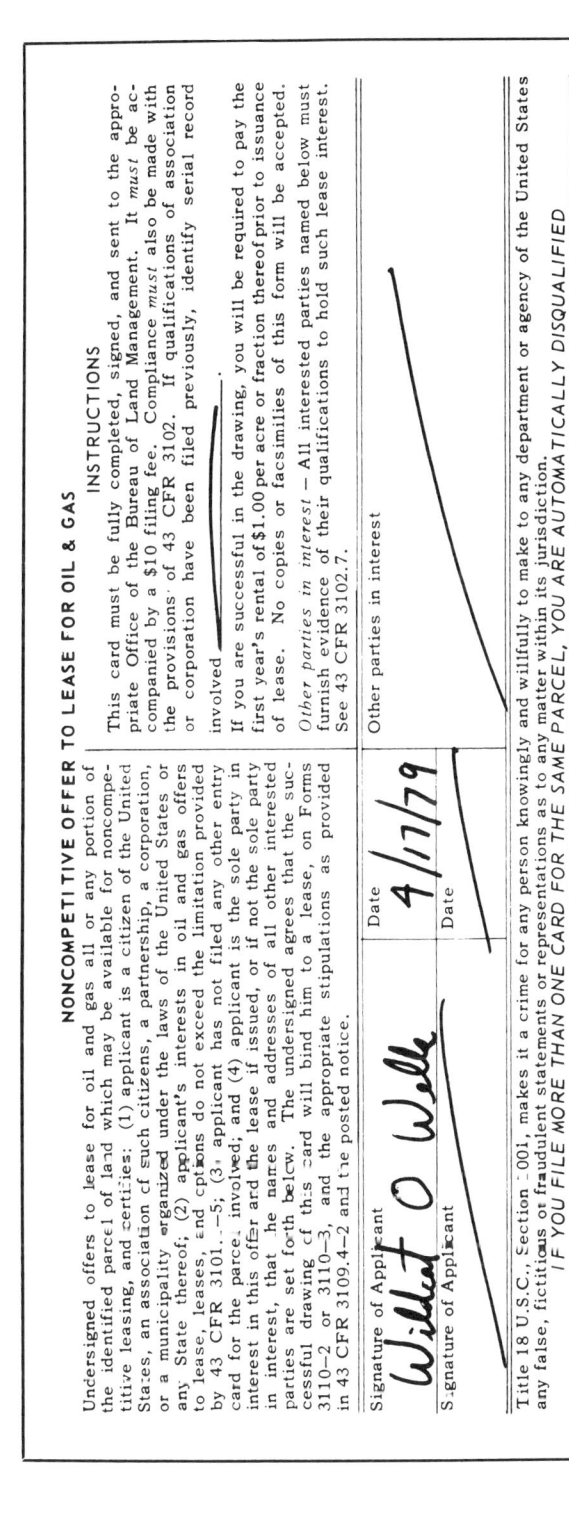

Figure 23. Drawing Entry Card—Back

rity numbers in the boxes on the front of the card. Both parties must sign and date the back of the card. If the parties do not share the same address, the second address may be given on the back of the card in the space marked "Other Parties in Interest."

The BLM plans to change the procedure to allow only one person to be listed as the applicant on an entry card. This revision is designed to aid the BLM administratively in alphabetizing the cards and in locating specific cards on microfilmed records. Additional persons, instead of being entered as joint applicants, would be treated as other parties in interest, and the entry card would be completed in the same manner as was described for joint applicants.

If there are additional persons having an interest in the lease offer, it is necessary for their names and addresses to be entered in the space marked on the back of the card "Other Parties in Interest." Other parties in interest must comply with 43 CFR 3102.7, which states:

> If there are other parties interested in the offer a separate statement must be signed by them and by the offeror, setting forth the nature and extent of the interest of each in the offer, the nature of the agreement between them if oral, and a copy of such agreement if written. All interested parties must furnish evidence of their qualifications to hold such lease interest. Such separate statement and written agreement, if any, must be filed not later than 15 days after the filing of the lease offer. Failure to file the statement and written agreement within the time allowed will result in the cancellation of any lease that may have been issued pursuant to the offer. Upon execution of the lease the first year's rental will be earned and deposited in the U.S. Treasury and will not be returnable even though the lease is cancelled.

What is considered to be an "interest" is defined under 3100.5 (b):

> An "interest" in the lease includes, but is not limited to, record title interests, overriding royalty interests, working interests, operating rights or options, or any agreements covering such "interests." Any claim or any prospective or future claim to an advantage or benefit from a lease, and any participation or any defined or undefined share in any increments, issues, or profits which may be derived from or which may accrue in any manner from the lease based upon or pursuant to any agreement or understanding existing at the time when the offer is filed is deemed to constitute an "interest" in such lease.

These regulations pertaining to other parties in interest are self-explanatory. Let me remind you, however, that prior to filing your offer you do not want to enter into written agreement or oral understanding with a filing service which could give the service an interest in your lease. If such an interest is deemed to have been created and you fail to show the filing service as a party in interest, your lease will be invalidated.

Filings by Associations, Corporations, Guardians, or Trustees

If you are filing as a corporation, company, partnership, association, guardian, or trustee, it is necessary to have a "serial qualification number" issued by the Bureau of Land Management. The serial qualification number is also referred to as a "serial reference number," "serial record number," "corporation qualification number," "partnership qualification number," and by many other similar names. To obtain a serial reference number you will need to file a "statement of qualification" with the BLM.

Associations, which includes partnerships, must file a certified copy of their articles of association or partnership, together with a statement showing: (1) that they are authorized to hold oil and gas leases, (2) that the members or partners executing the lease are authorized to act on behalf of the association in such matters, and (3) the names and addresses of all members owning or controlling more than 10 percent of the association. Additionally, each person owning or controlling more than 10 percent of the association must file a separate statement setting forth his qualifications to hold oil and gas leases and the extent of the direct and indirect interests held in oil and gas leases.

Similar requirements will need to be met to qualify a sole proprietorship.

To qualify a corporation, file a statement showing: (1) the State in which it is incorporated, (2) that it is authorized to hold oil and gas leases and that the officers executing the lease are authorized to act on behalf of the corporation in such matters, (3) the percentage of voting stock and the percentage of all the stock owned by aliens or those having addresses outside of the United States, and (4) the names and addresses of the stockholders holding more than 10 percent of the stock of the corporation. Where the stock owned by aliens is over 10 percent, additional information may be required by the BLM before the lease is issued or production is obtained. Additionally, each stockholder owning or controlling more than 10 percent of the stock of the corporation must file a separate statement setting forth his qualifications to hold oil and gas leases and the extent of direct and indirect interests held in oil and gas leases.

Guardians or trustees filing offers on behalf of minors also need to obtain a serial reference number. The guardian or trustee must file a certified copy of the court order authorizing him/her to act as such and to fulfill in behalf of the minor or minors all obligations of the lease or arising thereunder. Additionally, the guardian or trustee must file a statement with the BLM setting forth his qualifications to hold oil and gas leases and the extent of direct and indirect interests held in oil and gas leases to include leases held for the benefit of other minors. The statement must also include the citizenship and holdings of each of the minors.

Forms and instructions for filing statements of qualification may be obtained from any BLM office. When requesting forms be specific as to the category of statement you intend to file. The forms differ for each filing. Statements may be filed at any of the State offices of the Bureau of Land Management.

Once you have received the serial reference number it may be used for filing oil and gas lease offers and assignments at any BLM office. When filing for a lease the serial reference number must be entered in the appropriate space on the obverse side of the drawing entry card. Make sure that you do not violate the multiple filing provisions of 43 CFR 3112.5-2. See chapter twelve for the text of this regulation.

Filings and the Privacy Act of 1974

There has been an increasing concern by the public lately for their rights to privacy. Computer technology and teleprocessing have reached such a level of sophistication today that it is possible to maintain a central data bank on every U.S. citizen, to include health records, educational profile, résumé of business activities, jobs held, salaries earned, property owned, driving records, family data, names of spouse, children and relatives, banking history, violations records, etc. Some government and private agencies have already compiled central computer files on the public. In some states the highway patrol has computerized data on all of their resident motorists. They need only to radio in your license number to central processing and by the time they pull you over they already know a lot about you, your driving record, and outstanding citations you may have. Insurance companies are collectively maintaining a centralized medical history on all of their clients in order to minimize claims for "preexisting" conditions.

How much information should be maintained, what type of information, who should maintain it, and who has the right to access the information are some of the salient factors for which there is no easy solution. Few people will disagree that the IRS should have the right to maintain tax records on wage earners, but should the IRS also be able to coordinate this data with other government agencies who each have a piece of information about you? At what point does the accumulation and use of data about an individual violate his rights to privacy? There are probably as many opinions about rights to privacy as there are individuals concerned.

On the other hand, the public has the right to obtain information about the workings of its government, how it spends its money, allocates resources, makes decisions, etc. Giving the public the right to information requires that some agencies' and individuals' privacy will be compromised. For example, all filings and assignments for oil and gas leases become a matter of public record. Anyone can find out the history of lease ownership and filing activity for a given parcel or area. This accessibility of information works to the oil-lease speculator's advantage. By carefully examining the public records you can gauge the action in the lottery. Take for example, the following information which was compiled from the microfilm record of a recently drawn parcel in Wyoming.

Name of Filing Service	Number of Entries Filed
Energy Group of America	528
Federal Oil & Gas Leases, Inc.	522
Oil Income Lottery	228
Resource Service Company	384
Stewart Capital Corporation	325

There were other filing services who also filed their clients on this parcel. The filing services may not like this type of information being spread around since from it you can piece together their filing strategy and also be able to estimate the filing revenues of any service. This compromises their privacy. Nevertheless, you have a right to know about the filing activities on public domain lands. Likewise, other individuals also have the right to know about filing activities, to include your filings. If you win a valuable lease, a lot of people are going to know about it, the IRS for one, the filing services, of course, perhaps the news media, and we hope, the oil producers, who may be interested in buying your lease. And don't be surprised if you get a call from some salesman who used the winners list to locate prospective clients for his business investments.

Pursuant to the Privacy Act of 1974 and the regulations in 43 CFR 2.48 (d), the Bureau of Land Management publishes the following notice regarding the information required to be completed on the simultaneous oil and gas drawing entry card:

AUTHORITY: The various statutes under which applications are filed are listed in the regulations in Title 43 of Code of Federal Regulations.

PRINCIPAL PURPOSE: The information is to be used to process your application for a right or interest in Natural Resource lands and resources.

ROUTINE USES: (1) The adjudication of the applicants' rights to the land or resources. (2) Documentation for public information in support of notations made on land status records for the management, disposal, and use of National Resource lands and resources. (3) Transfer to appropriate Federal agencies when concurrence is required prior to granting a right in Natural Resource lands or resources. (4) Transfer to the U.S. Department of Justice in the event of litigation involving the records or the subject matter of the records. (5) Transfer, in the event there is indicated a violation or potential violation of a statute, regulations, rule, order or license, whether civil, criminal or regulatory in nature, to the appropriate agency or agencies, whether federal, state, local or foreign, charged with the responsibility of investigation or prosecuting such violation or charged with enforcing or implementing the statute, rule, regulation, order or license violated or potentially violated.

EFFECT OF NOT PROVIDING INFORMATION: If you do not furnish all the information required, your application may be rejected.

You give up some of your privacy for the privilege of participating in the government's oil and gas lease lottery, but it is a small price to pay for the freedom of opportunity to share in our nation's wealth. At least in this case, Big Brother is working to your advantage.

12
What Not to Do

Tricks to Avoid

A principal objective of this book is to thoroughly examine the oil and gas lease lottery system in order to be able to develop various strategies which would improve your odds of winning. To this end you should do whatever you can, so long as it is both legal and morally right. The legalities for participating in the lottery are well defined by the Bureau of Land Management, but what about moralities? There is no established set of moral principles for participating in the lottery. Morality begins where the legalities leave off. (Actually, legalities begin where moralities leave off.) Moralities are self-governing principles which come from within each individual, to one extent or another. Unfortunately, a few persons, lured by the chance for a fast buck, compromise their moral principles or disregard them completely when playing the lottery. A typical example would be the unscrupulous filing agent who uses his clients for the sole purpose of enhancing his own gain, or who files phantom-name entries to stack the odds in his favor. Do not compromise your integrity. It is far better to maintain a high code of personal ethics and not win a parcel, than to win a bonanza at the expense of personal integrity. Avoid using phony names and other similar gimmicks to file multiple entries. Do not use several variations of your legal name to make it appear to the BLM that different members of one family are filing on the same parcel. Some of the so-called lottery pros dust their entry cards with chalk powder, or lightly sandpaper their entry cards, or bend the corners of the cards, or otherwise alter their entry cards in order to increase the chances of having their cards drawn. The BLM is on to these cheap tricks and closely examines the cards before and after the drawing. Entry cards that show signs of being intentionally altered are disqualified. Entry cards which are bent, folded, or mutilated without undue visible external damage to the envelope in which mailed will not be included in the drawing. To help safeguard your entries fold a couple of 8½-by-11 sheets of paper around the cards before inserting them into the envelope. If the entry cards are damaged in the mail at least the BLM clerks will be assured that you did make an effort to keep the cards in good order.

If you organize a filing club, or a filing service agency, or if you use the services of a filing agent, make sure that your filings comply with the multiple filing provisions in 43 CFR 3112.5-2, which state:

> When any person, association, corporation, or other entity or business enterprise files an offer to lease for inclusion in a drawing, and an offer (or offers) to lease is filed for the same lands in the same drawing by any person or party acting for, on behalf of, or in collusion with the other person, association, corporation, entity or business enterprise, under any agreement, scheme, or plan which would give either, or both, a greater probability of successfully obtaining a lease, or interest therein, in any public drawing, all offers filed by either party will be rejected. Similarly, where an agent or broker files an offer to lease for the same lands in behalf of more than one offeror under an agreement that, if a lease issues to any such offerors, the agent or broker will participate in any proceeds derived from such lease, the agent or broker obtains thereby a greater probability of success in obtaining a share in the proceeds of the lease and all such offers filed by such agent or broker will also be rejected. Should any such offer be given a priority as a result of such a drawing, it will be similarly rejected. In the event a lease is issued on the basis of any such offer, action will be taken for the cancellation of all interests in said lease held by each person who acquired any interest therein as a result of collusive filing unless the rights of a bona fide purchaser intervene, whether the pertinent information regarding it is obtained by or was available to the Government before or after the lease was issued.

This regulation should be sufficient to guide you in the legalities of multiple filings. If you have a specific filing strategy for which you need an interpretive opinion you can always contact the Director, Bureau of Land Management, Washington, D.C. 20240. If you need an opinion on the morality of a filing strategy I suggest that you contact and listen to your own inner self, the highest authority on such issues.

Filing Deadlines

They are very simple, but many people are confused about filing deadlines. At 10:00 A.M. on the third Monday of each month, each state land office of the Bureau of Land Management posts its list of the available, noncompetitive oil and gas leases. The time and date of the posting begins the filing period which runs for seven days (five business days) until 10:00 A.M. the following Monday. In the event there is a holiday within the filing period, one more day is added for filing. Filing cards *received* after 10:00 A.M. on the closing date of the filing period are not accepted for entry into the drawing. It is important to note that the BLM does not pay attention to the date your entry was postmarked. Your entry card must arrive at the BLM office within the designated filing period for the drawing.

The Bureau of Land Management is considering changing to a quarterly schedule for its drawings. This would enable expanding the time allowed for the filing of entry cards from 5 to 15 business days. The BLM believes this change would overcome the difficulties which applicants experience in meeting existing deadlines. There is much opposition to this from independent oil companies as well as from within the ranks of the BLM itself. What will finally happen remains to be seen. Perhaps a compromise will result in a bimonthly drawing. In any event, you will always know the schedule since the filing period and deadline are indicated on every issue of the BLM's list of available oil and gas leases.

Usually, the BLM offices will mail their lists of available lands to their subscribers before the actual posting time. This enables subscribers to receive the lists approximately at the official date of posting. Depending upon the mails you could receive the lists within one or two days after the posting date, or even a couple of days before the posting date. The late receipt of your list does not extend the filing deadline.

All things considered you do not have much time to research the parcels on the list. From the time you receive the availability list to the time of the filing deadline is generally a matter of a few days. From this you must subtract sufficient time for the early mailing of your entries so that your cards arrive at the BLM office on time. Mail service varies between different locations. Check with your post office for their pick up and the estimated delivery schedules, then add a day's time as a buffer. Weather conditions, mail volume, and a variety of other factors, will effect your mail service. Consider using Special Delivery or Express Mail service as an added safeguard to your time and cost of research. Depending upon points being served these services could reduce delivery time by one or two days.

To safeguard their businesses and their clients' interests some of the filing service agents personally hand-deliver their clients' entries to the BLM offices. This allows the agents a couple of days extra for receiving and processing entries. Since you will not be dealing in the high volume of entries that filing agents do, it won't be economically feasible for you to hand-deliver your applications. You will therefore need to make a careful estimate of the time it takes for you to receive the availability list, your research time, and the time it takes for the mails to deliver your entry cards to the BLM offices. If you act promptly and mail your cards early there should be no problem in meeting the filing deadline. If you feel that you need more time for research you can always obtain a preliminary abridged listing of available lands free through most filing services. These lists will provide you with one to three weeks' additional time to do your research. In any event, if you miss the deadline you are out of luck.

Why Filings are Rejected

After several months of research and waiting, the type of parcel you have been looking for has just appeared on the availability list issued by the BLM office in, say, California. The 320-acre parcel offsets an existing oil field. You figure it to be worth around $35 to $50 per acre, plus a small overriding royalty of about 3 percent. Based on the analysis of prior drawing results you estimate that there will be about 100 to 200 entries filed for this parcel. A $10 gamble at roughly 150 to 1 odds for a potential payout of around $15,000, plus override, is too good a deal to pass up. You complete your entry card and mail it. The next several weeks you spend eagerly waiting for the Bureau of Land Management to mail you a notice that you won. You check the mailbox daily. Finally, a letter comes from the BLM. In great anticipation you nervously tear open the seal. You remove the contents—your drawing entry card along with a notice. First bewilderment overtakes you, then anger, as you read the notice:

"Your Simultaneous Oil and Gas Drawing Entry Card is returned for the reason indicated: Incorrect parcel number." "What are those turkeys talking about?" you blurt to yourself as you snap your entry card over to check the number. "There, the number's right there just like ..." Then it dawns on you. You forgot to include the state prefix code as part of the parcel number. To add insult to injury the BLM is retaining your filing fee as a service charge. You're galled and discouraged. You *know* you would have won that parcel if it weren't for your filing error!

Each year thousands of people lose in the oil and gas lottery even before the drawing is held. For one reason of defect or another their entry cards are rejected. The Bureau of Land Management will reject simultaneous oil and gas lease offers having any of the following defects:

(1) Unacceptable remittance: not signed, not dated, postdated, improper payee, no payee, no amount.

(2) Insufficient filing fees: e.g., ten offers with one check for only nine offers; *all* entries will be returned.

(3) Premature or late filing.

(4) Parcel deleted from list by BLM.

(5) Entry card filed in wrong state office.

(6) Entry not on authorized Form 3112-1.

(7) Duplicate filing on the same parcel.

(8) Entry card failed to indicate the parcel number for which offeror was applying.

(9) Parcel number incorrect or incomplete: no state prefix indicated, proper state not shown.

(10) Entry card indicated a parcel number not on current filing list.

(11) Entry card contains an illegible parcel number.

(12) Failed to complete the entry card by omitting: signature, date, address, or social security or taxpayer number (indicating that such a number has been applied for is not sufficient). Note: In practice the BLM state office in *Wyoming* has been assigning an arbitrary number for entry cards without social security numbers. If you do not wish to disclose your social security number, you may use the BLM assigned number on your entries.

(13) Entry card does not show clearly the name and address on the face of the card.

(14) Signature differs from name on face of card.

(15) Reference to corporate qualifications or number not shown on back of card.

(16) Uncollectible remittance submitted for the filing fee.

(17) Entry card shows signs of being intentionally bent, folded, altered or mutilated.

The Bureau of Land Management will return the filing fee for any of the first five defects indicated above. For any of the others, the BLM will retain the fee as a service charge.

Use the foregoing list as your final check list. It is easy to make a costly mistake. Double check your filing to assure that your filing card becomes a valid entry in the drawing.

13
Winning and Losing

Computerized Drawings

In 1972 about 200,000 entries were filed in the Wyoming State office of the Bureau of Land Management. By 1977 this figure jumped over eight-fold topping 1.7 million entries. The BLM personnel were manually processing the applications and were working about 250 hours of overtime per month to keep pace with the increasing workload. With increasingly more entries anticipated it became apparent that a new processing system had to be implemented. The use of a computerized system was the obvious solution. By August 1978 a computerized system was implemented which automated much of the simultaneous filing system. Under the new system the same Drawing Entry Card Form 3112-1 is used and completed as usual. After the standard process of receipting the filing fees the entry cards are encoded with magnetic ink similar to the encoding used by banks for identification. The encoding includes the parcel number, your identification number, and a sequence number. (The entry cards are numbered in sequence as they are received). The encoded data is stored on magnetic tape cassettes. The entry cards are also microfilmed and then stored in sequence order in locked cabinets for safekeeping until after the "drawing." The data on the magnetic tapes is transmitted by a minicomputer in the Cheyenne office via telephone interface to a large-scale host computer in Denver. The host computer temporarily stores the telecommunicated data for processing.

During processing the host computer checks for, and generates a printout of, duplicate filings, missing information, and possible illegal or improper entries. The printout is manually verified for accuracy. Defective entries are purged and nondefective entries are reentered into the computer for inclusion into the drawing.

Unlike the manual drawing system the computer system provides for the random selection of entries based on a mathematical formula for random number generation. These "drawing" results are then transmitted via telephone from the host computer back to the minicomputer at the state office in Cheyenne, and immediately made known to the public. The BLM claims that a number of checks and balances have been built into the system to ensure integrity and security of the drawings. The complete winners list is generated on the day of the drawing in the same format as in the manual system. In addition to the winners list the host computer provides an alphabetic list of all applicants and a listing of all applicants by parcel number. A paper copy of each page costs fifty cents, and it takes about 200 pages to furnish the data for one month's filings. For only one dollar you can obtain the equivalent information on a microfische card. Do not confuse the microfische record, which is slightly larger than a postcard and currently available only for filings made at the Wyoming Land Office, with the microfilm rolls available from all BLM land offices.

Is this a better system for conducting oil lease lotteries? To the BLM it is. It saves processing time and labor costs. But to the oil lease speculator who attends the drawings at the public room, there is no longer the glamor of watching the cards loaded into a drum, watching the drum spin scattering the cards, seeing someone reach in and pull out a card, then hearing the winner's name called. The computerized system has other drawbacks. It breaks down. A failure in the minicomputer, telephone interface, or the host computer could delay the drawing upwards to several days. And, contrary to marketing propaganda, computers do make mistakes, and big ones at that. A computer can make the same mistake in a few minutes that would take ten people a week's time to make. Also, the people using the automated system are subject to making errors as they are learning and use a system that is more complex and more abstract than the manual forerunner.

How does a computerized drawing effect Lady Luck? With the human factor no longer directly involved in the selection of leases, is the use of amulets, charms, and silent prayers to influence the computer's random number generator of naught? It is something to consider if you are superstitious.

Regardless of the drawbacks, on balance, the computer serves as a tool for providing a faster and more efficient lottery system.

There are already some signs that its use will be expanded in the lease lottery. A new filing card design is on the docket to be used when filing for leases in computerized drawings. The new cards will enable the computer to optically scan and read entrants' handwritten marks on the filing cards, thereby eliminating the time it now takes to key entry data into the computer. Also, plans are in the works to enable a person to use one card to file for many parcels. I believe that within a few years the BLM drawings for all states will be made by a centralized computer. The host computer in Denver will serve as the central service bureau for all of the BLM state offices. Each office will transmit their list of available parcels to the host computer. All filings for parcels will be mailed by the entrants directly to the Denver center where all of the entry cards will be encoded and the data loaded into the computer for the "drawings." The host computer will pick winners at random and transmit a list of winners to each respective state office for posting and distribution.

Some day we will all have a keyboard terminal attached to our telephones for transacting our business. Then, no longer will we need to complete filing cards, write checks, and rush to the post office with our entries. Instead, we will simply dial the BLM office, key in our personal number, the transaction code, and the parcel numbers. The BLM will electronically credit our bank accounts and load the computer file with the parcels of our choice. After the drawing we will receive a winners list transmitted to us via telephone and printed on our home-teletype. By the time such a system is part of our way of life, however, we probably will not have an oil lease lottery system. Instead, perhaps we will be simultaneously filing for wildcat sections of the sky to acquire lease rights for the potential wind and sunshine.

Unsuccessful Entries

As Alain Rene Le Sage observed, "The blanks as well as the prizes must be drawn in the cheating game of life."

There is no way around it; there can be only one winner for each drawing. Unfortunately, losing is very much a part of the oil lease lottery system. Some 2.5 million filings each year do not make it to first place. It would be nice if you could win every time you entered, but the game of chance doesn't work that way even if you have an "in" with Lady Luck. The lady is fickle; her game is playing the field, showering her favors on the least suspecting.

During the month following the posting of the list of available lands the drawings are held. There is no set date for the drawing each month. It depends upon the amount of time required to process all entry cards. The date, time, and place are announced by the BLM at least 24 hours before the drawing. Successful applicants are notified shortly after the drawing, a topic discussed below. Unsuccessful applicants, commonly referred to as "good sports" for their ability to withstand being rejected by Lady Luck, are notified of their loss by the return of their respective entry cards. All entry cards are retained by the Bureau of Land Management for five working days following the drawing. This allows the public some time in which to examine the cards. After the five days the BLM delivers the cards to the post office for distribution. It takes the post office several days to sort the cards and return them to the applicants. If you do not receive the return of your entry card within approximately two to three weeks following the drawing you can assume one of the following: (1) Your filing never made it to the BLM office in the first place. (2) Your entry made it to the BLM office but was accidentally misplaced either before or after the drawing. (3) Your entry card had an illegible or inadequate address and therefore could not be returned. (4) The BLM mailed your card but the card became delayed or lost in the mails.

Regarding the first assumption: Your best verification that your application was received by the BLM is the return of your cancelled check. If your check does not clear the bank your application most likely did not make it to the BLM office. Your application could have been lost in the mails, though that's unlikely. Maybe you forgot to mail it. Did you give it to your husband to mail on the way to work? He could have tucked it out of view over his car's visor and forgot to retrieve it in his rush to get to the office.

Regarding the second assumption: With the volume of entry cards that the BLM processes annually it is likely that some mistakes will be made, cards will be misplaced or even lost. To verify whether your card was entered into the drawing you would need to order a copy of the microfilm records, or in Wyoming, the computerized listing of entrants. The BLM photographs the front and back of each and every card whether it wins or not, just like the banks do with checks.

Regarding the third assumption: The BLM reports that numerous cards are returned to them marked "undeliverable" by the post office. These cards contain illegible or incomplete addresses and zip codes.

Regarding the fourth assumption: The entry card does not look like a piece of mail. It looks more like an enclosure that fell out of an envelope. Also, the face side of the entry card has a lot of extraneous information on it that camouflages the name and address. When I first examined the entry card I did not realize that it also served as a postal card. It is unlike any piece of mail that I had ever seen. I guess to the discriminating glances of postal clerks it must appear as mail. Nevertheless, it is difficult to read and process, factors which could contribute to the delay or loss of entry cards.

When you receive your returned entry card you will notice that it may or may not have been stamped "received" by the BLM. Generally, the BLM time-stamps the entry cards upon receipt. The BLM is not required by law, however, to stamp the cards, merely to return them. So do not feel that your card was not processed correctly or that you were not in the drawing if your card is returned unstamped.

Protests and Appeals

With the millions of entries that are filed with the Bureau of Land Management each year occasionally processing mistakes are made. To err is human, the BLM staff not excepted. Sometimes entry cards are disqualified for obviously incorrect reasons: "Parcel number not on the list"—when in fact the parcel number did appear on the availability list. A first-place winner may be informed that his offer to lease was rejected due to a (not-so-obvious) "technicality." The applicable lottery rules and regulations are "guidelines" which might not always be appropriately interpreted by the BLM officials when reviewing the circumstances of a filing. Further, the BLM is not able to monitor each and every offer and does not check into the credentials of offerors. Someone may have pulled a fast one to win that lease you were after. If you feel that your entry was incorrectly disqualified or rejected, or that you were otherwise wronged in the lottery process, or maybe you just disagree with an administrative policy, you have the right to appeal. You should feel free to exercise this right since you are entitled to an accurate and fair lottery. The protest and appeal procedure is outlined below. The chances are that you will not have to use it. Even so, someone else might attempt to challenge your winning entry and therefore you should be aware of the appeal process.

To submit a protest, merely write a letter stating the basis for your protest and mail it to the appropriate BLM state office. There is no prescribed format for submitting a protest. Upon receipt of your protest, the BLM office will make a review and issue its decision. Sometimes, in instances regarding disqualified or rejected entries, the BLM will automatically issue its decision without the need for you to file a protest. If you disagree with a decision you have the right to appeal. You do not "protest" a decision, you "appeal" it. Appeals of State office decisions are taken to the Interior Board of Land Appeals (IBLA) which speaks for the secretary of the interior. All appeals of decisions must comply with 43 CFR Subpart 4.400 through 4.478, which is paraphrased, in part, as follows.

Within 30 days of being served with a decision, file a notice of appeal in the BLM office which issued the decision. The notice of appeal must give the serial number or other identification of the case—the BLM parcel number and drawing date will suffice. If you desire, you may state your reasons for appealing and provide any arguments you wish to make. If your notice of appeal did not include a statement of the reasons for the appeal, such a statement must be filed with the Board of Land Appeals, Office of Hearings and Appeals, 4015 Wilson Boulevard, Arlington, VA 22203 within 30 days after notice of appeal was filed.

Within 15 days after each document is filed—a document is not considered as filed until it is actually received in the proper office—you must serve each adverse party named in the decision with a copy of the notice of appeal, the statement of reasons, and any other documents, such as written arguments or briefs, that have been filed.

Within 15 days after any document is served on an adverse party, file proof of that service with the Board of Land Appeals, Office of Hearings and Appeals (same address as given above). This proof of service may consist of a certified or registered mail return receipt card signed by the adverse party.

Any party served with a notice of appeal who wishes to participate in the proceedings on appeal, must file an answer within 30 days after being served. The answer must state the reasons why the appeal should not be sustained. If an answer is not filed and served on the appellant within the time required, it may be disregarded in deciding the appeal.

If the hearing involves a question of fact, either you or the adverse party may request that the case be assigned to an administrative law judge for such a hearing.

The final decision of the IBLA may be appealed to federal Court if such contest of decision is taken within 90 days after the final decision has been made.

A case history illustrating a reversal by the IBLA of a decision made by the BLM's Montana state office is given here as Appendix G.

You Win!

It's a Wednesday morning in April. It could just as well be any weekday of any month of any of the last 18 years. Except for the weather, the time Pipsi gave birth to a litter of kittens, and the day the newsboy smashed the morning newspaper through the living room window, it has been the same routine for the Lanskis day in and day out. The Big Ben alarm jolts them to wakeful attentiveness at 6:00 A.M. While Walter washes, shaves, and dresses, his wife Carolyn fixes the usual breakfast: sausages, toast, two sunny-side up, and coffee. She then retrieves the newspaper from the porch in time for Walter's 6:20 arrival at the table. While he reads and eats, Carolyn nibbles her breakfast at the kitchen counter as she prepares a box lunch. At 6:40, running a bit late for work, Walter hastily sips the last of his coffee while alighting from the table. He tucks the newspaper under his arm. Carolyn hands him his lunch box. They exchange a routine mechanical kiss. Walter heads for the door starting his half-hour commute to the machine shop.

Today, however, Walter's exit is interrupted by the telephone ringing, beginning a new scenario for the Lanskis. Carolyn, lifting the receiver, hears an unfamiliar voice query in a businesslike manner, "Is this Mrs. Lanski?"

"Yes," she says, looking quizzical.

"May I speak with your husband please?"

Carolyn nods to her husband to indicate that the call is for him as she replies, "Yes. Who may I ask is calling?"

"Mr. Burt Taylor of Shell Oil."

"Just a moment." Carolyn covers the telephone mouthpiece to tell her husband of the caller.

Walter frowns with painful recollection that he forgot to make his overdue credit card payment. He pauses, considering not taking the call, then changes his mind, sighing, "I'll take it.

"Hello. This is Walter Lanski," he says with anticipation of receiving a hard line back.

"Congratulations Mr. Lanski. Our office noticed that you are the first drawee on a 2,119-acre lease in Converse, Wyoming. Shell is prepared to pay you $145,000 and a 5 percent overriding royalty for the rights to your lease. Would you be interested in transferring the ownership of...."

The moment of "truth" had arrived for the Lanskis.

Although this story and the names are fictional the circumstances are not. Each month, by the luck of the draw, many people from all walks of life get the surprise of their life when they learn that they won it big in the oil lottery. For many of the winners it means freedom from the doldrums of a routine job and life. Most of the winners are laymen who know little about the oil and gas business and oftentimes even less about the lottery itself. That winner could just as easily—or more easily, now that you are in possession of this book—be *you*.

If you win a hot lease you will undoubtedly be contacted by telephone or in person by commercial enterprises before the BLM sends you a notification of your win. Corporation representatives and private investors attend the drawings and are after the big winners as soon as the drawing results are announced. The BLM may take several days before mailing winners their notices. Then, the postal service adds a couple of days or so to the time it takes to get the notices into the winners' hands. Your first communique from the BLM of your new status as an oilman comes in the form of a certified letter, which is sent in duplicate.

You have been aggressively filing for many months now, and in spite of the long odds against you your patience and strategy paid off. You won the big lease that you have been after. It's worth a small fortune. You don't know exactly how much. Anyway, at this point you are no longer thinking in terms of dollars. A new car, maybe two, a paid off mortgage, college expenses for the kids, a luxury vacation every year, or maybe two homes, one in Maui and one in Switzerland.... Your fantasies race on. Within seconds you spend ten times what the lease will bring. You think of quitting your monotonous job, and contrive a half-dozen resignations. You can't wait to see the expression on your boss's face when you tell him you quit.

"Mr. Flabberhast, er, Gus, I am no longer going to be in the employ of your corporation. I am in the oil business now."

"What? You can't even keep the stockroom tidy. What oil business? You going to pump gas at some service station?"

This time you do not have to shrug off his condescending remarks. You see yourself having the last word, and laugh. With a valuable oil lease backing you up there is no more need for you to tolerate that irate old toad. You're free to do anything you want. . . .

But just a minute. Read that notice from the BLM again. What does it say? It does not tell you how much money you won, does it? So far, any thoughts of profit from your lease are conjectured, unless you received some offers already. Even then, you still haven't signed an assignment or received any payments. You do not even have the lease yet. Maybe it is best not to count those chickens before they hatch. Read that letter once again. Does it say that you will be issued a lease, even if you pay the rental due? No. It says, "You are the drawee who *may* be *considered* to receive an oil and gas lease. . . ." It appears from the letter that the only condition that remains to be met before the lease is issued to you is payment of the rental due. This does not always hold true. After you submit the payment with a copy of the Notice of Rental Due, the BLM requests the United States Geological Survey to issue a KGS report on your hoped-for parcel. The USGS takes around 10 days to a month to issue its determination. If the determination indicates that the parcel is a known geological structure, you will receive a letter from the BLM politely rejecting your offer to lease the parcel. The parcel will be reoffered under competitive bidding as is done with all KGSs. Usually, the USGS report is negative, the parcel considered not to be a KGS. Then, if all else is in order, your payment has been made, you are qualified to hold a lease, your entry is valid, nobody is contesting your win, etc., the BLM will issue you a lease which will indicate the legal description of your parcel, your name as lessee and a serial identification number. This process may take from one to three days. The completed lease form is your legal title to the lease. Generally, there are no additional forms for you to sign. The drawing entry card that you signed is your application for and agreement to the lease itself. (Sometimes you may be required to sign a separate agreement to special stipulations that are made part of the lease.) You may obtain sample copies of the noncompetitive oil and gas lease from any BLM office. Ask for Form 3110-2.

Becoming a first-place winner on a parcel is only the first big hurdle you will need to get over. The second hurdle is to get the lease issued to you. The BLM holds strictly to the 15-day limitation in which to get your rental payment in. Therefore, make sure that you meet this deadline. The 15 days begin from the date you sign receipt of your certified letter. If you expect to have difficulty coming up with the rental payment by the deadline you can stall for some extra time by avoiding the mail carrier. Do *not* flatly refuse the certified letter, otherwise it will be marked "refused" and sent back to the BLM. And you will have a rough time explaining your way out of (or, rather, back into) that one. By not making yourself available to sign for the letter you will cause the mail carrier to leave a claim check in your mailbox and take the letter back to the post office where it will remain for fifteen days while the post office sends you a second notice and then a final notice of attempted delivery, after which time the letter will be returned to the sender as "unclaimed." When you get the third and final notice and you still need more time in order to make the rental payment you can call the post office and ask them to hold the letter for you as you will be able to come pick it up in a few days. By using the post office procedure to your advantage you can gain up to three weeks additional time in which to make your rental payment. This gives you some time to test the market for your lease before deciding to make your rental payment. Some speculators incorporate this strategy into their game plan. They file on most any lease without doing much research. If they win, they use delays to gain time for testing the market for their lease. If they cannot find anyone interested in the lease they do not make the lease payment. The advantage to this approach is that their risk never exceeds the $10 filing fee. The disadvantage is that they might forfeit a good lease on the erroneous assumption that lack of immediate interest in the lease means that the lease is worthless.

The BLM wants to increase the time period allowed for the submittal of the first year's rental from 15 to 30 days in order to allow lease winners sufficient time to make payment. This provision, coupled with the BLM's proposed increase in the maximum size of noncompetitive leases from 2,560 to 10,240 acres, would provide you with an excellent speculative opportunity. For a $10 filing fee you would have the chance to obtain a lease worth over $1 million (assuming 10,240 acres at $100 per acre) plus potential millions in royalties, with 30 days (plus three weeks stalling time via the Postal Service) in which to find a buyer and to obtain financing for the lease. Try beating that for leverage!

When making your rental payment to the BLM mail it registered, return receipt requested. Registered mail is treated much like cash and under tight security. Human nature being what it is, certified mail is not given the same treatment as registered, since the risk of loss is not assumed by mail handlers to be as great. Mail your payment sufficiently early so that it is *received* by the BLM by the deadline.

If you won your lease through a filing agent, acting on your behalf, make sure that you are the one who is paying for the lease. The BLM proposes to implement rules prohibiting other parties from paying rentals on behalf of winners. The BLM finds this procedure a necessary precaution because in the past some services have advanced the first year's rental and obtained leases which have then been assigned without their clients' knowledge. Relying on someone else to pay your rental for you puts you at their mercy.

Once you have been issued the lease you still have another major hurdle to clear—selling your lease. It is the profiting from a lease that turns a novice into a pro. Anyone can file for, and acquire, a goat pasture lease. It is the ability to acquire and sell a marketable lease that makes the difference. Thus far, we have considered the various aspects of selecting and acquiring marketable oil and gas leases. In the next section we will consider the aspects of selling your lease.

Part IV
Selling Your Lease

14
Reevaluating Your Lease

Once you win a lease you need to determine its value if you intend to be prudent in selling it. Over the last few months of playing the lottery you had some general ideas about the value of leases you were filing for. In the interim some circumstances may have changed which could have affected the value of your lease. Also, if you are like most speculators your ideas of value were probably magnified by pipe dreams of oil riches and what those riches could buy. Now you need to get to the reality of the situation. You won a wildcat oil lease which *may* be valuable. How valuable? There is no easy answer. Many factors influence the value of a lease, and the factors are in constant flux. (Review the end of chapter four on the value of leases.) What you need to do is to determine from your continual research a range between a minimum and maximum amount you feel you could reasonably obtain for your lease. There is no precise formula which you can use to determine this range. After checking the trade newspapers and magazines, and reviewing prices paid for other leases, you will still, at best, have only a general gut feel for what you can expect to obtain for your lease. Filing service agents who boast maintaining surveillance of oil and gas activity to include reviewing reports of exploratory wells, dry holes, discoveries, new pays, extentions, stratigraphic geology, production, geophysical surveys, and leasing and sales activities often disagree among themselves about the values of leases. For example, Wyoming parcel number 77, measuring 2,120 acres, offered in July 1978, was assigned the following estimated values by five leading service agents:

Agent	Estimated Value
A	$170,000 plus ORR (no estimate on ORR)
B	$30,000 to $50,000 plus 3% to 5% ORR valued at $950,000

Agent	Estimated Value
C	$60,000 to $100,000 plus ORR valued at $300,000
D	$210,000 plus ORR valued at $2 million
E	$70,000 to $130,000 plus 3% to 5% ORR valued at $950,000

The estimated value of this parcel ranged from $30,000 to $210,000 plus an overriding royalty ranging anywhere from $300,000 to $2,000,000. This is quite a spread. If we eliminate the highest and lowest estimates we come up with a better idea of what the parcel is worth; $60,000 to $170,000 plus an ORR valued at $300,000 to $950,000. This still leaves a large spread, but at least gives you some figures to work with. I eliminated the highest and lowest estimates because in light of the norm of the other services' estimates they appeared unrealistic. Some service agents may exaggerate the value of a parcel in order to attract more clients and stimulate more filing interest. Other agents may underestimate the value in order to not disappoint their clients at the time of sale, or, if the agent is dishonest, to precondition the client into thinking that the parcel is worth less than it really is so that the client will sell it cheap, hopefully to the agent's associate. One honest agent estimated a North Dakota lease to be worth $10 per acre and later was able to get $60 per acre for his client. A Wyoming 2,500-acre lease estimated to be worth about $30 an acre by another agent sold for $130 per acre. You can see that you cannot totally rely on the estimated value service agents place on parcels. Get as many agents to send you their tip sheets as you can. Review their estimates of parcel values. Eliminate the extreme estimates. Then chart the prices on a map and make sure to date your entries.

Keep in mind that oil and gas lease prices are also related to inflationary trends in the general economy. Oil and gas leases have been increasing in value by 10 percent to 12 percent each year. The escalating price of oil has a direct impact on the value of leases.

Read trade newspapers and magazines to get another source of input on lease values. Figures obtained from these sources are likely to be more reliable than the estimates found on filing services' tip sheets. Review articles on lease sales and chart and date the prices on your map.

In the classified section of the trade publications you will often find advertisements of lease sales. Some individuals advertise around a dozen parcels at a time which indicates to me that they are not rank novices. They advertise consistently and are always coming up with new leases. I assume that these pros know the oil lease market from months of testing and negotiating, and therefore, their advertised prices truly indicate the maximum value of their parcels. Record the prices on your map.

The public records of the BLM offices do not indicate prices paid for simultaneous oil and gas leases. Selling prices of wildcat leases are private transactions between the buyers and sellers. The BLM does, however, keep records of the prices it receives for leases it offers under competitive bidding. Known geological structures are sometimes bid as high as several thousand dollars per acre. You cannot expect to get a KGS price for a wildcat lease. Still, competitive bid prices are another input of data by which to judge the value of your lease. If your lease is in the same geology and location as a KGS and the KGS sold for $100 per acre, all other circumstances being equal, you realistically cannot expect to sell your wildcat lease for $300 per acre. So also chart and date bid prices on your map.

After a few months you will have a very good indication of the market value of leases. When charting lease prices on your map use a code to identify the source of the price. In this way you can give a weighted value judgement to your subsequent final evaluation.

Some filing service agents specialize in evaluating oil and gas lease properties. They provide maps identifying your lease in relationship to surrounding past and current exploration, drilling, and development trends. Their evaluation report includes an opinion on the potential of the acreage along with an estimate of the lease's cash and override value. The cost of the evaluations vary, but expect to pay in the neighborhood of $30 to $100. Two firms offering this service are: Southwest Leasing Service, P.O. Box 14518, Albuquerque, N.M. 87111; and Petroleum Investment Co., 654 South 9th East, Salt Lake City, Utah 84125. I have not used these evaluation services and therefore cannot comment on the accuracy of their reports—you are on your own.

Lease price is a function of demand. Get a copy of the microfilm records of all entry cards that were filed on the lease you won. Find out who filed on your lease. Do not be misled by the number of applicants. A large number of filings could be due to the touting efforts of filing agents. You may find that most of the entries were from amateurs who would have no desire to acquire a lease from a winner; they just want to win their own. Scrutinize the microfilm to find out how many oil companies filed for the lease. This will give you an idea of the commercial demand. Also, you may want to check the filing data on parcels adjacent to the one you won. Do you spot a trend of anyone attempting to accumulate leases in the area? The higher the demand the higher the price you can expect to get for your lease. Of course, you cannot determine the value of a lease just by knowing how many oil companies filed for the lease. The type of company, its other holdings, resources, development plans, etc., all figure into what a company may offer. However, once you have determined a high and a low estimated value for your lease you will know to favor the high estimate if many oil companies filed for the lease, and vice versa.

As mentioned earlier, your telephone is an excellent tool for obtaining information. Obtain the BLM winners list from a few months back. Call the information operator to obtain the telephone numbers of winners who hold parcels near yours. Point blank tell winners that you also won a lease and ask them if they will be willing to help you. Tell them that you are not sure of what to ask for your lease. Ask if their lease has sold, how long it took, and how much they got for it. As can be expected in this paranoid world of ours, you will find some people defensive, evasive, and quick to hang up. But, if you are up-front and sincere it will be transmitted in your voice and you stand a good chance of getting some excellent advice. Figure any prices that you are told as the minimum values. No oil company would have paid more for a parcel than it is worth, they certainly would pay less. If you live near a winner go pay them a visit. Incidentally, do not bother contacting winners who are oil companies. They will not tell you anything.

Of course you have been keeping track of the leasing, exploration and drilling activity in the neighborhood of your lease. You were doing this as part of your research for lease selection. Data on oil strikes, dry holes, planned drilling, lease acquisitions, etc., have all been inputed into your mental computer on a continuing basis. Other than common sense, there is no formula to follow to use this data. Figure that if exploration activity increases near your lease you should favor the maximum amount you think your lease is worth. If a nearby wildcat tests dry consider lowering your sights a bit. Instead of the 36-foot yacht you were going to sink your lease profits into, you may have to settle for a 28-footer.

How much cash payment you receive for your lease also depends upon how much overriding royalty interest you retain in possible future production from the lease. The higher the cash payment, the lower will be the ORR that you will receive; the higher the override, the lower the cash amount paid. Before settling on a figure consider what you want. Do you want to take less or even no cash up front for your lease and let your gamble ride on the prospect that a larger override might make you much richer? A 5 percent override royalty on a hot lease could yield a million dollars or so in payments to you over the next twenty years. According to the U.S. Bureau of Mines the average life of an oil well in the United States in 1976 was 25.5 years, which is about what it has been since the early 1930s. Before you favor a long-term payment in oil royalties and settle for less cash up front, consider the fact that oil companies have millions of acres of wildcat lands under lease most of which will never be drilled. The Bureau of Land Management states that 90 percent of the tracts won in their lottery are not drilled. Companies plan their drilling activities years ahead of time. So even if your parcel is drilled it may not be for some time yet. Then, from the time a parcel is drilled to the time production starts could be another year or so. And, if the oil company should decide not to drill on your lease and drops the lease your override is forfeited as well. The override, which is a gamble on a future potential windfall, *might* make you rich—tomorrow. The cash payment you get for your lease is a known amount, and although it may not make you as rich, if you are lucky enough to win a hot parcel, you will not notice the difference. Note that the overriding royalty is paid free and clear of expenses. It is computed on the basis of actual gross production. Even if the tract turns out to be a low-yielding one, where it might take fifteen to twenty years of production to cover the cost of the well, you would still be receiving your payments on the gross production and from the time that production began. Another factor to consider is that the difference of 1 to 2 percent in ORR (e.g., a 5 percent ORR instead of a 3 percent ORR) could be a couple of hundred thousand dollars.

"A bird in the hand is worth two in the bush." How much cash up front you will want in lieu of an override will depend on whether you are short-term oriented or long-term oriented. How do you see the future economy? A long-term paying override can be an excellent hedge against inflation for many years to come. As oil prices move upwards, so will your overriding payments, assuming production remains constant. Weigh this against having immediate cash at your disposal and how that cash can be leveraged and pyramided over the next few years. I personally prefer a higher cash up front. Our economy is subject to quick, short-term fluctuations. Who knows what lies beyond these fluctuations, ten or twenty years from now?

After figuring what the lease is worth on the market you have to consider your own personal circumstances to determine what you are willing to accept for the lease. The amount you decide on may be lower than the market value, if for example, you need the money for some urgent use and even getting half the amount the lease is worth may suit you fine if you can negotiate a quick deal. A primary factor to consider when deciding on a price for your lease is your personal tax circumstances. Due to the provisions of the capital gains tax you could obtain more cash-in-pocket by accepting less money at a later date than by taking a higher offer now.

Since taxes play an important factor in determining the amount of cash you net from the sale of your lease, I have devoted the following separate chapter to this topic.

15
Tax Considerations

> *Over and over again courts have said that there is nothing sinister in so arranging one's affairs as to keep taxes as low as possible. Everybody does so, rich or poor; and all do right, for nobody owes any public duty to pay more than the law demands; taxes are enforced exactions, not voluntary contributions. To demand more in the name of morals is mere cant.*
>
> JUDGE LEARNED HAND

A Mr. Fred Carpenter won a 520-acre lease located in Eddy County, New Mexico. Five months later, in December 1978, he sold the lease to an oil company for a lump sum cash payment of $50,000 plus a 4.5 percent ORR. What Carpenter failed to take into consideration was the cut the Internal Revenue Service was soon to demand. The $50,000 added to Carpenter's $18,000 taxable salary income placed him in the 64 percent tax bracket. His federal income tax for 1978 computed at about $30,000, over $26,000 of which was attributed to the sale of the lease. Hence, the $50,000 lease netted a cash-in-pocket of only about $24,000 ($50,000 less $26,000).

Had Carpenter done some pre-tax planning he could have arranged his business affairs so as to take advantage of the tax laws. For example, he could have incorporated and done all of his filings through his company. His corporate tax would have been 20 percent on the first $25,000, 22 percent on the next $25,000, and 48 percent on taxable income in excess of $50,000. Hence, the tax on the $50,000 lease sale would have been $10,500, leaving a cash-in-pocket of about $40,000. The tax on Carpenter's $18,000 personal income would be just under $4,000 at a tax bracket of 34 percent. By not considering the tax aspects of his lease sale Carpenter gave away $16,000 to the IRS, an amount he could have used to build up his estate. If nothing else, for $16,000 Carpenter could have filed 1,600 entry cards in subsequent BLM drawings. From a statistical viewpoint he would have stood to do well with such an aggressive filing effort.

Additionally, by filing in the lottery as a business, Carpenter could have set off his expenses against the gross income. His tax write-offs could have included: filing fees; lease rental payments; fees paid to filing agents and consulting firms; expenditures for maps, books (e.g., this book) and other references; costs of subscriptions to trade and technical publications; geology or other related courses; depletion allowance (for producing wells); home office expenses; and costs incurred in the sale of the lease such as attorney fees, brokerage fees, costs of advertising, travel, and even entertainment expenses.

Even if Fred Carpenter did not incorporate before participating in the lottery he could have incorporated after winning the lease. He could then have transferred the lease to his company, which would then have sold it. Or, instead of incorporating, prior to participating in the lottery, Carpenter could have established a sole proprietorship or a partnership for the purpose of acquiring and selling oil and gas leases. Either of these two approaches could also have reduced his taxes.

Further, Carpenter should have considered the *timing* of his sale. If he decided to use his oil lease profits to, say, go to graduate school in 1979, during which time he would not have any earnings, he would have been better off from a tax standpoint to have waited one month, selling his lease in January 1979. With no other income in 1979 to escalate his tax bracket, his tax rate would have been 55 percent. He would have paid just over $18,000 in taxes (as an individual). By waiting one month in order to sell his lease in the subsequent tax year when he expected no other income Carpenter could have saved $8,000 in taxes.

Timing can also be used to establish the sale as a long-term capital gain (held over one year) rather than a short-term gain (held less than one year). Short-term gains are fully taxed as ordinary income. We have already seen the tax consequences of a short-term sale. It was the first example given. By holding his lease for a full twelve months before selling, Carpenter would have been allowed to deduct from his gross income 50 percent of the amount he received for his lease. Only the remaining 50 percent would have been taxed as ordinary income. Assuming Carpenter earned an $18,000 taxable salary in the year in which he sold his lease for $50,000, he would have had a total income of $68,000. From this amount he could have deducted 50 percent of his long-term capital gain, $25,000, giving him a net taxable income of $43,000. Using the 1978 tax tables, his tax bracket would have been 55 percent, and his tax liability would have dropped to roughly $15,000, $11,000 attributable to the sale of his lease. By holding his lease for one year and then selling it, Carpenter would have paid about $11,000 in taxes on his lease sale instead of $26,000. By timing his lease sale to establish a long-term capital gain Carpenter would have netted a cash-in-pocket of $39,000 for his lease, $15,000 more than the $24,000 cash-in-pocket he made with the short-term sale.

(Note: Where I indicated tax-bracket percentages, I did so for comparative purposes only. The tax bracket is the percentage of tax paid on the *last* taxable dollar earned. Tax treatment of earnings is not a linear relationship. That is why in the examples given above you are not able to take the tax rate and multiply it by the taxable income to derive the tax. To compute Carpenter's tax in the above examples I used the 1978 IRS tax tables for single taxpayers.)

Another tax-saving strategy that Carpenter should have considered is the creation of a short-term trust. A short-term trust would have enabled him to assign a portion of his income and the related tax liability thereon to another person in a lower tax bracket. Upon termination of the trust, generally after a minimum period of ten years, the trust principal would have been returned to Carpenter. The short-term trust is a useful tax savings device if, for example, you have a minor child for whom you want to accumulate funds for the payment of future college expenses. Or you could use the trust fund to provide support payments for your aged or other dependent relatives.

For maximum tax benefit, a trust account should be set up before participating in the lottery. The trust documents need to specify that the trust funds may be used for filing entries in the simultaneous oil and gas lottery, paying lease rentals, selling leases, etc. Any monies gained from winning and selling leases would thus not be taxable to you as your personal income. Instead, the profits would be taxable to the trust under the lower tax rates of the trust. Trusts may also be used to create a fund to set up a child in business or to provide a dowry when a child marries. There are many aspects to trusts and many uses.

Keogh Plans and Individual Retirement Accounts (IRAs) are other forms of trust accounts which may be used to file for, acquire, and sell oil and gas leases. The federal Securities and Exchange Commission considers oil and gas leases to be securities. The IRS allows Keogh Plans and IRAs to be used to acquire and sell securities. Taxes on funds accumulated in these two types of trust accounts are deferred until funds are dispersed at retirement. Only the amount disbursed is taxed, and it is taxed at personal income tax levels, which at retirement are likely to drop.

The BLM proposes to amend its policy and disallow use of revocable trusts as a means of participating in the lease lottery. By law, the BLM must approve all transfers of lease interests and assure that the transferee is qualified to hold a lease. A power of revocation allows a lease to be transferred by operation of law without consideration by the bureau. Before establishing a trust, contact one of the BLM land offices for the latest policy on trusts. It is also wise to have the advice of an attorney when establishing trust accounts.

Perhaps you are one of those people who knows little about business affairs and do not want to hassle your way through setting up a corporation, trust funds, or the use of tax strategies. You simply want to file your entry and, if you win, will be glad to give a cut of your winnings to the IRS. Fine. Nevertheless, the very minimum that you should consider is the deductibility of your expenses when filing your personal income tax. According to Revenue Ruling 71-191 costs incurred in participating in the simultaneous oil and gas lease program are fully tax-deductible from ordinary income as "miscellaneous" itemized deductions. In the event of winning a lease your expenses in the particular filing would be considered an acquisition cost and would be recoverable by depletion (Rev. Rul. 67-141). Revenue Ruling 56-252 further provides that the first year's rental fee paid upon winning a lease is an ordinary and necessary deductible business expense for income tax purposes. It should be itemized as a miscellaneous deduction.

Tax considerations should be an important integral of your overall lottery strategy. What is the sense in filing against 2,000 to 1 odds for a lease valued at $50,000 and then giving half of the proceeds to the IRS? It would be more advantageous to file for a lease worth $25,000, at half the odds, and give nothing to the IRS. If you do not plan your tax strategies before you win, at least consider the tax aspects when you win. Through careful tax planning you can materially reduce your taxes, and even reduce them down to nothing. There is no reason other than tax naiveté why a person who wins $50,000 in the lottery can't keep all of his gains without incurring a tax liability.

Do not get me wrong. I am not advocating tax evasion. I do believe, however, that you have a right to plan your business affairs in a manner which will minimize your tax liability. Granted, planning business affairs for maximum tax advantage can be a complicated matter. It is not the scope of this book to detail a tax planning program suitable for each and every individual; it would take volumes to provide that information. However, you should have gained sufficient insight from this chapter to realize that there are various legal tax strategies that can be and should be used to minimize or negate your tax liabilities. Unless you are familiar with the tax laws or have a mind that can sift through many pages of legal jargon I urge you to consult with a tax attorney or a tax accountant in order to maximize the cash-in-pocket you obtain from the sales of your leases.

16
The Buyers

If you are one of the more fortunate winners who has bagged a hot parcel, interested buyers will come out of the woodwork looking for you. You will not have to find them. Expect to be swamped. If you get a half-dozen calls, letters, or visits, consider yourself swamped. Suppose you were not so lucky, still you have what you estimate to be a fairly good lease. Who do you sell it to? Theoretically your lease may be valuable, but realistically it is not worth much more than a tax write-off unless you can find a buyer for it. Generally, for the less valuable leases, buyers will not beat a path to your door. They are too busy wheeling and dealing in their daily business activities to search you out. They are giving priority attention to developing their current leases and acquisitions for future development are easily postponed. Anyway they have a backlog of leases they need to review. If you do get a call from an interested buyer it is likely to be from someone who hopes you are naive enough to be sweet-talked into selling your lease for a song. So, it is going to be up to you to search the marketplace, find the buyers, and call their attention to your lease.

There are four general markets in which you can sell your lease. They are: oil companies, independent operators, oil and gas lease brokers ("landmen"), and private investors.

Oil Companies

This is one of your most important markets for your lease. Oil companies are faced with windfall profits which they need to offset before taxes. Some of their best investments are oil leases, and exploration and development programs. The oil companies like to acquire a large area of leases around their current producing fields. This keeps competition away and gives the oil companies potential for future expansion. The oil companies are also interested in acquiring leases in virgin areas for future consideration, and near their competitors' current or planned operations in order to get in on the action. Although the oil companies have a lot of leases in the Rocky Mountain Region they do very little of their own wildcat drilling in this area. Instead, they rely on the independent operators.

Independent Operators

This is another important market for your lease. According to American Petroleum Institute statistics for the first six months of 1978 the independents drilled 89 percent of all the wildcat wells in the United States. The oil companies will usually farm out a fractional interest in a lease to the independent operator as part of the drilling agreement. The independents want to widen and protect their interests around their test drilling and therefore are also interested in building an inventory of strategically located leases. In addition to drilling for others the independent operators also test drill their own parcels. Hence, there is a continual demand for leases by the independents.

Oil and Gas Lease Brokers

The brokers are often referred to as "landmen." They may trade in oil and gas leases for their own account or act as commissioned agents for others. The brokers have a communications network established with a number of oil companies and independents. Their business is to know the market. The better brokers know with certainty what they can sell, where they can sell it, and how much they can get for it. They will have a buyer lined up for the lease before they acquire the lease from a winner. Most leases won by laymen are purchased by the brokers who often make more profit and override on the sale of the lease than they paid the winner. As commissioned agents, the brokers, at least the honest ones, represent their clients in the sale of the leases. They negotiate the best price they can on behalf of their clients and receive commissions for their service. Commissions average around 10 to 15 percent of the sale price. Some lease brokers buy leases as long-term personal investments.

Private Investors

Like the oil and gas lease brokers who buy leases for their own account, the private investor is on the lookout for a good deal. He may watch the development trends of a few areas and buys leases on the prospect that wildcatting may prove fruitful. He also hopes to find a naive winner who is willing to sell the lease for below its market value. Some private investors buy leases, then form partnerships and underwrite drilling programs.

These four markets often overlap. You may find an independent operator who is also a broker, or a broker who is also a private investor, etc.

Locating Prospective Buyers

To locate the names and addresses of prospective buyers use the resources described below.

USA Oil Industry Directory. One of the best references, this volume lists every major oil company and independent operator in the United States. Included are subsidiaries, affiliates and divisions. The listing provides addresses, telephone numbers and the names and titles of all key operating personnel. This 116 page directory, which costs $45, is published annually in September by the Petroleum Publishing Company, P.O. Box 1260, Tulsa, Okla. 74101.

Walter Skinner's Oil and Gas International Yearbook. This reference lists the principle oil exploration and production companies operating in the United States. Included are the principal subsidiary and associated companies. Each listing indicates the business involvement of the company, production figures, capital, revenues, location of lease-holdings, and exploration activities. The book is indexed geographically with a cross-referenced company index. It is published by the Financial Times, Bracken House, Cannon St., London, England EC4P4BY.

Dun and Bradstreet Million Dollar Directory. For our purposes this reference is not as good as the first two mentioned. Nevertheless it is useful if the others are not available. Use the volume which lists businesses by product classification. Find section 13, "Oil and Gas Extraction." Look under subsections 1311, "Crude

Petroleum and Natural Gas," and 1381, "Drilling Oil and Gas Wells." You will find, listed in alphabetic order, by state, the names and addresses of hundreds of oil companies and independent operators.

Classified Telephone Directory. Generally, use the directory from the principal city nearest to the location of your lease. If necessary widen your search by using directories from the next closest principal cities. Check listings under these headings: "Oil and Gas Exploration and Development," "Oil Land Leases," "Oil Operators," "Oil Producers," and "Oil Properties." Larger libraries maintain a collection of telephone directories for principal cities. If they are not available at your local library, you, of course, can order the directories from your telephone company. If you are in good with the secretary at your place of work ask her to order the directories for you. There is no charge to businesses for the telephone directories they order.

BLM Microfilm Records. Microfilm records of simultaneous filings made on parcels are an excellent source of information on who may be interested in your lease. Contact the appropriate BLM land office for this data.

Lease Ownership Maps. Maps which show the ownership of leases are available from private sources and from some BLM offices. By checking the maps you can determine who owns leases near yours. These are good prospective buyers for your lease. Commercial sources for maps are provided in Appendix E.

Notices to Drill, Rework or Abandon. These reports are issued periodically by State oil and gas agencies. Reports include the name of the operator, and the nature and specific location of the operator's activity. These operators are good prospective buyers. For a listing of state oil and gas agencies refer to Appendix E. Some of the agencies publish annual summary reports of the drilling activities in their state. The reports often mention which are the most active oil companies in the state.

Trade Publications. One trade publication which deals almost exclusively with issues and data of interest to the BLM lottery participant is *Southwest Oil & Gas News*, mentioned several times in this book. Brokers and private investors occasionally run classified ads in this paper to indicate their interest in buying leases. Some of the advertisers have been: Sublette County Land & Royalty Co., 2681 West Park Drive, Baltimore, Md. 21207; Eagle Realty, 4147 Portola Dr., Santa Cruz, Calif. 95062 (call Mr.

Eagle collect at 408/476-6591); and G. Klurfeld, 55 Liberty Street, New York, N.Y. 10005.

Having considered the market areas and where to search for prospective buyers, let's now consider some tips to keep in mind when selling your lease.

17
Some Selling Tips

As the owner of 100 percent of record title to an oil and gas lease you are permitted to sell or assign your lease rights to another party. You are faced with several options:

(1) You may sell the lease outright for a flat cash payment. You would have no further interest in the lease and would not receive any additional monies if the lease later proved to be fruitful.

(2) You may transfer the lease for an overriding royalty payment only. The assignee picks up the lease payments. You retain a percentage interest in any oil or gas which *might* be produced. Overriding royalty payments are computed on actual production and not on the basis of discoveries and estimated reserves. Should the assignee fail to continue the lease payments, the lease will expire and so will your rights to any override. If the assignee transfers the lease to another party your override would remain valid, as long as the new assignee continues making the annual lease payments.

You may transfer or sell your overriding royalty rights. For example, you could transfer the ORR to your child's trust account. Or, you can sell your rights to the ORR for a flat cash payment.

(3) You may combine options (1) and (2), receiving both a cash payment and retaining an overriding royalty interest.

(4) You may subdivide your lease and then sell the rights to one or more of the subdivisions. You might use this procedure if you have a large tract for which you have obtained a firm offer that you believe is too low, there are no other offers, and you are forced to sell because you cannot afford to make the second year's rental payment on the entire tract. Also, some lower-valued leases may sell easier if they are first subdivided. Private investors may chance rental payments on a small tract while steering clear of the larger acreage.

Sometimes a buyer will want you to subdivide your tract since he may be only interested in making an offer for those certain portions of your lease which he feels are worthwhile.

(5) You may assign a fractional undivided interest in your lease. For example, retain a one-quarter interest in your lease and sell a three-quarter interest to an oil company. This gives you a 25 percent interest in the entire tract. If significant quantities of oil are found anywhere on the tract, your interest could become very valuable. If you desire, you can later sell or assign all or part of the fractional interest which you have retained.

Which of the above options you use will not always be a matter of your choice. How much flexibility you will have will depend a lot upon the value of your lease and the demand for it. If you have a highly sought-after parcel you will most likely be able to obtain your terms. The lower the value and demand for a parcel the less chance you will have for negotiations. Keep your desired terms simple and reasonable. Too many complicated maneuvers, although technically accurate, will label you "bush league," and you will lose ground in negotiations. I know of one man who wanted to subdivide his 1,782-acre lease, retain a 3 percent ORR on one portion, and assign an oddball 72 percent fractional undivided interest in the remaining portion. The last I heard he was still looking for a buyer—over two years after he won his lease. Who would bother with him?

Be patient when selling your lease. Generally, someone will not pop up at your door with a check the day you win a lease, although this may happen for a choice parcel. Expect to spend some time negotiating. Usually the first contact and offer is a "feeling out." The buyer is testing you to see how anxious you may be to sell and if you are naive enough to sell at a bargain. Expect the prospective buyer to probe for information about you and the lease. He will want to know how long you owned the lease. If he did not already find this out from the BLM records he will ask you for this input. The number of years remaining on the lease will affect the offer you will receive. Also, the buyer will want to know how close you are to the rental due date. If your lease covers a couple thousand acres or so, the buyer will figure that you might be pressured into a quick deal at a lower price in order to avoid laying out a couple more grand for another year's rental. The buyer may also want to know how you acquired the lease. For all he knows you could have bought it from a private party, inherited it, or obtained it through an open land filing. If you bought it the buyer may classify you to be at least a notch above a novice. If you won it, inherited it, or otherwise got it cheap, he may figure that maybe you will sell cheap.

Have you had any offers for your lease? The buyer would love to know this so he could size up the competition. Obviously, you do not want to give out specific information which can be used against you. Do not tell anyone the names of the companies you have contacted or what offers you have had, if any. Be vague. Say something to the effect that you have been shopping around and you know that you can get at least X dollars per acre for your lease but are searching the market a bit more since you feel you can do better. There is a kinship within each business trade. If you drop a name you are giving your prospective buyer the opportunity to contact his "competition." They will not bid against each other if they can avoid doing so.

Expect to be probed for why you want to sell the lease. The probe may be as subtle as, "Well Mrs. Jones I guess you will soon be able to buy that dream house of yours." The buyer hopes that you will reply with the real reason. If you reply, "Oh, no. I need the money to get my Aunt the best medical treatment possible for her cancer," this tips the buyer off to the fact that you are likely to go for a quick, and maybe a low deal. If in fact you are anxious to sell make sure you do not communicate that fact to the prospective buyer. It is nobody's business what you plan to do with the money. If pressured and if you want to keep negotiations friendly you can say something to the effect that you have not decided yet, or say that you plan to start a foundation to help humanity in some way, maybe to help save the platypus from extinction. The buyer will figure you do not need the money for yourself, you are not pressed for time, and that you are probably radical enough to hold out until you get your price.

Never volunteer any information. This is one rule of selling that every professional salesman knows. When negotiating the sale of your lease consider yourself a salesman, or a saleslady as the case may be. Never let your guard down. Keep a poker face with your hand a secret. The fewer cards you reveal to your opponent (and the buyer is your opponent), the stronger will be your position. At the same time be sincerely friendly, like you would be with your neighborhood pals during a high-stakes poker game.

If you are fortunate enough to get an offer for your lease you will probably be pressured into accepting the offer. The professional negotiator knows that people are motivated to action by the possibility of gain and by the fear of loss. Once establishing the possibility of gain the buyer will face you with the fear of loss to get you to respond. It may go something like this: "Mrs. Jones, we feel that we have made you a very fair offer, considering the speculative nature of your lease, the dry wildcat six miles away, etc. Our principals are also considering other leases, and as you know we are limited by law to the number of acres we can hold. We need to finalize our purchases for this fiscal year. Why don't you think about it and let us know the first thing tomorrow morning?" It appears that you are faced with a take-it-or-leave-it proposition. And, in fact, you may be. If the offer is within your estimated high-low evaluation of your parcel, and your parcel is not a choice one, and you have been having difficulty selling it, do not put off a deal. Take it. Holding out for a couple of more dollars per acre may lose the deal. If, however, you feel that you have a fairly good parcel and the offer seems low based on your evaluation, do not be afraid to wait it out. Call the buyer's bluff. Counter the offer by stating what you are asking as a minimum offer, which should be a little on the high side so that you can come down in price if necessary during negotiations. State some positive facts about your lease; its location near some wildcat testing, that geology is similar to that of the nearby oil fields, that nearby parcels have sold for at least the amount you are asking, etc. The buyer will realize that he is not negotiating with a novice, that you know the value of your lease and that you expect to be paid the fair value. How well you negotiate will depend upon how well you have done your homework in reevaluating your lease. The more knowledgeable you are about the history, current plays, and future prospects of the tracts surrounding your lease the more confident you will be in your negotiations. The knowledge and confidence you project will have a positive correlation to the amount you will be offered for your lease. There is plenty of money floating around. Oilmen are literally tapped into the source. They can afford to pay you a fair price for your lease. It is a tax write-off for them anyway.

Exposure is important when attempting to sell your lease. If your lease is not one of the top ten you will need to do some canvassing, like any salesman. Some novices use the shotgun method, sending a flurry of letters to a hundred prospective buyers at one time, hoping to score a hit. Such wide coverage is not generally recommended. It tips off every oil man to the fact that you are eager to unload your lease. Oilmen communicate among themselves, especially the independents. They try to help each other out. Picture this telephone conversation between two oil men:

"Hi Curly, Tom here."

"Hey, Tom! How's it going? Haven't heard from you in a while. What's cooking?"

"Curly, I just got a letter from a guy who wants to unload a lease near your proposed wildcat test. It's in Emery, T 17S R 14E, Sections 8, 11 and 14, about 1,200 acres."

"That's that Jacobson guy, isn't it Tom?"

"Yah."

"Tom, you're the second person to call me about it. I'll give Jacobson a call and see what I can work out. Thanks for the tip anyway. Hey, if I get wind of a deal in your neck o' the woods I'll let you know."

Why should the independents compete against each other when they have enough headaches with competition from the majors? Of course, not all independents are working together as friendly competitors. Still, there is enough comradeship out there to make it difficult to sell a lease competitively. What position did Jacobson place himself in? Some buyers will not even bother making an offer on a parcel if they know that every Tom, Dick, and Harry is getting a crack at it. It is not worth their time and effort to try to outbid other parties by a few cents per acre for a low-valued lease. If the word is out that you are beating the bushes for a buyer you are likely to chase most of the prospects away. In the above example Curly will probably call Jacobson with an offer and try to close a fast deal before Jacobson gets others. If Jacobson doesn't grab the deal, Curly might not waste any more of his time trying to land the parcel. Let's say that Jacobson is considering the deal which is $12 per acre plus a 3 percent ORR. But he hedges, thinking that maybe if he waited for replies to his other letters he could do better. Apparently Jacobson was right.

The following morning he gets a call from a lease broker who says that he has a buyer for the lease at $20 per acre plus a 5 percent ORR. This is more than Jacobson figured the lease to be worth. He's excited as he and the broker subsequently go through some preliminary motions to close the deal. Meanwhile Jacobson manages to get another offer from a third interested party at $13 per acre plus a 3 percent ORR. He does not respond to the new offer since he is expecting to sell the lease to the broker any day now. What Jacobson doesn't know is that the $20 offer was a ploy used by the broker to stave off his competition. Jacobson begins to suspect the deal is sour after being stalled with one story after another by the broker. The buyer is waiting for his other lease to sell, or that CD to mature, or the funds to clear out of trust. Jacobson catches on too late. He has jilted the solid offers. He gets the coup de grace when the broker calls with the bad news that his client had trouble with his partners who will not make the deal. "But don't worry," the broker says, "I have another client eager to pick up your lease at, ahem, $10 per acre plus 2 percent ORR; not as good as the last prospect, but for the location of your lease, and so on, it's not a bad offer. But, she needs to know right now." Zonk! Jacobson is boxed in. If he tries to go back to Curly or the third offerer they will suspect his predicament and may offer him less, if they are still interested. Having attempted to test the entire market simultaneously and having been outwitted in his attempt to play the ends against the middle Jacobson is left with little bargaining power. His full hand exposed, he is in a tough position to sell his lease.

In selling a lease I prefer "sharpshooting." It takes more research to determine which specific companies or individuals are the most likely to be interested in your parcel, but it gives you something to fall back on if your first attempts at a sale are unsuccessful. Find out what companies are active in the area surrounding your lease. Who owns the nearby leases and who is doing the drilling in the area? Contact two or three of the most likely prospective buyers. Also, try to determine what company, not operating in the area, might be interested in expanding into the area, and write them. When writing, type each letter neatly and accurately as you would expect a professionally typed business letter to look. Handwritten letters, photocopy submissions, or letters with typos are marks of amateurs. By being selective in submitting your letters you are able to test the market and learn in the process. If a deal falls through you have many more companies remaining whom you can contact.

Sometimes, time is of the essence and you cannot hold your fire while you take careful aim at each of a handful of prospects. Your lease payment may be coming due or you might suspect that the wildcat test near your parcel may come up dry. You want to unload your parcel as quickly as possible. Then, shotgun, but be prepared to take the first halfway decent offer, and be wary of any offer that sounds too high and which comes with a "story."

My preference also is to deal directly with the principals and not use broker middlemen. By dealing directly you will have to be knowledgeable of lease values and be able to do your own negotiating. You will have to write your own letters and develop your own contacts. It could take you dozens of letters and many months' time before you locate a buyer and finally sell your lease. Your first sale will be the hardest. After that you will be rubbing shoulders with the pros. If you do not have the time or do not want the involvement of tracking down a buyer and negotiating price then consider using the services of a commissioned broker. Nevertheless, to protect your own interests you should still have a good idea of what your lease is worth. Make the broker earn his commission. Expect him to get you what you consider to be a good price for your lease.

The lease broker will undoubtedly want you to sign an agreement to give him exclusive rights to sell the lease. Make sure that you know what you are signing. Some brokers ask for exclusive rights for as long as five years. Would you give a real estate broker a five-year exclusive sales contract to sell your home? The more options you keep open for yourself the better off you will be. A reminder; it is best not to give a power of attorney to anyone to sell your lease for you.

Sometimes an oil company or an independent who knows that there is little or no competition for a lease may make you sit with the lease, even if it is valuable. This explains why some very valuable leases do not sell immediately. Companies know where their competition is active, and if no one other than they are leasing in the area of your lease, what's the rush to buy it from you? They will let you pay the annual rentals until they need the lease. This places the companies in a better negotiating position since you will probably be more eager to sell and they can argue that the lease is worth less because it is closer to its 10-year expiration date. If you are left sitting with a valuable lease, file a notice of intent to drill. This should build a fire under the oil companies! If your lease is adjacent to an oil field or to a prospective oil field there is always the fear that you could drill and tap, from your parcel, the same pool that they tap from their parcel. The chances are that you will soon sell your lease.

If all of your marketing efforts fail and you are left holding a goat pasture, but feel that there is some long-term potential to the lease you might try advertising your lease in a trade paper. Running a classified ad to sell your lease is a valid marketing strategy. It brings you into contact with thousands of people, many who might be willing to buy your lease. However, you run a risk when attempting to sell a lease by advertising. As indicated earlier, many states' securities laws define oil and gas leases as securities. As such, any sale of or offer for the sale of oil and gas leases must comply with the securities laws. Usually this means registering the proposed offering and selling the offering through a registered securities dealer. Being in violation of the securities laws when attempting to sell your lease is not in itself a problem. I do not think that any state securities commissioner, who might notice your ad, would come down on you, even if you were continually advertising and trading in leases, except if somebody stoked his coals. What if the buyer of your lease files a complaint? A person who bought your lease on the speculation that he could resell it at a profit and then finds that he is unable to sell it could come back to you with a request for a refund. If you do not make a refund the buyer could file a complaint with the state securities commissioner claiming that you misled him about the value of your lease, that you did not give him written full and fair disclosure about the risks of buying the "security" from you, and that you are not even licensed to sell securities. Even though you sold the lease with all good intentions you would be hard put to come up with a convincing reply, securities commissioners being as hard-nosed as they are. Anyone who is attempting to market his oil lease to the general public in the mass media is potentially exposing himself to a lawsuit by the buyer. Further, anyone who wants to give you a hard time can also file a complaint against you just for running your ad. If you plan on advertising your lease for sale make sure that you comply with your state's blue sky laws, and the blue sky laws of the state of residency of the buyer. And to be on the safe side make sure that you also comply with the securities laws of the federal Securities and Exchange Commission. If you do not take these precautionary measures you may find that you sold your lease with an open-ended deal where the buyer has a technical way out of the deal should he choose to take it. An unscrupulous buyer could use this technicality to prey upon innocent, well-meaning, but naive sellers.

Since most people want some idea in order to plan their finances, and after ploughing a thousand dollars or so into a lease they naturally want to know when to expect to reap their harvest, I am often asked, "How long will it take me to sell my lease?" The shortest time that I am aware of in which a lease has been sold is two weeks, the longest time is a couple of years, or more. Leases not sold within a couple of years, that are attempting to be sold, are usually dropped. Leases held for longer periods are usually intentionally being held as long-term speculations or are being held by companies as part of their inventory. Only a die-hard would continue holding a lease for three, four, five years, and more while his aggressive marketing efforts continue in vain. There are many factors which influence the time that it takes to sell a lease. The demand for the lease, and your asking price are two of the more salient influencing factors. The circumstances of each transaction are different and so I cannot state exactly how long lease sales will take. The following historic data provided by three popular oil lease brokers, however, should give you some general data to work with.

Broker A stated, "Our 'highly recommended' leases are usually sold within ninety days."

Broker B stated, "Most leases are sold within 30 to 90 days." He was referring to the "hot" parcels on his monthly list of recommendations.

Broker C provided specific examples: one month to sell a 1,320-acre Utah lease for $98,000 plus a 6 percent ORR; one year to consummate a deal at $62,910 plus a 5 percent ORR for an 839-acre lease in Wyoming; and six months to negotiate a price of $123,500 plus a 5 percent ORR for a 2,560-acre lease in Wyoming.

Whether it is two weeks or one year your negotiations will finally bring you to the moment of truth, when you receive payment in exchange for your lease. The assignment of your lease to the buyer completes your sale. If it is not handled properly you may find that you gave away your lease instead of selling it. The following chapter provides you with some helpful tips to remember when assigning your lease to the buyer.

18
Assigning Your Lease

The assignment of your lease to any person or persons is effected by completing a simple form, the Assignment Affecting Record Title to Oil and Gas Lease (BLM Form 3106-5), which is then filed with the Bureau of Land Management. You complete part one of the form, wherein you state what part of your record title interest and overriding royalty or production payments you want conveyed to assignee. Your signature on the form authorizes the BLM to assign and transfer the specified rights in your lease to the assignee. This authorization is what the assignee needs in order to become lessee as to the assigned interest. Your endorsed assignment is a negotiable document, therefore, you do not want to relinquish it to an assignee unless you can be assured of receiving payment for your lease.

Mrs. R. D., a switchboard operator from Selden, New York, was the lucky winner of a 520-acre lease parcel located in Chaves County, New Mexico. After writing many letters she finally managed to contact a broker interested in buying her lease for $5.25 per acre plus a 3.5 percent ORR. The broker telephoned his offer to Mrs. R. D., assuring her that he would make his payment as soon as her endorsed assignment was approved and on file with the BLM. She completed the assignment and mailed it to the broker as instructed, but her payment never came. At first she thought that the mail service was responsible for the delay in payment; maybe the broker didn't receive her assignment, or maybe he got it and sent the check, but the payment was lost en route. After repeated efforts, she finally got through to the broker, who informed her that the Bureau of Land Management takes "a couple" of months to process and approve the assignment. Mrs. R. D. whistled for her money for an entire year before she finally accepted the fact that she was robbed. Her lesson cost her $2,730, at a minimum. Had she taken precautionary procedures she would not have presented the broker with the opportunity to rip her off.

When selling your lease the minimum you should obtain from the buyer is a written offer which states that upon the Bureau's approval of assignment you will be paid a certain sum for your lease. Without a written commitment from the buyer how can you prove what amount you were to be paid for your lease? When dealing with a reputable, well established corporation, such as one of the major oil companies, a written offer specifying the terms of payment should be sufficient protection for you, especially if the transaction is for a relatively small amount of money. Mail your completed and signed assignment along with a respective copy of your lease to the assignee, registered return receipt requested. Retain a copy of the assignment and the original lease for your records.

If you are dealing with an "unknown," a written offer from the assignee is not sufficient. The assignee could skip town or fail to pay as promised and you would have to "go fish." To protect yourself, consider using the collection services of your bank's note department. For a nominal fee—the Bank of America charges four dollars—you can deposit your documents at your bank with instructions to the collection clerk that the documents are to be surrendered to assignee only when they have in their possession a cashier's check of a certain amount. If the assignee is from out of town, the bank will mail the documents, registered, to their correspondent bank in the assignee's home town. The assignee will be contacted and able to examine the documents which will be released to him when he fulfills the terms of the collection. This procedure is excellent protection for you, but places the assignee at a disadvantage since your endorsed assignment needs to be approved by the BLM before it becomes valid. The assignee will be releasing payment to you before being assured that the lease is approved. But, let that be his problem.

Once the assignee receives your endorsed assignment, the assignee must complete part two of the assignment form, "Assignee's Request for Approval of Assignment." The assignee certifies that he is qualified to hold the lease; that is, that he is of legal age, a U.S. citizen, etc. He pays a $25 filing fee and must file the form within 90 days of your date of endorsement. If all is in order the BLM will authorize the assignment.

If a collection is not acceptable to your buyer, request that the buyer put up a letter of irrevocable credit with his bank in an amount equal to the purchase price of your lease as guarantee of payment for your lease should the buyer fail to meet the terms of your written agreement. The agreement should stipulate the price and terms, and should specify that the agreement is null and void if the assignment is not approved by the BLM; but, if approved, then payment is due by a certain date. This procedure is a bit more costly (about $5 per $1,000) but places you both on an equal footing.

An alternate procedure is to set up an escrow to transact the sale of your lease, as is typically done with real estate sales. The mechanics of an escrow are similar to those of a collection. A third party receives the assignment and delivers it to the assignee only upon fulfillment of the specified terms of the escrow.

How much precaution and safeguards you need to take depends upon the value of your lease and to whom you are assigning it. If you are dealing in more sizeable figures (you decide what is a "sizeable" amount) and you do not feel comfortable with the transfer of assignment, then consider using the services of an attorney to assist you.

19
Thinking Big

Why sell your lease? If you sell your lease you have no assurance that the buyer will ever drill on the tract. The chances are that he will not. He might even drop the lease after a year, or two, cutting off your potential for any overriding royalty. Even if the buyer would successfully develop the lease all you would receive is a few percentage points royalty on production. Admittedly, the cash up front that you can make from the sale of your lease may be a sufficient windfall for you. And the intent of this book is to bring you to that point.

But now, addressing my fellow gamblers, I present the ultimate challenge to you in this oil and gas lottery game. Consider the prospects of retaining your lease rights, not cashing in your chips, but letting it ride on an all-or-nothing proposition, that of joining the ranks of wildcatters and drilling your own wells. Your 87.5 percent retained interest (remember, the U.S. government gets 12.5 percent) may have a potential worth in the millions. I am assuming, of course, that your 87.5 percent interest is in a "decent" lease. At the end of chapter four we saw a conservative example of how a 5 percent royalty on a dozen small wells could be worth close to $2 million. Now, weigh the prospects of gain against the risk involved. If your drilling operation is in vain, your lease will lose value, and could even become worthless. And you would have nothing to show for the tremendous effort and expense that you put forth.

To succeed as a wildcatter, or even to break the ice as one, you will need imagination. You have to conceive of, and to believe in, yourself as a wildcatter. Then, you will have to conceptualize plans, schedules, and the likely whereabouts of oil pools. You will also need a business acumen, complemented by a strong personal magnetism. You will be working with experts in oil exploration and drilling, financing, and accounting. You will also be working with legal counsel. You will have to decide if you will enter into a joint venture with a driller or an oil exploration company. This will require assigning a fractional undivided interest in your lease, which could be a large piece of the action, one-fourth, one-half, even three-fourths. Assigning an undivided interest gives the owner of such interest a full voice in the conduct of the operations of the venture. It generally also gives him unlimited liability for the debts and obligations of the venture. Maybe you will prefer to establish a limited partnership, retaining full control of the venture as the general manager. In either event you will need to consider the financial aspects of your planned enterprise. The cost of drilling a well today runs an average of around $45 per foot. A 5,000-foot test would cost in the neighborhood of $225,000—excluding "completion" money to prepare the hole for production. You can raise venture capital by selling partnership or undivided interests in your lease. You can do this privately with a small group of people (usually under 15) or, you can go public by filing a securities offering with the federal and state securities commissions. Even drilling on a worthless tract can be financed in this way, as long as you disclose the complete facts to the investors. Having personally prepared several securities offerings for sale I can attest to the fact that it is one of the more frustrating business projects that you could undertake. Hiring an underwriter to package and sell the deal for you could run you 15 percent of the total amount of the offering. As is necessary in any major business venture, wildcatters also require virtually unlimited energy and stamina coupled with a high frustration tolerance. You may experience costly delays which threaten to bankrupt you. Weather, strikes, equipment failures, challenges by environmentalists, ability to raise venture capital, disagreements with partners—all these can cause havoc to your wildcatting efforts. To succeed as a wildcatter you will also need considerable technical expertise in several fields. At minimum, you should be able to understand financing, geologic reports, and drilling and production problems. An additional element which you cannot overlook in your wildcatting venture is luck. Whether you think in terms of Lady Luck, or her consort the chief of the genii, or the statistical law of averages, you cannot escape the influence luck plays in the lives of wildcatters. The odds of drilling a commercially productive wildcat are about one in four. Even then, the wildcat may have tapped a low grade oil pool which could require 20 years of production just to recover the initial investment. Therefore, finally, every wildcatter also needs to have the humility to accept the blow of defeat.

In spite of the odds and the possibility of defeat there is no limit to the level of success that you can achieve by playing the oil and gas lease lottery. Regardless of your national origin, race, color, creed, or sex, the chance for you to become an oil magnate is there for the taking. The lottery is one of the few bona fide avenues available for realizing the American Dream. For a $10 filing fee, anyone can literally move from rags to riches overnight. It all begins with thinking big.

Appendix A
Filing Agents' Recommendations for the July 1978 Wyoming Posting

This appendix lists the Wyoming parcels recommended by each of eight major filing agents for the August 1978 drawing. Notice the greater total number of filings received by the BLM for those parcels recommended by more than one filing agent.

BLM Filing No.	#1	#2	#3	#4	#5	#6	#7	#8	Parcel Size (acres)	Total Filings Received by BLM, All Sources
WY-22								X	480	963
WY-28								X	600	1,049
WY-35				X	X	X	X		1,361	2,950
WY-39								X	1,520	2,100
WY-45								X	560	1,233
WY-50								X	637	1,409
WY-51						X			1,480	2,419
WY-52	X					X			1,160	2,349
WY-53								X	160	517
WY-61	X	X				X		X	1,200	2,854
WY-62	X							X	760	2,563
WY-65	X	X				X	X		1,896	4,024
WY-66	X	X				X			1,120	3,109
WY-70								X	640	1,932
WY-73	X								920	2,366
WY-75	X	X		X	X	X			1,040	3,689
WY-76	X	X	X		X				639	3,039
WY-77	X	X	X		X	X	X		2,119	6,776
WY-78	X								320	1,283
WY-80	X								320	1,348
WY-84	X								345	1,202
WY-87				X				X	1,200	1,082
WY-92					X				357	1,612
WY-93								X	621	629
WY-110	X								359	1,071
WY-113	X								1,751	1,476
WY-124	X	X	X		X				1,555	2,982
WY-126	X	X	X	X	X	X	X		2,141	6,431
WY-134	X			X	X				640	2,436
WY-136	X	X		X	X		X		560	3,142
WY-144		X							2,520	2,054
WY-153	X	X	X	X	X		X		600	5,144
WY-164		X							2,561	2,494
WY-165							X		1,911	2,042

219

BLM Filing No.	#1	#2	#3	#4	#5	#6	#7	#8	Parcel Size (acres)	Total Filings Received by BLM, All Sources
WY-168		X							1,122	1,656
WY-172					X	X		X	1,280	1,684
WY-184						X	X		1,600	2,714
WY-185		X		X	X	X	X		2,398	3,322
WY-188		X				X	X		1,175	2,548
WY-190				X	X	X			1,531	2,296
WY-191	X			X	X				625	2,783
WY-194	X								613	1,424
WY-195						X	X		1,599	2,219
WY-199	X		X		X				640	3,830

Eight Filing Agents' Recommendations

Appendix B
U.S. Crude Oil and Natural Gas Production by State, 1975

State	Oil (bbls) All Lands	Rank	Public Land Only	Rank	Gas (mcf) All Lands	Rank	Public Land Only	Rank
AL	13,477,000	18	3,661	16	37,814,000	20	—	—
AK	69,834,000	7	9,078,072	5	160,270,000	9	58,009,581	3
AZ	635,000	27	—	—	208,000	27	604	14
AR	16,133,000	17	146	17	116,237,000	11	768,993	12
CA	322,139,000	3	17,972,545	3	318,308,000	6	10,994,437	7
CO	38,039,000	12	12,475,578	4	171,629,000	8	55,959,719	4
FL	41,877,000	11	—	—	44,383,000	18	—	—
IL	26,057,000	14	—	—	1,440,000	25	—	—
IN	4,632,000	22	—	—	346,000	26	—	—
KS	59,106,000	8	435,485	10	843,625,000	5	11,441,083	6
KY	7,556,000	20	—	—	60,511,000	16	—	—
LA	650,840,000	2	538,024	9	7,090,645,000	2	2,707,313	10
MD	—	—	—	—	93,000	28	—	—
MI	24,420,000	15	—	—	102,113,000	12	—	—
MS	46,614,000	9	25,104	15	74,345,000	15	—	—
MO	57,000	30	—	—	30,000	29	—	—
MT	32,844,000	13	7,315,336	7	40,734,000	19	9,530,579	8
NB	6,120,000	21	104,465	13	2,565,000	24	1,278,232	11
NV	115,000	29	111,243	12	—	—	—	—
NM	95,063,000	6	26,610,101	2	1,217,430,000	4	607,709,974	1
NY	875,000	25	—	—	7,628,000	22	—	—
ND	20,452,000	16	1,341,619	8	24,786,000	21	370,472	13

Appendix B (Continued)
U.S. Crude Oil and Natural Gas Production by State, 1975

State	Oil (bbls) All Lands	Rank	Public Land Only	Rank	Gas (mcf) All Lands	Rank	Public Land Only	Rank
OH	9,578,000	19	—	—	84,960,000	13	—	—
OK	163,123,000	4	172,035	11	1,605,410,000	3	12,419,400	5
PA	3,264,000	23	—	—	84,676,000	14	—	—
SD	472,000	28	30,299	14	—	—	—	—
TN	682,000	26	—	—	27,000	30	—	—
TX	1,221,929,000	1	—	—	7,485,764,000	1	—	—
UT	42,301,000	10	7,674,832	6	55,354,000	17	5,857,995	9
VA	3,000	31	—	—	6,723,000	23	—	—
WV	2,479,000	24	—	—	154,484,000	10	—	—
WY	135,943,000	5	79,173,197	1	316,123,000	7	165,363,432	2

Sources: U.S. Bureau of Mines, *Petroleum Statement, 1975*; U.S. Bureau of Mines, *Natural Gas Annual, 1975*; Geological Survey, *Federal and Indian Lands Oil and Gas Production, Royalty Income, and Related Statistics, 1975.*

Appendix C
Federal Land Acreage

State	Total State Land Area	Total Federally Owned Land Acres	Percent of State	Federally Owned Land Administered by Bureau of Land Management Acres	Percent of State
Alabama	32,678,400	1,097,317	3.4	636	0.002
Alaska	365,481,600	348,467,343	95.3	295,445,187	81.1
Arizona	72,688,000	32,432,513	44.6	12,787,929	17.6
Arkansas	33,599,360	3,155,407	9.4	2,309	0.007
California	100,206,720	44,393,881	44.3	15,192,493	15.2
Colorado	66,485,760	24,152,057	36.3	8,443,254	12.7
Florida	34,721,280	3,392,455	9.8	1,093	0.003
Illinois	35,795,200	523,994	1.5	None	None
Indiana	23,158,400	424,863	1.8	None	None
Kansas	52,510,720	666,874	1.3	1,515	0.003
Kentucky	25,512,320	1,230,727	4.8	None	None
Louisiana	28,867,840	1,042,410	3.6	3,089	0.011
Maryland	6,319,360	189,700	3.0	None	None
Michigan	36,492,160	3,316,286	9.1	3,249	0.009
Mississippi	30,222,720	1,569,320	5.2	1,237	0.004
Missouri	44,248,320	1,882,360	4.3	None	None
Montana	93,271,040	27,654,289	29.6	8,217,414	8.8
Nebraska	49,031,680	728,260	1.5	7,923	0.016
Nevada	70,264,320	60,725,334	86.4	48,067,092	68.4
New Mexico	77,766,400	26,388,272	33.9	13,269,085	17.1
New York	30,680,960	232,626	0.8	None	None
North Dakota	44,452,480	2,119,375	4.8	75,120	0.167
Ohio	26,222,080	263,134	1.0	None	None
Oklahoma	44,087,680	1,423,669	3.2	8,190	0.019
Pennsylvania	28,804,480	597,758	2.1	None	None
South Dakota	48,881,920	3,408,408	7.0	277,834	0.568
Tennessee	26,727,680	1,699,438	6.4	None	None
Texas	168,217,600	3,003,996	1.8	None	None
Utah	52,696,960	35,060,194	66.5	22,994,581	43.6
Virginia	25,496,320	2,192,116	8.6	None	None
West Virginia	15,410,560	987,811	6.4	None	None
Wyoming	62,343,040	30,059,522	48.2	17,464,699	28.0

Source: GSA real property inventory records for agencies as of June 30, 1968.

Note: States with federal land but no oil or gas production are *not* included in this listing.

223

Appendix D
Bureau of Land Management Offices

Alaska	555 Cordova Street
	Anchorage, Alaska 99501
Arizona	2400 Valley Bank Center
	Phoenix, Arizona 85073
California	Room E-2841, Federal Building
	2800 Cottage Way
	Sacramento, California 95825
Colorado	Rm. 700, Colorado State Bank Bldg.
	1600 Broadway
	Denver, Colorado 80202
Idaho	Room 398, Federal Building
	550 West Fort Street
	P.O. Box 042
	Boise, Idaho 83724
Montana	Granite Tower, 222 N. 32nd Street
North Dakota	P.O. Box 30157
South Dakota	Billings, Montana 59107
Nevada	Rm. 3008, Federal Building
	300 Booth Street
	Reno, Nevada 89509
New Mexico	U.S. Post Office and Federal Bldg.
Oklahoma	South Federal Place
Texas	P.O. Box 1449
	Santa Fe, New Mexico 87501
Oregon	729 N. E. Oregon Street
Washington	P.O. Box 2965
	Portland, Oregon 97208
Utah	University Club Building
	136 East South Temple
	Salt Lake City, Utah 84111
Wyoming	2515 Warren Avenue
Kansas	P.O. Box 1828
Nebraska	Cheyenne, Wyoming 82001

Arkansas, Iowa,
Louisiana, Minnesota,
and all states east of
the Mississippi River

Eastern States Land Office
7981 Eastern Avenue
Silver Spring, Maryland 20910

National Office, Bureau
of Land Management

U.S. Department of the Interior
18th and C Streets, NW
Washington, DC 20240

Appendix E
Resource Index

This appendix provides reference sources for the 13 states identified in chapter seven.

Agencies	References

Arizona

Oil and Gas Conservation Commission
1645 W. Jefferson, Rm. 420
Phoenix, Arizona 85007

Geologic reports, drilling results, maps, well locations, production statistics, charts, catalogs, etc. (Ask for Price List No. 8—order/invoice form.)

California

California Division of Oil and Gas
1416 9th St. Rm. 1316-35
Sacramento, California 95814

Weekly listing of notices to drill, rework or abandon wells; monthly and annual reports; history of wells drilled; maps, etc. (Ask for Oil and Gas Publications Listing PR2S.)

Colorado

Oil and Gas Conservation Commission
State Centennial Building
1313 Sherman St. Rm. 721
Denver, Colorado 80203

Only sells annual report of oil and gas statistics.

Idaho

Oil and Gas Conservation Commission
Department of Lands
State House
Boise, Idaho 83720

Maintains and publishes a drilling register of all oil and gas drilling activity.

Agencies	References
Idaho Bureau of Mines and Geology University of Idaho Moscow, Idaho 83843	Geological Publications and data.

Montana

Agencies	References
Board of Oil and Gas Conservation Division Office 325 Fuller Ave. Box 217 Helena, Montana 59601	Publishes three reports: *Annual Review*, *Valuation Report*, and *Monthly Statistical Bulletin*.
Board of Oil and Gas Conservation Technical Office 15 Poly Drive Billings, Montana 59101	Maintains well records for all wells.
Centralized Services Dept. of Natural Resources 32 South Ewing Street Helena, Montana 59601	Provides individual well production data.

Nevada

Agencies	References
Department of Conservation and Natural Resources Capitol Complex 201 S. Fall Street Carson City, Nevada 89710	Maintains drilling and production records.
Nevada Bureau of Mines and Geology Publications Office University of Nevada Reno, Nevada 89557	Publishes geological bulletins, reports and maps. (Ask for List No. 6—Publications Listing.)

New Mexico

Agencies	References
Energy and Minerals Dept. Oil Conservation Division P.O. Box 2088 State Land Office Building Santa Fe, New Mexico 87501	Maintains updated oil and gas maps in their office, for onsite public inspection only.

Agencies	References
New Mexico Bureau of Mines and Mineral Resources Socorro, New Mexico 87801	Geologic Oil and Gas publications are provided.

North Dakota

North Dakota Geological Survey University Station Grand Forks, North Dakota 58202	Provides reports of investigations, production statistics, maps, etc. (Ask for their list of publications.)

Oregon

State of Oregon Dept. of Geology and Mineral Industries 1069 State Office Bldg. Portland, Oregon 97201	Provides reports and papers of oil and gas investigations and geologic surveys. (Ask for list of available publications.)

South Dakota

South Dakota Geological Survey USD Science Center Vermillion, South Dakota 57069	Provides reports of investigations, geologic reports, maps. (Ask for their publications list.)
South Dakota Geological Survey Western Field Office 308 West Boulevard Rapid City, South Dakota 57701	Provides annual report of well drilling activity.

Utah

Division of Oil, Gas and Mining 1588 West North Temple Salt Lake City, Utah 84116	Publishes weekly reports of notices of intent to drill, abandon, and convert. Publishes monthly oil and gas production reports.
Utah Geological and Mineral Survey 606 Black Hawk Way Salt Lake City, Utah 84108	Provides oil and gas field studies, maps, geologic reports, etc. (Ask for their list of publications.)

Agencies	References

Washington

Department of Natural Resources Olympia, Washington 98504	Publishes a history of oil and gas exploration.

Wyoming

Oil and Gas Conservation Commission Box 2640 Casper, Wyoming 86202	Offers: Energy resources map; statistical publication of oil and gas production; reports of wells drilled, etc. (Ask for a listing of available data.)
Wyoming Geological Survey P.O. Box 3008 University of Wyoming Laramie, Wyoming 82071	Provides oil and gas maps and publications.

For a detailed listing of reports and maps published by the Geological Survey relating to the geology and mineral resources of each state, write to the Public Inquiries Office, U.S. Geological Survey, Room 7638, Federal Building, 300 N. Los Angeles Street, Los Angeles, California 90012. Ask for the free booklet, *Geologic and Water-Supply Reports and Maps,* for the state of your choice. Geologic bulletins, papers, and reports are for sale by the Branch of Distribution, U.S. Geological Survey, 1200 S. Eads Street, Arlington, Virginia 22202, and maps, folios, atlases, and charts are sold by the Branch of Distribution, U.S. Geological Survey, Building 41, Federal Center, Denver, Colorado 80225.

Many of the publications and maps of the Geological Survey, including out of print material, are available at your local public libraries and at geological libraries of colleges and universities.

Supportive geological services are also available from some of the Bureau of Land Management state offices. Inquire to the appropriate office of jurisdiction (see Appendix D).

The American Association of Petroleum Geologists, Box 979, Tulsa, Oklahoma 74101, publishes a series of geological books and maps. Map sections include: stratigraphic column, tectonic map, physiographic map, a source-of-information listing, area cross-sections, regional geologic history, and a mileage chart. Maps are overlain by a standard highway map. Request the AAPG Publications Catalog.

Some commercial firms specialize in providing geological data. These include filing services, discussed in Appendix F, and mapping companies. Check your local classified telephone directory under "Oil Land Leases," "Oil Reports," and "Maps" for leads on additional sources. Some commercial mapping firms are listed below:

Interstate Map Company
P.O. Box 896
Scottsdale, Arizona 85252

Petroleum Information
P.O. Box 2612
Denver, Colorado 80201

MAPCO
P.O. Box 1891
Denver, Colorado 80201

Petroleum Investment Co.
231 West 800 South
Salt Lake City, Utah 84101

New Mexico Land Maps
P.O. Box 1797
Santa Fe, New Mexico 87501

Roswell Map Company
Box 1381
Roswell, New Mexico 88201

A series of out-of-print geological publications are available through Xerox University's Books on Demand program as paper- or cloth-bound photocopies. For further information and prices write to Books on Demand, University Microfilms International, 300 North Zeeb Road, Ann Arbor, Michigan 48106.

Appendix F
Directory of Filing Services

This directory of filing service organizations represents about 8 percent of the total services in operation today. No special criteria were used to determine which filing services to include in this report. The service firms chosen were those which came to my attention through newspaper advertisements, articles, telephone directories, and referrals. The listing is representative of the wide range of services that are available. Some of the service organizations are large and well-publicized, others are relatively small and unknown. The information provided on each of the services is believed to be correct, having been gleaned mostly from the services' advertising circulars, and to a lesser extent from newspaper and magazine articles. I have wirtten more about some services than I have about others. This was entirely due to the amount of information that was readily available, and is not meant to imply that one service is better or more comprehensive than another. Further, the information provided about a service organization may not be complete. A service may offer options additional to that which I have indicated. Finally, before committing your funds to a service, reread the comments on filing services in parts one and two of this book. Caveat emptor!

Canyon Energy Service, P.O. Box 2205, Albuquerque, New Mexico 87103. This service does research and evaluation of lease parcels through its field agents to determine potential value of parcels. The service asks you to sign an agreement which authorizes the service to file entry cards with the BLM on your behalf, at their discretion, but as near as possible to the instructions which you provide. Your instructions can indicate the range of values of the parcels for which you wish the service to file, i.e., $200 to $300 per acre, $100 to $200 per acre, $25 to $100 per acre. You may also indicate the parcel size you would like the service to file for; 40 to 320 acres, or 320 to 1,300 acres. They will try to accommodate any other special instructions you may wish to provide regarding the type of parcels for which you want to file.

Their fee is $6 for the first card and $3 for each additional entry made within the same month, plus the $10 BLM filing fee per card. If you win, this service will loan you the first year's lease rental which you reimburse when the lease is sold. They do not in any way hold or take any financial interest in any lease drawn by a customer. Their sole financial interest is limited to the fees charged for filing BLM entry cards. Parcel winners receive free advice on how to sell their leases.

Energy Group of America, Inc., Suite 3308, Empire State Building, New York City, New York 10001. The person representing this organization is "Wildcat" Ed Axel. Telephone: 212/279-4480. This company provides a free advanced list of recommendations of 15 to 20 parcels from which you make selections. The recommendation list includes parcels only from New Mexico and Wyoming—the company indicates that its best research resources and information are from these states. The list includes information on size of parcel, township and range location of parcels, the number of anticipated entries per parcel, and a conservative estimate of the market value of each parcel. You file entries through the company, noting on a separate form the parcel for which you wish to file. If you desire, they will make the parcel selections for you. The company completes the card for you and then forwards the entry cards on your behalf to the BLM. EGA charges $10 plus the $10 BLM filing fee per card. Occasionally, service-fee discounts are provided. These vary with the number of filings requested, e.g., 1 for $10, 2 for $15, 3 for $15, 4 for $20, 5 to 10 for $25, 11 to 15 for $30—*plus* the $10 BLM filing fee per card.

If you wish, EGA will loan you the advance lease rental fee, which you must reimburse to them after you have sold and been paid for your lease.

Energy Research and Marketing Services, Petroleum Center, Suite E116 (P.O. Box 17249), San Antonio, Texas 78217. This service retains geological consultants in several of the Rocky Mountain states. Based on their consultants' recommendations this service compiles a monthly list of leases considered to be the most valuable. The list includes the legal description, BLM parcel number, acreage, and the estimated market value of each lease. The list of selected leases is sold on a subscription basis; 1 month for $15, 3 months for $36, 6 months for $66, and 1 year for $120. The list is sent special delivery mail. For $2 more per month customers have the option to receive the list by mailgram, or, for the additional $2 per month plus the cost of a telephone call, you can have the list dictated to you over the telephone. The lists are sent only after the BLM offices release the official parcel numbers. This fast service gets the list to you in time for you to file your own entry cards directly with the BLM. This service does not do the filing for its customers. Following each month's drawings subscribers receive a newsletter posting the winners. Incidentally, this service accepts Master Charge or Visa. In addition to issuing lists, this service is in the business of selling oil and gas leases. They loan you the first year's lease rental, which is reimbursable after the lease is sold. They charge a sales commission of 10 percent on all lease sales they make. They cannot sell leases on a commission basis for residents of California until the company's registration is completed with the state department of corporations. For further information call their marketing director, Jack D. Liston, at 512/822-0855.

Federal Oil & Gas Leases, Inc., 2995 L.B.J. Freeway (P.O. Box 29646), Dallas, Texas 75229. This service was incorporated in Texas in 1967, and Tom B. Boston is president and director. Telephone: 214/243-4253 or, toll free, 1/800/527-2654 (outside Texas). The company, which has its own staff of geologists and landmen, offers three participation plans: Plan A—you receive a free advanced list of recommendations of about 18 parcels from which you make selections. The company files entries on your behalf. The cost of this service is $25 per selection, which includes the BLM filing fee. Plan B—you sign a contract authorizing the service company to select and file a minimum of one entry per month for six months. The cost is $25 per entry which includes the BLM filing fees. Under either plan, if you win a recommended parcel, the company will loan you the first year's lease rental, which you must reimburse to the company after you sell your lease.

Plan C—you subscribe to a list of monthly recommendations, which includes a selection of about 50 to 100 lease parcels. The list costs $40 a month or $300 a year. The list is sent to you late enough to include the BLM's official parcel numbers, but early enough to give you sufficient time to file. You complete the filing cards in full and file them directly with the BLM. You pay the BLM filing fee per card, plus the rental if you win. All three plans provide a list indicating the winners of each parcel the company recommended. The winners list also includes the total number of applicants received by the BLM for each of the parcels. The list of recommendations provide a legal description of parcels, size in acreage, location in respect to producing oil fields, and a commentary regarding oil company interests or explorations in the vicinity. Parcel winners receive free advice and assistance in marketing their lease. Lessees are put in direct contact with oil companies or lease brokers. The service company does not participate in any way in the profits you receive for your lease.

Federal Oil and Gas Leases of California, Inc., 1130 Camino Del Mar, Suite E (P.O. Box 520), Del Mar, California 92014. Federal Oil and Gas Leases of California is a wholly owned subsidiary of Federal Oil and Gas Leases, Inc. It was incorporated in 1975 for the purpose of conducting business in California for its parent corporation. For additional information you may call collect: 714/481-8167.

Federal Simultaneous Associates, U.S. Federal Building, P.O. Box 2852, Santa Fe, New Mexico 87501. Telephone: 505/982-3742. FSA is in the business of offering its clients technical assistance in participating in the Government lease drawings. Each month FSA analyzes the list of parcels being offered by the BLM and selects the top 10 parcels based on potential for development and relation to present production sites. Selections are limited to the states of New Mexico, Oklahoma, and Texas. FSA prepares its list of 10 recommendations to include the township and range locations of each parcel, the acreage, estimated cash and royalty value, the BLM official parcel numbers, and the anticipated number of entries expected to be filed with the BLM for each parcel. FSA files entry cards on behalf of its clients.

For its services FSA charges an annual fee of $100, payable at the time of your first filing, plus a monthly per-card filing fee as follows: $20 for 1, $40 for 2, $55 for 3, $65 for 4, $75 for 5, $90 for 6, $105 for 7, $120 for 8, $135 for 9, and $150 for 10. The filing-fee schedule includes the BLM's $10 per card filing fee. There are no additional fees to pay. Lease winners are required to pay the annual rental fee to the BLM.

If you wish FSA will assist you in the sale of your lease by recommending locally active oil and gas lease brokers who will sell your lease on a commission basis. All applicants receive a copy of the winners list.

F. Milligan, Inc., 600 Manhattan, Suite C12 (Lock Box 3408), Boulder, Colorado 80307. President of the service is Frank T. Milligan, and the manager is Doris M. Sotter. Telephone: 303/499-1562. This company provides a free advanced list of 12 parcel recommendations in Wyoming. The list includes the township and range location of each parcel, acreage, anticipated market values, and a comment about oil company activities in the vicinity of each of the parcels. To participate you indicate the parcels for which you wish to file, and the company files entry cards to the BLM on your behalf. Milligan also provides filing services for parcels in New Mexico, Colorado, Utah, Montana, and North Dakota. However, no descriptive list of parcels is provided for these states. Instead, you advise the service of the lease values that interest you, and Milligan chooses the parcels and completes and files your cards.

The fees charged are $25 for the first entry card and $20 for each additional card that is filed during the same month. The fee includes the $10 per card charged by the BLM. Should you win a lease, this company guarantees that you will be able to sell it for at least 1,000 times the amount you paid the company for its services, or they will refund your fees in full. If you wish, the company will loan the first year's rental to you which is repayable when you sell the lease. To assist you in the sale of the lease the company will provide you with a list of lease brokers. F. Milligan, Inc. does not participate in any way in the profits you receive for your lease. This company also sells large-scale maps of Wyoming or New Mexico at $10 each. The maps show oil and gas fields and are marked with township and range so that you can locate the leases. The company's literature did not indicate if maps were current or if oil wells and dry holes were posted. Inquire first before ordering.

Government Oil Lease Investments, Inc., 8365 N. E. 2nd Ave., (P.O. Box 38-0759) Little River Branch, Miami, Florida 33138. Martin E. Schor is President, Merle Schor is the Executive Vice President. Telephone: 305/757-1561. This company provides parcel selections, filing services and lease disposition for its clients. Their sales literature did not indicate the states in which parcel selections are made. By inference, however, I believe they are in the Rocky Mountain area. The company does not issue advanced lists of recommendations. Instead, they use their discretion to select, based on geological advice, those "hot" parcels which show the greatest potential for immediate profits. Entry cards are filed by the company on behalf of clients.

Fees for this service are: 1 filing $25, 2 filings $45, 3 filings $67.50, 4 filings $90. They also offer discounted annual filing rates: 1 filing per month for $275, 2 filings per month for $535, 3 filings per month for $750, 4 filings per month for $985. Payment by Master Charge or Visa is accepted.

If you wish, you may telephone the company on the third Tuesday of any month and they will give you the BLM parcel numbers from which you can make your selections (after you have paid your fees). Thus you have the option of mailing your entries directly to the BLM. Although not specifically stated in its literature, the company's filing selections appear to be limited to four parcels. If you win a lease, the company guarantees that it will be able to sell it for at least 1,000 times the amount you paid the company for its services, or they will refund your fees in full. If you wish, the company will loan you the first year's rental, to be repaid when you sell the lease. You are under no obligation to use their services to sell your lease. All participants receive a newsletter announcing the winners.

J. P. Allenbright, 10917 Huston St., N. Hollywood, California 91601. This service, operated by the author of this book, evaluates geologic reports on various leases offered by the BLM and files entries on your behalf. Within specified ranges you select the acreage and values of the parcels for which you wish to enter. The available range in acreage is: 40 to 350, 350 to 650, 650 to 1,250, and 1,250 to 2,560. The available range in value per acre is: $5 to $15, $15 to $35, $35 to $50, and $50 and up. Allenbright will also accommodate any additional special instructions you may wish to provide regarding the types of parcels for which you want to enter.

After filing entries on your behalf, the service sends you a postcard informing you of the parcel numbers for which your entries were filed. After the drawings, you receive a winners list for all leases on which Allenbright has filed for subscribers.

This service makes a "best effort" to spread subscribers' entries over a wide selection of leases in order to minimize the competition among his clients. Depending upon the quantity and types of leases offered and the number of subscribers and their instructions, lease filings are made, at the service's discretion, with one or more of the following BLM offices: California, Colorado, Montana, New Mexico, Utah, and Wyoming.

The filing service fee is $15 plus the $10 BLM filing fee per card. Discounted annual service rates are available. They are: one filing per month at a service fee of $13 plus $10 BLM fee per card for a total of $276; two filings per month at a service fee of

$12 plus the $10 BLM fee per card for a total of $528; three filings per month at a service fee of $11 plus the $10 BLM fee per card for a total of $756.

Allenbright unconditionally guarantees that if at any time you are not satisfied with the service you may cancel your subscription and receive an immediate refund for the full balance of unused service and BLM fees.

This service does not compete against its customers in the BLM lottery. Lease winners are required to pay the annual rental fee to the BLM. Free advice on selling leases is provided to winners. This service does not in any way, either directly or indirectly, participate in any monies realized from the sale or assignment of winners' leases. J. P. Allenbright's financial interest is limited to the fees charged for filing BLM entry cards. Write for free information.

Max Wilson, Inc., Oil Producers (P.O. Drawer 1978), Roswell, New Mexico. Telephone: 505/623-0507 or, toll free, 1/800/545-7955. Max Wilson, president of this company, claims a background of over 30 years in the oil business. His services are primarily the selection and recommendation of about 20 parcels located in New Mexico and Wyoming, filing for the parcels, and negotiating parcel lease sales to an oil company. The list of recommendations is sent free of charge and without obligation. It includes information concerning the township and range location of the parcels, size in acreage, number of applications anticipated to be filed with the BLM, the approximate values of the leases, and the official BLM parcel numbers. The list is mailed just after the BLM releases the official filing numbers. The value assigned to each parcel is what the lease is worth to Wilson personally, should you decide to sell the lease to him.

To file, you complete the BLM entry cards in full and either send the cards directly to the BLM office with your check for $10 per card or send $20 per card to Max Wilson and have him file the cards for you. In addition to the filing service, if you win, Wilson will lend the first year's lease rental to you, which you repay upon selling your lease.

If you wish, Wilson will assist you in negotiating the sale of your lease. For this additional service you pay a 10 percent commission based on the price paid by the purchaser. The commission charge does not apply to your reserved overriding royalty.

Oil & Gas Corporation of America, 1642 South Parker Road, Suite 310, Denver, Colorado 80231. The firm's president is Joseph

G. Pite. Telephone: 303/750-2616 (collect). OGCA has a staff geologist who evaluates the parcels that become available for lease each month in the Rocky Mountain area. Based on geological analysis and market information OGCA compiles an advanced listing of "highly recommended" parcels. The listing provides information which includes a detailed legal description of each parcel, acreage, profit potential, and a commentary on oil company exploration and purchasing activities in the area.

The filing procedure for this firm is as follows. On a separate form you indicate the parcels for which you wish to file, and the company files your cards to the BLM on your behalf. OGCA charges $25 for each card submitted. If you win a lease, the company guarantees that you will be able to sell it for at least 1,000 times the amount you paid the company for its services or they will refund your fees in full. If you wish, OGCA will loan you the first year's lease rental, which is repayable when you sell the lease. All profits and royalties that you make from the sale belong to you. All participants receive a newsletter announcing the winners.

Oil and Gas Leasing Services, P.O. Box 1343, Cheyenne, Wyoming 82001. The contact person at this service agency is Betty B. Shaffer. Telephone: 307/638-6144. Shaffer's services consist of preparing lists of parcels in Wyoming only. She provides a preliminary listing of all those parcels in Wyoming which are expected to be offered by the BLM the following month, thus providing her clients plenty of time to research parcels before the BLM filing deadline. The price of this preliminary list is $15 per month. At posting time, Shaffer offers the official BLM filing list, but with this additional information: the past lessees and respective lease dates for each parcel. This list costs $15 per month.

Petroleum Investment Company, 231 West 800 South (P.O. Box 27156) Salt Lake City, Utah 84101. Telephone: 801/363-3941. This firm provides a comprehensive service package consisting of maps, filing services, assistance in the sale of leases, and evaluation of leases. Their services cover most of the states which are included in the BLM lottery. Through its affiliated personnel in the various states, Petroleum Investment receives an advanced listing of lands that will most likely be offered by the BLM. The lists, which are made available to subscribers three to seven days before the BLM list is posted, indicate the description of the land, acreage, the serial number, previous lessee, and the year the lease was released or terminated. A geological and recommendation list is also provided, usually in advance of the BLM list. This list provides a geological analysis of parcels. Each of the parcels is rated excellent, good, fair, or poor. Coincident with the rating is an estimate of value of each lease and a comment about the exploration activity in the area of the lease and the possibilities of oil and gas being found in the land. A final list is issued immediately after the official BLM list is posted. The final list provides the necessary parcel numbers for each leasing unit.

After each monthly drawing Petroleum Investment issues a results list. In addition to the usual indication of first-, second-, and third-place winners, and statistics on the total applications filed per parcel and the total number of filings in the state, this company provides a compilation of all the significant applicants that filed for each parcel, such as oil companies and lease brokers. They also publish a list of each lease assignment, which includes the names of the assignor and assignee for most of the more active states. And finally, they provide a monthly list of open land lease filings for each state. This provides the speculator with information on the latest wildcat leasing activity and the name of the lease applicant. The list price schedule runs between $25 and $55 per state.

If you do not wish to do your own filing, Petroleum Investment will select the parcels for you, complete your filing cards—using your address—and mail the cards on your behalf to the appropriate BLM office. Their fee schedule for this service is: $15 for each single filing, $10 each for 2 to 5 filings, $5 each for 6 to 22 filings, and $4 for each filing over 22—plus the $10 per card fee charged by the BLM.

Tectonic maps showing oil and gas fields, anticlines, synclines, pipelines, etc., are sold for $25 to $50 per state. Oil and gas development maps showing drilling activity, producing fields, etc., are available in large scale at prices of $25 to $50 per portion.

For a fee of $100 Petroleum Investment will provide you with a comprehensive evaluation of your oil and gas lease. The evaluation report includes development trends in the area, local filing interest, prices paid for ambient leases, dry hole data, etc. For an additional fee, which varies depending on the circumstances, the company will assist you in the sale of your lease.

Petroleum Leasing Services, Inc., P.O. Drawer 8, Ruidoso, New Mexico 88345. The person representing this organization is Tom McRae. Telephone: 505/257-5357 (collect). This company has been in existence for four years. Their primary activity is selecting marketable parcels and providing filing services thereon. Each month PLS obtains geological information on parcels being offered by the Bureau of Land Management in Wyoming and New Mexico. The company selects 14 parcels it believes to have the highest chance for profitable performance and sends a free advanced listing of these selections to prospective clients for their review. The listing provides information to include: the township and range location of the parcels, acreage, a conservative estimate of the market value of the parcels, and the number of entries they estimate will be filed with the BLM for each of the parcels listed. To file, on a separate form you indicate the parcels for which you wish to file. Send the form to PLS along with a payment of $25 per card, which includes the BLM filing fee. PLS files entry cards to the appropriate land office on your behalf.

Through its affiliated organization, Westates, Inc., P.O. Box 210, Alto, New Mexico 88312, the company offers a program whereby you can do your own filing with the BLM. For a subscription cost of $25 per month, for a three-month minimum term, you can receive a monthly listing of the 14 "most profitable" leases. The listing is sent by mailgram on the Friday before the third Monday of each month. By having the parcel numbers you can file directly with the BLM. In addition to the subscription cost, you must pay the BLM filing fees. For additional information call 505/257-2900.

With either of the two organizations, if you win, arrangements will be made to loan you the first year's rental at no cost. You must repay this amount when your lease is sold. Assistance in selling your lease is also provided. PLS states that its clients' winnings belong solely to the clients; that PLS never profits from its winners' leases. I assume that the same holds true for Westates, Inc.

PLS also sells large scale maps of Wyoming and of the New Mexico Permian basin at $10 each. The maps show oil and gas fields and are marked with township and range so that you can locate the leases which are offered each month. PLS literature did not indicate to what date the maps were current or if oil wells and dry holes were posted. Inquire before purchasing.

Reliable Leasing Service, P.O. Box 27234, Denver, Colorado 80227. The person representing this organization is Forrest B. Gilman. This service, which has been operating for 10 years, provides a monthly advance listing of about 30 recommended parcels and files entry cards for its clients. Parcel recommendations are limited to Wyoming.

The recommendations include the township and range location of each parcel, size in acreage, estimated market values, and comments on oil company activities in the proximity of each parcel. You make the selections from the list, and on a separate form, you indicate the parcels for which you wish to file. Send your order to the service agency along with payment as follows: $10 for one entry, $15 for two entries, $20 for three entries, and $25 for four, five, or six entries. The fee for seven or more entry cards is $25 plus $2 for each card. In addition, you must pay the $10 per card filing fee charged by the BLM. A schedule of winners for the parcels RLS recommended will be mailed to you immediately after the drawing has been concluded.

RLS uses the services of another agency, which is located at RR2, Colby, Kansas 67701. This agency handles the mailings for RLS. RLS advertises that they do not compete against their customers in the BLM lottery. Their policy prohibits RLS employees from filing on any parcels the service recommends.

Resource Service Company, 9200 West North Avenue, Milwaukee, Wisconsin 53226. Mr. Fred L. Engle operates RSC, which he founded in 1973. RSC evaluates the various parcels offered for lease by the BLM offices and files entries on behalf of clients pursuant to endorsed service agreements. A variety of service agreement plans are available, differing only in the number of entries filed for you each month. Plan A provides one filing each month for 12 consecutive months at a total cost of $216, which includes the monthly BLM filing fees. Other plans provide for multiple drawings per month over a 12 month period, with the average cost per card discounted for increased filings. Also available is a single drawing plan for $20, which includes the $10 BLM filing fee.

If you win, RSC will loan you the first year's rental. If you win parcels that RSC recommended, the service guarantees to sell them within five years for at least $10,000 gross in aggregate or they will process up to 300 additional applications for you free of charge. Any final negotiated price for your lease is subject to your approval. Their commission for marketing your lease ranges from 12 to 16 percent depending on the sale price of the lease. For further information call 414/453-8080.

Robert Whisenant, 2916 West Rancho Drive (P.O. Box 27571),

Phoenix, Arizona 85061. Telephone: 602/242-1892. The company also uses this mailing address: P.O. Box 15051, Phoenix, Arizona 85060. Whisenant's services include parcel selections, filing, and marketing of leases. Each month he selects eight top parcels from either New Mexico, Wyoming, Montana, Colorado, Utah, Texas, Oklahoma, Louisiana, Mississippi, or Alabama. Generally, clients do not get a listing of these eight parcels. Instead, Whisenant prefers to use his discretion to decide on which parcels he will file for you. The filing procedure he uses is as follows: You indicate how many parcels you wish to file on and mail your instructions to Whisenant with your payment: $25 for a three months' subscription or $50 for a six months' subscription plus a $10 fee per card payable to the BLM. The subscription fee pays for the service of filing up to eight cards per month for the duration of the subscription. For no additional service charge Whisenant will permit another member of your family to file with you. Whisenant completes your cards and sends them to the appropriate BLM land office. If you win, he will loan you the first year's rental, which is repayable upon sale of your lease. He guarantees that he will find a buyer for your lease. If he doesn't, Whisenant will forfeit the rental loan he made to you.

At your request, Whisenant will permit you to select the parcel numbers on which you wish to file. For further information call 602/242-1892.

U.S. Oil & Gas Information Service, P.O. Box 61-0455, Miami, Florida 33161. The manager representing this service agency is A. Coleman. Telephone: 305/895-2464. This agency provides evaluation, filing services, and lease sales assistance to its clients. Parcel selections are limited to Wyoming. Each month this agency's geologists recommend the 12 "hottest" parcels of the month, those parcels that are considered to be the best for immediate profits. The agency claims that its parcel selections are also made based on other confidential data that is available directly to them for the area in which the leases are located. Their required filing procedure is as follows: You must sign a form which authorizes the service agency to use its discretion in selecting hot parcels and to make filings to the BLM on your behalf.

The fees charged for this service are: $10 for one filing, $18 for two filings, $24 for three filings, $30 for four filings, and an additional $7 for each additional entry, all plus a $10 charge per card to cover the BLM filing fee.

If you wish, U.S. Oil & Gas will loan you the first year's lease rental. This amount is reimbursable to them upon sale of your lease. This service guarantees that if you are not able to sell your lease for 200 to 1,000 times the $20 you spent winning it, they will refund your $20 in full and you will not be liable to repay the rental loan.

Appendix G

Decision of the Department of Interior Board of Land Appeals Reversing a BLM State Land Office Rejection of a Winner's Offer in a 1978 Oil and Gas Lease Drawing

IBLA 78-549   Decided September 29, 1978

Appeal from a decision of the Montana State Office, Bureau of Land Management, rejecting appellant's offer in a simultaneous oil and gas lease drawing. M-40282.

Reversed.

1. Oil and Gas Leases: Rentals

    The rent for oil and gas lease rights obtained in a simultaneous oil and gas lease drawing must be received in the proper office of the Bureau of Land Management within 15 days from the date of receipt of notice that such payment is due. Where there is no proof that service of the notice that payment is due was made upon offeror [*sic*] more than 15 days before the payment is received by the proper office of BLM, such payment will be deemed as timely made.

APPEARANCES: Kathleen A. Rubenstein, *pro se*.

OPINION BY ADMINISTRATIVE JUDGE HENRIQUES

Kathleen A. Rubenstein appeals from a decision of the Montana State Office, Bureau of Land Management (BLM), rendered June 22, 1978, rejecting her offer M-40282 in the simultaneous oil and gas lease drawing conducted in March 1978.

Appellant's offer was selected first and accorded first priority for oil and gas rights to Parcel MT-649.

The case file discloses that a notice was mailed to appellant by certified mail on April 7, 1978, informing appellant of her successful offer and of the requirement that she pay the first year's rent for the parcel within fifteen (15) days of receipt of the notice.

Although this notice was sent with a return receipt requested, no receipt was ever returned to BLM.

Thereafter, on May 23, 1978, BLM mailed a second notice and again requested that a return receipt be returned showing the date of appellant's receipt. No such receipt was ever returned to BLM.

On June 12, 1978, BLM received appellant's check for the first year's rent and also a number of stipulations which bear the signature of appellant under date of June 8, 1978.

BLM rejected appellant's offer as untimely inasmuch as it had not been received within 15 days from date of receipt of BLM's notice, but allowed appellant 30 days to furnish evidence of the date of receipt of the notice. BLM further notified appellant that it would make final its decision to reject appellant's offer if no evidence were forthcoming.

It is worthy of note that BLM bases its decision solely upon the alleged failure of appellant to pay rent within 15 days of receipt of the *second* notice; BLM does not rely for its decision on the first notice mailed April 7.

Rubenstein appeals from this decision and contends that the obligation to show the date of her receipt of the notice belongs to BLM. Appellant maintains that this is proper, because BLM chose the U.S. Postal Service as its agent for delivery of the notice and hence must bear the responsibility of the Postal Service's failure to furnish proof of receipt of the notice.

[1] The pertinent regulation, 43 CFR 3112.4-1, provides the law applicable to the facts at hand:

> Rental must be received in the proper office of the Bureau of Land Management within fifteen (15) days from the date of receipt of notice that such payment is due. The drawee failing to submit the rental payment within the time allowed will be automatically disqualified to receive the lease, and consideration will be given to the entry of the drawee having the next highest priority in the drawing.

We reverse the decision of BLM and do so without regard to the question of who has the burden of producing evidence of the date of appellant's receipt of the notice. As set forth above, BLM mailed its notice to appellant on Tuesday, May 23. Appellant's rental check was received by BLM on Monday, June 12.

If BLM's notice to appellant had been received by her on May 26, or thereafter, the rental check received by BLM on June 12 would be timely. The case file discloses that a certified letter mailed from the BLM in Billings, Montana, on June 22, 1978, required 5 days to be delivered to Ms. Rubenstein in Denver, Colorado. If, therefore, the mails were operating in due course, the notice mailed by BLM on May 23 might not have been received by appellant before May 30 because of the Memorial Day holiday, Monday, May 29. The available evidence contradicts BLM's assertion that appellant's check was not received in a timely fashion.

Therefore, pursuant to the authority delegated to the Board of Land Appeals by the Secretary of the Interior, 43 CFR 4.1, the decision appealed from is reversed.

Index

Alabama: federal land acreage, 223; oil and gas exploration, 82, 83, 221, 244
Alaska: Alaska Native Claims Settlement Act of 1971, 84; Alaska Statehood Act of 1958, 84; federal land acreage, 223; oil and gas exploration, 39, 82, 84, 221
Allenbright, J. P., 238–39
Amerada Hess Corporation, 27
American Association of Petroleum Geologists, 230
American Petroleum Institute, 40, 132, 199
Annual Reviews of Oil and Gas Activity, 105
Anschutz Corporation, 97
anticlines, 72–73
Appalachian Forest Reserve Act, 28
"Aquarian Age" parcel selection, 149–51
Arizona: federal land acreage, 223; oil and gas exploration, 52, 53, 82, 84, 88, 97–98, 108–109, 152, 221
Arizona Oil and Gas Conservation Commission, 19, 227
Arkansas: federal land acreage, 223; oil and gas exploration, 82, 83, 221
Arkansas Oil and Gas Commission, 19
Atomic Energy Commission, 14, 20

Bank of America, 213
Barkdull, James, 49
"basinal" areas, 85, 90–94, 95–96, 100, 101, 133–34
Bell, Bryan, 50
Better Business Bureau, 124
Bierlein, John W., 47

Billings Energy Corporation, 16
Blakemore, B(ruce) A., 48, 63
Board of Land Appeals, 111–12
Bolger, E. Perry, 50
Books on Demand, 105, 231
Bradshaw, F. J., 49
Brown, Russell W., 44
Buell, E. C., 49
Bureau of Land Management (BLM), ix, 23–24, 25, 26, 28, 29, 30, 31, 32, 33–35, 38, 39, 40, 41, 42, 43, 45, 46, 51, 52, 53, 56, 57, 58, 59, 62, 64, 66, 81, 83, 84, 106, 107, 108, 110, 113, 114, 116, 120, 122, 123, 128, 129, 130, 167, 180, 191, 226, 230, 240, 244, 247–49; amendments in leasing rules, 118, 126–27, 182–83, 196; Assignment Affecting Record Title to Oil and Gas Lease, 212–14; "BLM Lottery Winners Report," 140; entry cards, 111, 119, 124–26, 127–28, 130, 140–41, 157–64, 166, 167–69, 170–72, 173, 176, 177, 189, 219–20, 233–34, 235, 236, 237, 238–39, 240, 241, 242, 243, 244; microfilm records, 201, 204; "Notice of Lands Available for Oil and Gas Filing," 33, 38, 130, 133, 147, 236, 240–41, 242; "Regulations Pertaining to Oil and Gas Leasing as Contained in Title 43 of the Code of Federal Regulations," 21, 144; results list, 139, 141, 174, 190, 236; special stipulations, 134–36
—categories of land: known geological structures (KGSs), 25–28, 181, 189; lands in conflict, 25, 30–33; open land, 25, 28–30, 141, 204–205
—district offices: Alaska, 225;

251

252 INDEX

Arizona, 225; California, 138–39, 225; Colorado, 157, 158, 173, 175, 225; Idaho, 225; Montana, 158, 225; North Dakota, 158, 159, 225; South Dakota, 225; Nevada, 225; New Mexico, 225; Oklahoma, 225; Texas, 225; Oregon, 225; Washington, 225; Utah, 225; Wyoming, 121, 158, 173, 174, 176, 225; Kansas, 225; Nebraska, 225; Arkansas, Iowa, Louisiana, Minnesota and states east of the Mississippi River, 226. See also United States Department of Interior
Burgess, Warren K., 45

California: *An Introduction to the Energy Resources of California*, 77; *Exploratory Wells Drilled Outside of Oil and Gas Fields in California*, 144; federal land acreage, 223; oil and gas exploration, 52, 59, 76–77, 82, 84, 85, 88–91, 98, 99, 106–107, 108, 109, 110, 119, 123, 129, 133–34, 137, 139, 221, 238
California Division of Oil and Gas, 77, 98, 106, 143, 227; Map Revision Bulletin, 143; Weekly Summary of Notices to Drill, Rework, and Abandon, 143
Campbell, John H., 50
Cantine, S. A., 48
Canyon Energy Service, 233–34
Cardinal, Floyd, 103
Carpenter, Fred, 193–94
Chambers, Merle C., 49
Champion Oil, 27–28; Alaska Supreme Court decision, 28
Classified Telephone Directories, 201, 231
Clement, W. and Napoleon Hill (*Success Through A Positive Mental Attitude*), 152
Code of Federal Regulations, 38
Colorado: federal land acreage, 223; oil and gas exploration, 19, 36, 52, 82, 84, 88, 91–92, 98, 100, 108, 221, 237, 238, 244

Colorado Oil and Gas Conservation Commission, 98, 100, 227
Cone, Marilyn, 47, 48, 63
Connell, Elizabeth, 44, 63
Connell, Robert L., 47, 50, 63

Diboli, Collins C., 44
Dippel, Nola M., 48
Dun and Bradstreet Million Dollar Directory ("Oil and Gas Extraction"), 200–201
Duncan, Annamarie, 49

Energy Group of America, Inc., 234; Ed Axel, 234
Energy Research and Development Administration, 15
Energy Research and Marketing Services, 234–35
Energy Reserves Group, 98

faults, 74
Federal Oil and Gas Leases, Inc., 235–36; Tom Boston, 235; Federal Oil and Gas Leases of California, 236
Federal Simultaneous Associates, 236
Fields, W. C., 111
Flanagan, Phillip E., 50
Florida: federal land acreage, 223; oil and gas exploration, 82, 83, 221
Fraker, Carol W., 50

Gains, Jack B., 50
Gaudet, Woodrow J., 50
General Electric, 15
General Mining Law of 1872, 21
General Services Administration (GSA), 223
Getty Oil, 27, 52; Western Exploration Division, 134
Gillis, Marvin B., 48
Goodman, Beverly B., 49
Government Oil Lease Investments, Inc., 237–38; Martin E. and Merle Schor, 237

INDEX

Graham, Charles E., 50
Green, Otto G., 48
Grynberg, Celeste C., 50
Gulf Oil, 103

Halperin, Bernard, 48
Hand, Judge Learned, 193
Harden, Dorothy G., 49
Harper Oil Company, 50
Harper, Ruth, 49
Harrah's Club, 61
Harris, Lawrence C., 49
Harrison, Randolph, 50
Herbert, George, ix
Hill, Napoleon, *(Think and Grow Rich)*, 152
Howard, Joann, 49

Idaho Bureau of Mines and Geology, 228
Idaho oil and gas exploration, 52, 53, 82, 84, 92, 100–101, 108, 109; Idaho-Wyoming Overthrust Belt, 92
Idaho Oil and Gas Conservation Commission, 227
Illinois: federal land acreage, 223; oil and gas exploration, 82, 83, 221
Illinois lottery, 46–47
Indiana: federal land acreage, 223; oil and gas exploration, 82, 83, 221
Internal Revenue Service (IRS), x, 165, 166, 206; Individual Retirement Accounts (IRA), 195–96; Keogh Plans, 195–96; Revenue Ruling 56-252, 196; Revenue Ruling 67-141, 196; Revenue Ruling 71-191, 196; short-term trusts, 195, 196; timing of lease sales, 194–95
Interstate Map Company, 231
Interstate Oil Compact Commission (IOCC), 97; "The Oil and Gas Compact Bulletin," 97–104

jojoba oil, 16–17
June Oil and Gas Company, 49

Kansas: federal land acreage, 223; oil and gas exploration, 82, 83, 221
Kentucky: federal land acreage, 223; oil and gas exploration, 82, 83, 221
Kerr-McGee Corporation, 98
Kirkwood, Viola J., 48
Kout, Robert D., 48
Kruse, W. N., 50

Lane, Marcia P., 48
Langley, Roger J., 47, 49
Lansdale, Dyke, 49
lease-lottery abuses, 112–13, 114, 119, 167, 177; "borrowed names," 114–15, 167; brochures, 124; computer tampering, 117; conflict of interest, 113–14; conspiracy, 116; "fly-by-night" filing, 117, 122; forging, 115; lease rental loans, 128; misuse of power of attorney, 115, 128; pre-lease contracts, 126–27
LeSage, Alain Rene, 175
Lindstrom, Jon P., 48
Logan, Harry R., 45
Louisiana: federal land acreage, 223; oil and gas exploration, 82, 83, 85, 221, 224
Lynch, Edmund C. Jr., 49

Mancillas, Arminda, 44
MAPCO, 231
Marathon Oil Company, ix
Maryland: federal land acreage, 223; oil and gas exploration, 82, 83, 221
Mask, John, 47
Master Charge, 235, 238
Max Wilson, Inc., 239; Max Wilson, 239
Mercedes-Benz, 16
Merriam, Louis T., Jr., 49
Michigan: federal land acreage, 223; oil and gas exploration, 82, 83, 221
Milligan, Inc., 236–37; Frank T. Milligan, 236; Doris M. Sotter, 236

Mineral Leasing Act of 1920, 21, 22, 23
Mississippi: federal land acreage, 223; oil and gas exploration, 82, 83, 221, 244
Missouri: federal land acreage, 223; oil and gas exploration, 82, 83, 221
Mitchell, Edwin W., 49
Mobil Corporation, 103
Moneysworth, 41–42
Montana: federal land acreage, 223; oil and gas exploration, 19, 52, 53, 82, 84, 88, 92–93, 94, 95, 101, 108, 221, 237, 238, 244
Montana Board of Oil and Gas Conservation, 228
Montana Department of Natural Resources, 228

Nakoa, Nancy S., 48
National Aeronautics and Space Agency (NASA), 15
National Petroleum Council (NPC), 13, 14–15, 18, 85, 88; Committee on Possible Future Petroleum Provinces, 18, 84–85; *Future Petroleum Provinces of the United States*, 84–85, 88–96, 104
Nebraska: federal land acreage, 223; oil and gas exploration, 82, 83, 221
Nevada: federal land acreage, 223; oil and gas exploration, 53, 82, 84, 93, 96, 102, 108, 221
Nevada Bureau of Mines and Geology, 228
Nevada Department of Conservation and Natural Resources, 228
New Mexico: federal land acreage, 223; oil and gas exploration, ix, 19, 52, 53, 82, 84, 88, 93–94, 102, 108, 109, 152, 212, 221, 234, 236, 237, 238, 239, 242, 244
New Mexico Bureau of Mines and Mineral Resources, 229
New Mexico Land Maps, 231
New Mexico Oil Conservation Department, 228
New York: federal land acreage, 223; oil and gas exploration, 82, 83, 221
New York State Lottery, 46
New York Stock Exchange, 150
North Dakota: federal land acreage, 223; oil and gas exploration, 82, 84, 88, 94, 95, 102–103, 108, 188, 221, 237
North Dakota Geological Survey, 229
Northwest Natural Gas Company, 103

Occidental Petroleum, 136–37
Ohio: federal land acreage, 223; oil and gas exploration, 82, 83, 221
Oil and Gas Corporation of America, 239; Joseph G. Pite, 240
Oil and Gas Journal, 26, 104
Oil and Gas Leasing Services, 240; Betty B. Shaffer, 240
Oklahoma: federal land acreage, 223; oil and gas exploration, 82, 83, 221, 236, 244
Olds, Evelyn K., 45
Oregon Department of Geology and Mineral Industries, 229
Oregon oil and gas exploration, 52, 53, 84, 94–95, 103, 108, 109
Organization of Petroleum Exporting Countries (OPEC), 13, 17, 18, 41, 56; Arab oil embargo, 19, 56
Outer Continental Shelf Lands Act of 1953, 28
overriding royalty rights (ORR), 40, 41–42, 44–45, 55, 63, 112, 113, 123, 132, 180, 187–88, 191–92, 193, 203, 204, 207, 208, 211, 212, 215
Oxnard, Henry, 50

Panos, Geoff, 49, 63
Panos, Greg, 44, 63
Park, Clifford, 48

INDEX

Pennsylvania: federal land acreage, 223; oil and gas exploration, 82, 83, 221
Pennsylvanian rock, 88, 95
Petroleum Exploration, 50
Petroleum Information, 231
Petroleum Investment Company, 189, 231, 240–41
Petroleum Leasing Services, Inc., 241–42; Tom McRae, 241; Westates, Inc., 242
Pittsford Oil Investors, 50
Prentice, Spelman, 49
Principles of Stratigraphic Nomenclature, 77
Privacy Act of 1974, 166
Public Land Law Review Commission, 18, 22
Puhl, John J., 47, 63
Pyramid Oil Company, 98

Reeder, Betty, 44
Reichold Energy, 103
Reliable Leasing Service, 242–43; Forrest B. Gilman, 242
Resource Service Company, 243; Fred L. Engle, 243
Rex, John, 103
Richards, Evelyn, 44, 45, 46
Rose, Arthur E., 48
Roswell Map Company, 231
Rubenstein, Irwin, 48
Rubenstein, Kathleen A., 247–49
Rucker, David, 44

Safeway's Bingo, 47
Securities and Exchange Commission, 210
Shell Oil, 179, 180
Sherrod, Blackie, 44
Sheverbush, R. B., 47
"Simultaneous Oil and Gas Entry Card," 34
Smith, Carl A., 44
South Dakota: federal land acreage, 223; oil and gas exploration, 19, 82, 84, 93, 95, 103, 108, 221

South Dakota Geological Survey, 229
Southwest Leasing Service, 189
Southwest Oil and Gas News, 42, 201
Standard Oil, 103
stratigraphic traps, 75–76, 88, 90, 94, 95, 96, 142, 187
Swenson, Richard J., 48
Swift, Donn R., 48

Taylor Grazing Act of 1934, 20
Tennessee: federal land acreage, 223; oil and gas exploration, 82, 83, 221
tertiary rock, 88, 94, 95, 96
Texaco, 103
Texas: federal land acreage, 223; oil and gas exploration, 82, 83, 221, 236, 244
Three Mile Island, 14
Trossen, C. D., 50
Truett, Jay L., 49

United States Bureau of Mines, 191, 221
United States Bureau of Reclamation, 15, 23
United States Department of Agriculture, 23; Forest Service, 23, 104; Roadless Area Review Evaluation, 104
United States Department of Defense, 20, 23
United States Department of the Interior, 23, 25, 226; Bureau of Indian Affairs, 83; Geological Survey (USGS), 14, 23–24, 25–26, 29–30, 32, 134, 181, 221, 230; Interior Board of Land Appeals (IBLA), 178–79, 247, 249; National Park Service, 23, 83; Second Land Ordnance, 144–46. See also Bureau of Land Management
United States Department of Justice, 166
United States Department of the Navy, 136

United States Fish and Wildlife Service, 23, 134; Endangered Species Act of 1973, 136
United States Postal Service, 125, 248
U. S. Oil and Gas Information Service, 244-45; A. Coleman, 244
USA Oil Industry Directory, 200
Utah: federal land acreage, 223; oil and gas exploration, 52, 53, 60, 82, 84, 88, 95-96, 97, 108, 221, 237, 238, 244
Utah Division of Oil, Gas and Mining, 229
Utah Geological and Mineral Survey, 229
Utah State University, 107

Virginia: federal land acreage, 223; oil and gas exploration, 82, 83, 221
Visa, 235, 238
Volz, Laurie A., 48

Wall Street Journal, 36
Walter Skinner's Oil and Gas International Yearbook, 200
Washington: federal land acreage, 223; oil and gas exploration, 84, 96, 103, 104, 108, 109, 221
Washington Oil and Gas Conservation Act, 104
Washington Oil and Gas Conservation Commission, 230
West Virginia: federal land acreage, 223; oil and gas exploration, 82, 83, 221
Western Oil Reporter, 26
Whisenant, Robert, 243-44
Wright, J. D., 47
Wyoming: federal land acreage, 223; oil and gas exploration, ix, 19, 41, 42, 44, 47, 52, 53, 55, 63, 82, 84, 88, 95, 96, 104, 107-108, 110, 114, 117, 119, 129, 130, 165, 173, 180, 187, 188, 211, 219-20, 221, 234, 237, 238, 239, 240, 242, 243, 244
Wyoming Geological Survey, 230
Wyoming Oil and Gas Conservation Commission, 230

Young, Clotilde, 49

Zuckerman, Harry, 48
Zweifel, Merle, 36-37